SUICIDE
BRIDGE

SUICIDE BRIDGE

A Book of the Furies

A Mythology of the South & East

Autumn 1973 – Spring 1978

IAIN SINCLAIR

SKYLIGHT PRESS

© Iain Sinclair, 1979, 2013

This expanded edition first published in Great Britain in 2013 by
Skylight Press, 210 Brooklyn Road, Cheltenham, Glos GL51 8EA

Suicide Bridge was first published in 1979 by Albion Village Press, London.

Many of the texts in this book, or earlier versions of those texts, were originally published in the following magazines or collections:
New Directions (10 English Poets, ed. Andrew Crozier); *Anthologie de la Nouvelle Poesie Anglaise* (ed. Paul Buck, Pierre Joris); *bal:le:d curtains*; *Grosseteste Review*; *Great Works*; *Meantime*; *Montemora*; *Ochre*; *Perfect Bound*; *Pod*; *Saturday Morning*; *The Human Handkerchief*.

Artwork by Susan Wood
Photographs (including cover photos) by Iain Sinclair
Designed and typeset by Rebsie Fairholm
Publisher: Daniel Staniforth

www.skylightpress.co.uk

Printed and bound in Great Britain by Lightning Source, Milton Keynes.
Typeset in Mr Eaves Sans, a font by Zuzana Licko.

British Library Cataloguing-in-Publication data:
A catalogue record for this book is available from the British Library.

ISBN 978-1-908011-61-9

'When a Manic Depressive escapes from his Furies he's irresistible. He captures History.'
    Saul Bellow, HUMBOLDT'S GIFT

'Plagiarism, fraud, perversion by pun, by reversal of values & displacement of content, of above into below, of male into female, left into right, before into after – all these Freud saw as operations of the unconscious.'
    Robert Duncan, THE H.D. BOOK

'To seek mysteries in the obscure, poking into magic and committing eccentricities in order to be talked about – This I do not.'
    Veronica Forrest-Thompson, ON THE PERIPHERY

offered to THE ENEMY

PUNK VORTEX
X FILE

INTIMATE ASSOCIATIONS: Myth & Place

Hands out of the entrails of time. Myths are lies. Out of the bucket. Retain those primary, first light dramas of aboriginal creation: getting, how here, dew freezing on the corpse, the erected land hurling star-sperm into the sky's belly, a moisture snaking among the dust to make the shape of the creature who must grow into his own shadow, male, containing female, put flesh into the morning. It is the length of what remains,

'It was the Kid who came in there on me,' Garrett told Poe, 'and I think I got him.'
'Pat,' replied Poe, 'I believe you have killed the wrong man.'

death, unburied defeat, poison-water despair of infected tribes, the dispossessed, then & now, the vegetal peoples made blind by brilliance cut out of stone: new gods with necklaces of corruption.

Which is the essence. The true flash. Of what myth is. Stolen from *The Collected Works of Billy the Kid* (Michael Ondaatje, Anansi Press 1970). That death is not a period to the heat of the man. Even in the sense of closing the text. Most often it opens. May instead be, signature. It has to be there: but not necessarily the death of the protagonist. The story is wound out of his head, a pigtail set with razors.

The land the animal. They have a location which is charged with an intense & continually reinforced personal magnetism, literally driven down into the granules of soil – so that each single grain is a charged particle of energy, forming a live carpet on which they stand & move, a cathode mosaic of infinitely detailed histories & archetypes. Past & present are coeval, equally radiant.

The birth flower is there & the distilled lights of all their suffering. They have Place made manifest in totemic animals, to be succoured & to be hunted, even to death; devoured, digested, taken back as the living body of what the tribe is. The circle is made: the nimbus, clearly visible around the standing shell of the man, is uncut. Demons of otherness cannot gain entry.

But this is recklessly ploughed under, is cleared, transported; & Place which is their own darkest, unspoken, identification of self, is damaged beyond recognition & forced to find other, alien forms.

It does have to be very simple to work. Narrative. And contain much that can be repeated. Was heard (over-) somewhere else in the first place. The bones are painted down the front of the suit, in lime. Burn through. Poe, prophet seer of American guilt, is deputy to Garrett. Whose watch-chain is bandage, not allowing the action to escape.

Pain is swallowed, with apparent ease, in tribal enactment. It does hurt: so much that it won't remain a mere irritation down the slope of the face & the inside of the skin. It shifts out. Lays hand on fate.

The essential myths of beginning are followed by myth as subversion. It will destroy the colonist, it will fatten in his cheek. He will haplessly pursue the past, will lie with ghosts, waste his essence on incubic shadowy movements.

Myth emerges as a weapon, a tool of resistance. It emerges in the hands of men wanting to maintain a contact with the previous, with the era of power & high function; men who know they must lie fallow in a time that is so distant from the plexus of their own unplanted sun. The memory fire

WALKING. WRITE THIS DOWN: KILL THE WORD. STIFLE ITS GROWTH TOWARDS LIGHT. SO THAT THE STRIDE, THE STEP UPON EARTH, CANCELS THAT IMPULSE. FOREVER. MOVE OVER THE GROUND. WITH THIS MOUTH

must at all costs be tended. They code what is left & they speak it secretly. They do not put it on paper. When the trader & the metallurgist shave out the stone, carve the earth faces, the unplaced tribesman borrows the stories of his animals, sleeps close to the fire, listening to the breath of the herd. Dreams are backtracked, names & symbols mated, cooked, released. It lies on the tongue like a grub. It climbs out of the book into a vertical energy called: FASCISM.

The need for the old myths is a confession of our failure to handle the world, to be on terms with the life-spill of this moment. We want back to what was never there. Immediate parentage is denied. Deeper & deeper into the sand.

Myth is breech: faces backwards. The siamese twin is place. They are sown together & cannot be separated, dependent systems. Man is the messenger substance between them. He is a raised tube, opened at crown of head & base of feet – so that it flows through him, conscious or unconscious, the power, the surge, the tachyonic voltage. He is erect. That is his vanity, to lift skull to the shafting sun. The wiser animal, the ally, travels with the ground in a relation of mutual benefit, low over the force-lines, guided in his essential journeying. But man is like plant. He is utterly possessed by what place is. He stands where a precisely defined exchange is consummated between star & ground. He is the saline medium. He marks place with a stone. But he is not rooted. He moves away, inflamed, into myth.

Myth is the living breath of place; is life. Place, in travesty, ordains & invests man. He gleams & glistens like the new born, he is

The story told fresh in an historical present. Live newsprint. If such a thing were possible.

Centaur. Man horse.

Episodic. You can add & fill your own (needs). You can begin anywhere. You can set it to music. Or spit it as venom. There are dogs.

mythic hero. The lives & virtues of many men, many cycles, are compressed into the one: Demi-God, Sword Bearer, Astronaut, or Suiciding Martyr. Place requires

Can you make it seem that he escaped the gravity earth. Kicked the lead. Can you.

that man become myth. A blood bond is contracted. A known place must hold within its definition, edge, the mythology of a known man. Blake tells it: 'PEACHEY HAD NORTH WALES.' It is a sex, a hunger. Man recognises his place by a lust in the skin, wants to go into the side of the mountain, come gold.

Make it seem there is a power detached from the facts of biography. It is all being taken down. But it won't be used.

Man needs, a blood cell imperative, continual extensions of place, extensions therefore of what mind is, extensions of boundaries, destruction of inhibitions & fears; always, more & more ground for the consciousness, & more consciousness for the ground. The colonists, getting-away-from as much as going-open-towards, have to push further & faster as space retreats in front of them, the known swallowing the unknown, the unknown regurgitating the known as something new: gobble it up, it isn't there. America, Africa, the Stars. Extending the metaphors of pain.

Where there is unclaimed space, unwritten land, there is the quest, & there is mining, a sickly clawing, not only for minerals, crops, dead artefacts, but also for mythologies. What tales the land holds buried. Drag them out with grappling-irons & tractors, record them. Hoard the images in mausoleums with chained wall; & uniformed attendants.

What we walk is myth flattened into space. Its hide

There is a man naked with a gun-belt. Weals. As if the skin were spontaneously tearing itself from the bones.

Who reaches for the knife in his boot.

stripped & ribboned, the thong wound out. This is or could be the Third Virtue. Not the celibate, fasting life, the eremite in his rocky sanctuary, nor the life of the materialist, forced to the service of his own goods, overstimulated into toxic inertia, but to reconnect with the migrant, the traveller of paths, in balance with natural forces arriving at the sacred sites at the most potent, & only workable, season, aligned with star & animal, searching for the star that is buried in the brain of the creature he hunts, taking on the qualities of that creature by eating his flesh.

Do you recognise the man shot across his own meat. As being close to those other (unnamed) heroes who left the quest early. So it was? Failure.

So place becomes active once more & this is the purpose of the walk – to keep track open, to lay hand on the 19 stones, to bear witness. Place trembles in you. Long Man moves out from your chest. The traveller is not

EMBRACING THE NETTLE TREES. ALL THE FACES TURNED UP. ALL UP TO FACE WHATEVER IT IS THAT IS, ABOVE.

TO WEAR THE FACE ON THE CROWN OF THE SKULL. PULL BACK THE WIND HAIR.

WHATEVER MOVES ABOVE.

BENDING BACK TO HOLD BALANCE ON THE CURVE. WALKING BETWEEN HEDGES. IT IS THE HEDGE, THE TREES, THAT MOVE.

THE TREE GATHERS IN, ACCUMULATES. MAN PRESENCE ALIEN. DRIVEN IN HIS TRACKS, TO SERVE. TO LIFT. THE STONES. MERE WORK.

the cultivator of crops or the butcher of domestic cattle. He is not dominated by a fixed concept of place, by boundaries set in scale to the geography of his own skull's cavern. Place does not go sour in his pocket or wither his sinew. He has escaped the fattening & over-informed vortex of centre where the city dweller, unravelled by centrifugal motions, has fallen victim to a weight, an ever-increasing density of myth, a black hole shrinking as it enlarges, cancerous, in terms of mere landscape. The city swivels on its axis, the sky is buried alive, buildings grow into the clouds, we carry the pains of architectural ambition on our shoulders.

Beyond this (seduction) is a poetry of mind, self-reflective, 'pure'. Where the consciousness (voice) is forever aware of its own timbre & includes fault as a crucial constituent in the irony. Which is also comic. In a swift vein. Includes knowledge. Those entry keys punched & in constant play. Disciplined.

Leaves the reader breathless, drawn remorselessly down through the layers of strategy to a new awareness of condition/impotence, & all its attractions.

And this is what we walk: the shape of the gods. We burn, by use, their outline into the turf. Cerne Abbas & the White Horse of Uffington are data: or, again, the precise number of steps that leaves you above the hidden spring beneath cathedral spire. The longer paths are less obviously marked & found by the ethical tuning of your personal compass. The track is the heated spoor of our own ancestral animal-host: hare, raven, salmon, wolf, or boar, whatever lives in the recesses of memory bones – the goat withering to the fish that is swallowed & leaps forth from the queen's womb. Energies put on the most convenient disguises. This is how we imagine them, this is how we divide up time & make it bearable. The shape is defined, given linear borders – as it intersects with time. We discover what the shape is by being forced to describe it.

In this same vacuum corridor the great secret was preserved, the sun. Men of power had the stock of myth all along: they knew where the trapped body was buried. Sun, Helios, Ely. 'SKOFELD HAD ELY.' Helios, Hyle. 'HYLE DWELT IN WINCHESTER.' These place/men, named energies, sons of the White Giant, lepers from excess of sun wisdom, these excavators of grave mysteries hid the socket of their potency, the furred spider of life, sun lion, yolking tawny beast, beneath vampire stakes, the rocks of Winchester & Ely, the Cathedrals. Chisels of partially-initiated Masons constructed the trap, wound the forbidden lore into a maze of earth & water. We have to circumnavigate that heat, walk wider & wider out into the surrounding meadows.

Place is a harpoon of the specific & has no name. It is not anonymous in the sense of withholding its location but is unknown & discovered only by a charge as powerful as death – in death-moment or some other heightened absolute, birth, climax, murder (that false trail of secret savage acts seeking to pin down place by isolated sacrifice, undirected hand, ritualists of the locked room hoarding their pathetic equipment, chainstore magic kits & cheap cameras.)

Place is shaved into a splinter, is tight as one wound

Myth's bullets. Trenching out the man. Eating larval galleries in the skull. Breeding. So the flesh dies. He cracks away, transformed. The vertical man crashes, is cut down. His sex seethes white, how, he is made female. Maggoty grubbing intelligences are in him. Invaded by unsuspected weakness.

The man who is named. Is myth. Who is accosted by death. Is not shaded into motivation. The inaugural force of will. Against the domestic, the shared. Against nature (other than his own.) Spits into the wind. And uses it.

or gash on earth's surface. Myth makes track in the hoof-prints of place. Lifelong quest for that unreachable singularity – to be reborn, re-energised by touch, by mutual ecstatic recognition of place & self. Myth is what place says. And it does lie. It spreads a seductive field of pits & snares. You go mad if you try to pursue place through myth: your path will disappear over the nearest cliff. Place is fed by sacrifice of the unwary – though the truly innocent, those born to innocence, according to myth, survive.

Place, finally, can be only one thing: where you die. Your own clenched spine secret. The motor word, **logos**, scorched into your chemistry; a sign on the ground that is yours & no-one else's. It is the elimination of absolutely everything, nothing remains, distance is wiped out, a total renunciation of all you have claimed as knowledge up to this moment. Your whole journey has been to find that place which you have dreamt, long before birth, glimpsed, snatched, visited – to find it & complete the story, which is the suicide bridge, which is the anticipation, sleep's rush on death, the forcing, the entry to something that is not yet, cannot yet be, known.

The wrong man steps through the empty grave like a door. The shadows of a timber house a heavy oil across his neck. The mountain is blue & you can see beneath the crust. Exposure/eye affected, shooting out of the slow dark, out of the palaeozoic into the astral. Fever shake in the rock. The use of man to stand between. They can call his presence 'love' if that is what they want. His purpose to conduct this transaction. Without him the system will wrench itself apart, ultimate density & ultimate light rejecting each other, travelling, where no contact can ever again be made.

A COSMOGONY FOR HAND & HYLE

I

'The 17th ray is that of the twins; in the African cults the Ibeji... were the shadowy companions of twin children... The tempest, Oro, also belongs to this ray, which is that of ominous appearances & screaming winds. Upon his feast day Oro appears in the shape of a monster in human form with face & lips smeared with blood. His bellowing resounds in all the cities, & the fetish priests celebrate his mass in the groves sacred to him. The terrible voice of Oro is simulated in the Mysteries by the rapid twirling of a wooden clapper attached to a string'

Kenneth Grant: *CULTS OF THE SHADOW*

hear it, mantled air divides like a skirt
                    look down

space-time, *M*
                    gravity, ☪
causing light,
                    the life rush,
                                rattling, streaming,
                    mountain reflector of leaf & small stone,
to deflect, bend inwards

no light escapes the surface
these great black suns
invisible gravel pits of time

'a region whose boundary decreases to zero'

singularities occur along the edge
the birth, the notice, of Hand & Hyle

'causality breakdowns in that
one could travel into one's past'

and so the observer,
                    the floating, detached cone
sees the formation of antimatter
sees the centre darken, the dark ring spread

until the whole ceases to be visible, discrete
THIS DOES NOT MEAN THAT IT IS NO LONGER THERE
it is there,
                    but the centre has lost definition
has lost its centrality

it is seen that the centre engrosses,
    engorges space;
the eye ring is forced
to lead consciousness outwards,
stretch the event horizon

                        unnoticed,
these suns, these pits of distortion
but with retained gravitational field
visible only by effect,
the turning of light in its purpose

                        shock waves,
possible sources of x-rays, radio waves,
voices on cheap transistors whisper
the annunciation of Hand & Hyle,
mixed with roar of coal gas, diesel traffic,
the engines of annihilation

amateurs of obsession spool the tape-loops,
oracular static, voices out of time,
dead star ramblings,
                    the force
that shrinks the walls of forbidden buildings

'the area of the boundary of a black hole cannot decrease with time, & if two or more black holes merge to form a single black hole, the area of its boundary will be greater than the areas of the boundaries of the original black holes'

fear: time

prisoner of the sharpened future cone
its narrowness & helmeted peak

space, the guardian element, presses
contains the pressure of evil
and, thus, is itself contained

'orbit of the Killing vector'
old question: is there death before life

M.D cut it into the accident elbow
of his glass, his black keyhole
refined into inertia
                              it was found
among the grinding mills, the cones
        a pattern
presented to him, trace elements
of the dying molecular equation
fuel'd his insight, brought his own decay
        the magnitude
of what he could not see

between the eye & the intention: horror

'for small cold bodies, self-gravity can be neglected & the degeneracy pressure will be balanced by attractive electrostatic forces between nearest neighbour particles arranged in some sort of lattice'

this descends, is forced down
on the neck of the city
is guided-in by the grid of the churches
is homed by 9th degree rituals
by the promise of Mass Murder
by the ovens
the opened veins of Whitechapel
surgeons inject the dust of white dwarfs
into the throats of will'd victims,
the cab jolts over the cobbles
shaking the stars in the window;

it is described by Rimbaud, years before the event,
swallowing the rod, writing with glass finger

*'the vehicle turns on the grass
of an obliterated highway: & in a blemish
at the top of the window on the right
swirl pale lunar figures, leaves, breasts ...'*

the sick moon of Hyle is dying, that Hand be born

shedding matter, supernovae, planetary nebulae
activating heat to work the nuclear reactions
     heavy gasses
white dwarf remains: the aura, the nimbic ghost

shadowy Hand rigid Hyle
falling out across the tumbled courtyards

time does not reach them, the red shift speeds

the ceiling of their death forces the father
deeper than ever into the mother's shame
shuddering, giving up his future
that they can be
that they must be, born again, anchored
to the fate, the corruption, of his island city

The quotations are taken from 'The Large Scale Structure of Space-Time' by S.W. Hawking & G.F.R. Ellis. (Cambridge University Press, 1973)

II

'An elemental is another of the creatures of the astral plane, which has many inhabitants beside the dead. It is populated by all sorts of beings, whether of human or independent origin – the gods, spirits & demons of outworn creeds & primitive beliefs, the astral bodies of animals, the astral simulacra of celebrated characters of fiction & legend, like Hamlet or Robin Hood, into whom sufficient human interest has been poured to endow them with long-lived astral existence'

Richard Cavendish: THE POWERS OF EVIL IN
WESTERN RELIGION, MAGIC & FOLK BELIEF

waking to become their own fathers,
sickle-handed, wolf-toothed to tear,
dribbling fetid, seeping acids;
grainy root juice
to burn & sizzle, to hollow out
the bone of dark:
the beginning was Mouth, & Mouth
was sealed, without knowledge of itself,
its separate, future parts, welded

'they form the foundation of the New Sexuality,
... combining ... to form a magical art –
the art of visualizing sensation, of
BECOMING ONE WITH ALL SENSATION,
& of transcending
the dual polarity of existence
by the annihilation of separate identity through
the mechanics of the Death Posture'

they have, they have
eaten the heart of the scattered child,
they have eaten his heat
for their pulse;
it is the unstopped bug of their time:
insect, hard shell, devours insect
swallows the spiked tail, smaller
with each bite the motive shrinking

repressed spirals fill Hand
Hyle is dark, the basis of mineral life

they copulate with their own fist, sin
against man & against animal,
lie with crocodile & bear, consume meat
dung, crow, sperm, slime,
frog, earth, fen, rock
bring forth hybrid mind forms
genetic double-takes, hundred headed
monsters & masks of naked greed

swollen & reduced they tumble
around the circumference of the wheel

mountain mad, dividers;
from the animal comes the divine,
to get out of ourselves,
possessed by what is swallowed,
milk teeth chip on stone & ring,
skull splinters chewed,
the avenging eye sucked down & held

Zagreus, Manson, Loki

disguised as woman to pass among women,
torn apart by their own mother:
courtesies & sentiments
of net curtain living rooms, wool
on the television cabinet, framed photographs
enshrine the dead child, tinted
bleached into a frieze of guilt

beyond the human into madness:
the restrictions of surgery,
rods in the bone pull free
he lurches towards us
with open kneecaps, gristle in the teeth
feathers his madness,
        the feather of flame,
out of it,
                into
the space beyond his father, sky

balance; balance on the raft,
the wafer of stiffened clay
between the fire pit
      and the retreating
reasoning warmth of stellar memorials

incubus, succubus:
Seth bearing the risen Osiris on his back,
sodomy, the rape of child Horus,
revenge, anger concealed in shell face,
this is Hand & Hyle, one creature
stumbling forward, weighted back
self-penetrated, blocked, death fertile
translated into medieval cathedral stone

Ahriman & Ohrmazd

*'the material world & finite time
had been made by Ohrmazd as a trap,
to lure Ahriman from the eternal Into the actual'*

fitted up, framed,
fitted the hand to the glove,
Hand within Hyle, disguised, double-eye
breaks the stare of gravity

star//   the grave of light
night//   the graveyard of the stars

'EVIL IS THE ACTIVE SPRINGING FROM ENERGY'

III

In which the aged and chair-condemned mother of the twins, of Hand & Hyle, falls asleep watching Raoul Walsh's HIGH SIERRA on the vast television window that her imprisoned sons have inflicted on her, by an act of conspicuous charity. A substitute presence for their loud absence (never to return). A slate mirror of American ghosts and deserts. Certain key images, playing on closed lids, lock her into an earlier viewing of this piece; an outing, when she was host to her unborn, parasitical sons. There was also the concentrated awe of her virgin glimpse of Walsh as a Klansman-hooded extra in the first film she ever saw, D.W. Griffith's THE BIRTH OF A NATION, in the Mile End Road. The primary and fatal invasion of her sleep.

'crashing out'
rushing towards the dog, death
like Dillinger, rushing towards you, weary of killing
STAR BUS ROUTES transport the subject
in crippled geometry, HIGH SIERRA;
no lateral track or smoky profile
but face out the car's fixed momentum
so that we are the window, or nothing
    into the cold,
              heart
ticking on the sleeve, deathwatch beetle
in badge or shield,
    stamped: WB
private made public; rheumatic
sentiment of iron-shod feet & gingham
mongrel emotionalism, crewcuts

death lurks in frame numbers, at margin,
unused sound, a jagged density
    without smell,
              cigarettes & marmalade &
suits & naked ties, black funeral shoes

where George Raft refuses, Hand is
    born,
            myopic
in the corner of Raoul Walsh's one good eye
Klansman-hooded
albino, or
revenging Whitechapel Elephant Man
in D.W. Griffith's THE BIRTH OF A NATION
viewed in the Mile End Road
by the live girl, Hand's mother

away from frontline, played straight
purple mixed in the dye
recognition of Jupiter's omen,
translated beyond hoarding she
dozes into a trance of forgetfulness
the awful death preparation
deathcage that is
            cinema;
her womb fills with sand

now sits late, in plant-
room with frenzy of caged birds
the colour set cuts her vision
into a blind tyranny of line
        the unborn at attention in the sac

California coastal shark spine
        is littered
with bones of white colonists buffing
the silver of Vegas
to found a new suburb in the ever-expanding
genetic chain that is Los Angeles,
                angel of death,
linking montage & warning
composed by early Don Siegel
with dissolving maps, route cards, trains,
fires, exploding calendars, the sacred

five-spoked wheel;
                                air so thin
car speeds in rapid-
cut segments, the enclosed capsule
the humpbacked tin coffin,
wheels towards the Drive-In, death,
but the man of destiny is not
in that car –
                        so what
happens to the time-wake? dust
is *real* & the flash of sunlight
on the rear window as he corners,
and the cancer is real, but
they are separated & mated
by technicians in haunted
movieolas of foetal experimentation

                Hand Hyle Coban Kox
on hooks or spooling
loose into waste bags
and these are the powers to be,
each frame a god to be jolted into life,
the powers that were and are
the whole history of this sad Kultur

BONE-MUSCLE

HAND & HYLE, ASCENDING: Narrative Track

*'THUS ALBION SAT, STUDIOUS OF OTHERS IN HIS PALE DISEASE,
BROODING ON EVIL ...'*

HAND & HYLE, shards
of Sumer, washed ashore
178 Vallance Road;
beyond the brick fields
to build a crimson-lake dynasty
of iron & blood knuckles

'dividing the space of love with brazen compasses'

HAND & HYLE, their disguise: sons
dutiful & hating women
who could trap
and bring forth children, their own assassins

'preferring unnatural lust to normal practice'

HAND & HYLE, damaged, kundalinic,
swallowing the serpent
down to magmatic halls
coupling with beasts
in fire-orgies of mud & slaughter

'at will contracting into worms or expanding into gods'

nerves aflood with molten metals
hog faced, shaved, order
the ghetto run on closed rails

Spieler opens its throat
the Voodoo Chile voices push them over

'aggression can be generated by material scarcity – anxiety by accelerating social change – psychological tension by contradictions between economic power & status'

cooked, the zygotic drama
twin ribs break
uniform heredity pattern

the way back is savage, & quite outside
the protection of any library

to recognise self
under this cowl of flesh
who is which is who

the structure of the head
is become a helmet
                red shift: as
face drags against the enfolding lips,
forward, last supper
at the Old Horns, Bethnal Green

beside the slatted barn,
gearpoint
in the nest of corpuscular magnetism

just beyond the geomantic limit
of the projected, the floating basilica

6 am arrest: cardiac

climb the hill

the breadknife goes in below the eye
opens the stomach
through the windpipe into the carpet

flesh disposal, ritual feasting

'A BUILDING OF ETERNAL DEATH, WHOSE PROPORTIONS ARE ETERNAL DESPAIR'

the stone vest no protection
Hand's cutlass slashes through
Hyle picks his spot
and breaks a knuckle
the light is in
room built vortex
no defence crack window
the hat falls Hyle's knife
grinds against the shaft of bone
where the eye-fish rests
no protection but it does connect
the buildings are bolts in this vest
only a giant can wear it
and bear the pain

'SOUTH STOOD THE NERVES OF HIS EYE'

nobody has spoken yet; Hand
will never speak. Hyle can whisper
   you may
tap his throat: the cards
are vibrating softly
                 as he moves.
it is not all despair, Horus
   finger to lips
marks the corners of the door.

the dome of the station
is comfort to many; particularly
those who are passing through
'*proleptic,*' said one,
              of the taxis.
the dry mailbags are stacked here
like artificial sheep,
& these are mummified by the pulsing
electric heat
          of the shape of this building:
by the frequency of the light strips:
by the funeral-bar songs of tape.
   no human voice:
not struck upon bone or skin.
it is a music to soften death
for those who await a planting.

the canvas over the gravehole
is an unerected tent,
expecting the faint excitement
of a corpse lay; the excusable
blush of worm bulbs.

heat is minimal. we have to think it.

'HE FORGED HIS HEAD & TAUGHT HIM TO READ THE LETTERS THAT ARE INSIDE'

Hand & Hyle at home

theta-driven
never knew the alpha waves

the blue spill

learnt from the ferocity of plants,
not living under the natural canopy
but keeping caged & potted specimens
in hot window corners
where they gave off a surly poison
      of hate,
a tangle of solar lusts.

'affected Plantations of venomous Vegetables'

doted, like Cato, upon the cabbage

then hit the dice & came up with indeterminate meanings

     one sequence ran:

ACE/ACE/ACE/QUEEN JACK/ACE/ACE/QUEEN/QUEEN/JACK
ACE/KING/QUEEN/JACK/NINE/ACE/ACE/JACK/TEN/TEN
ACE/KING/QUEEN/JACK/JACK/ACE/KING/JACK/JACK/NINE
ACE/KING/KING/TEN/NINE/ACE/ACE/QUEEN/QUEEN/QUEEN
ACE/ACE/JACK/TEN/TEN/ACE/KING/QUEEN/QUEEN/QUEEN
KING/KING/KING/QUEEN/JACK/KING/KING/JACK/JACK/TEN
ACE/JACK/ JACK/TEN/NINE/ACE/KING/KING/KING/NINE
ACE/ACE/KING/QUEEN/TEN/ACE/KING/JACK/TEN/TEN
JACK/JACK/NINE/NINE/ACE/ACE/ACE/KING/JACK
KING/TEN/TEN/TEN/NINE/KING/QUEEN/QUEEN/TEN/NINE

strange rituals for a potential mass murderer

(1) 'voices'; the hole (or plague pit)
(2) church pinnacle electro magnetics
(3) mesmerism, Borley Rectory
(4) table-tapping, Conan Doyle
(5) Besant, Ouspensky
(6) Peak District oracles
(7) West African sacrifice cults, wind worship

consulting the scapula in flame
as a map of action

the dots & cracks as it splinters
marking out the sacred places

'he was now past the healthful Dreams,
of the Sun, Moon, & Stars in their Clarity
& proper Courses. 'Twas too late to dream
of Flying, of Limpid Fountains, smooth
Waters, white Vestments, & fruitful green
Trees, which are the Visions of healthful
Sleeps, & at good distance from the Grave'

'DUPES'

Kotope: the Knitwear Anagram

'A Jew stole the grail the first time
And a jew died into it
That is the history of Britain'
          Jack Spicer: *THE HOLY GRAIL*

Kotope was thick with self-love
(despair, despair)
and when that was used & exhausted?

          the City, wealth
a casting of high diseases

defiant ghost pornographies
accosted his office-hour meditation,
unclean beast defilements bringing no correction;
humble clerk, with savage ambitions,
odeon land-dreams, born in the half dark,
the moon a bruise in his waistcoat
(control, control)
not easily expurgated, or worn down
they walk towards him, stretching
that cage of lines
they brand his forehead
(Cain's blood)
he suffers at his desk in man-made fibres

Kotope will climb above this
potential salesman, quits
the Road; chained to his room
& Mare Street Public Library

discovers the priapic masturbator godhead,
prophet, holy fire cockshot,
stuck with run of belly beard, gilded, rears
into folds & blind rushes, oracular woundings,
one of his own tribe, inspired publicist:
is led further – to Peachey

cabalistic secrets of power
THE FRUSTRATION OF DESIRE
hold it in check, inflame it, work it,
until the spring breaks loose
in some totally unpredictable quarter

(cell burst, trembling pavements)

he writes letters ('Forgive me for troubling you,
Dr Jung, but I have been thinking about what you meant
when you said ...'); wields an empire
of celestial velvet, lightweight
suits, mohair madness
of morning telephones, Fair Isle conspiracies

(Hokhmah, Father Adam betrayed)

'Mammon, the least erected Spirit'

KOTOPE: down the Clerkenwell corridor

'This art also visits the houses of merchants. They too can be found ascribing their successes in trade to the magicians, but reverses to ... failure to make all the proper sacrifices.'

Philostratus: THE LIFE OF APOLLONIUS

'What about Cathars?'

the question is slanted
across a brown & gold video-playtank

his bearded assistant's preserved smile
ruins his skeleton:
this deformity grinds beyond the grave

the wool-sweat Magus, tame poet-man, gasping, brow-mopping,
wreathed in pipe smoke, illusions, smouldering, skull on fire,
brandishes the fortune-casting coins,
takes the Book of Changes from the shelf,
feeds the fish & waits for the weekly envelope

'ON THE PAYROLL': shivering, corrupted sleep

Wilson, a philosopher of the keyhole,
comes forward from Cornish exile;
turkey smirk, a ferrotype, clubman,
knitted claw of tie:
                    'MAN WILL BE GOD'
evolutionary rocket theory,
man stretching to discover his potential

(shakti) the worm rises,
a good theory for worms

the court is at quest, witnessing
'unbelievable' guidance of the hand,
surely not random,
searching for the link
                    Pound/Cathars
that place? Mont Ségur

no reference Davie *('Ezra Pound: Poet As Sculptor')*
no reference Dekker *('Sailing After Knowledge')*
must be Kenner, no alternative,
flip open the great black book itself
& immediately confront:

'O Anubis, guard this portal
            as the cellula, Mont Ségur.
Sanctus
                that no blood sully this altar'

Kotope is not amazed, that smile,
the head turning,
minions have to react: awe
a magician,
this is it, & Anubis too
the jackal-headed one,
guardian of the mysteries
so lightly approached

for Wilson a simple matter:
mind discovering its power potential,
what you need you get;
for Kotope, the Way

'The four altars at the four coigns of that place,
But in the great love, bewildered
            farfalla in tempesta
under rain in the dark'

for the servants a Master

                        rediscovered

we must begin again: ROCK-DRILL

cross-section of the tree

the truth

grains of the Light
coming from under water

Kotope is forgotten, a messenger boy

mastery wounds the word;
it would be as great a thing
to read fully as to write fresh,
getting it down does not complete the process

Kotope is not amazed,

                        Wilson is not amazed,

the awe is our own

the old ones have been there, they have
suffered, & they said it

time is a fish bone, regurgitated,
the god plan,
                  we will surely
never become the god that Wilson claims

bend time & spring out
                      with the arrow

it ends as it begins

parachute down into the blue, the marble the sand
'if you go any faster you'll stop'

stop dead, split: the difference

II

Kotope, in fear, plunges through ancient systems,
his Rolls Royce Corniche cruises the eastern city,
climbs the path of hedgerow cures
with the window locked,
the heater fanning his ankle hairs

Saffron Hill to Herbal Hill
(spectre of Chatterton)
the domes of the city
                    hump him,
a spine running south from the Angel:
Penton Mound, Merlin's Cave,
                              Percival Street,
St John Street, Old Bailey, The Temple

crusade routes & masonic handshakes
cross-grip of bandage
fires of Smithfield
(the mould in the ground, the trapdoor)
retained slow drip of architect power

Mitre Court, Rahere,
St Bartholomew's Hospital

these enclosures relating back once more
to St Cross & Winchester

'mysteries
            that made my heart
too small to hold its blood'

(know that they did locate the Grail,
that it was here & the stones are flushed with it;
the septic water of Holy Well cellars
        prepares the pilgrim
before he moves out West, to where the Grail came from
& was again:
                lifting, crown over Warminster, Bodmin,
disguised as sighting, in floating dull-sky moisture,
        seen only when gone,
retrospective seizure of nostalgic terminals)

but this is all too specific
too active for Kotope

what he requires is something
that can be folded
to fit the pocket without a bulge

the truth is kept for the few

who speaks to the Great Publick
speaks to me

Kotope's movements are erratic & fear
sets in east of the money line,
say, Southampton Row/Kingsway, even perhaps
east of Charing Cross Road & Watkins Bookshop;
        original memory plasm
lurks in fur shadows, eighties pogroms,
soft-core sentiment for childhood's ghetto, bountiful visits

curtail the past, spurn city food
no smoke, no dope, no booze,
senses deranged by their own appointment

'What about Gurdjieff?' 'Steiner?'
'Castaneda?' 'Eliade?' 'John Michell?'
'Borges?' 'Black Holes?' 'Guirdham?'

to speak is not to know:

'DON'T SAY IT'

Kotope stares at the lowlife,
a jugular twitch, something dirty
is under his nails:
he arranges for a small assassination
stays at home a week
& orders a pouch of Tibetan chants
a hand-set story by DH Lawrence
reissues a necrophile novel
sells a corduroy jacket, with matching boots

but under it, the obvious
mantle of paranoid tremble & rush,
is some peculiar blade of accuracy,
self-proclaimed Zen Master dishing out
    sharp lessons,
re-aligning the collapsed Dunn's hatters
(by Secret Pyramid Mensuration)
so that they flee into gardens & harsh
sessions of ego-murder, so that
they turn face to the naked weather

'I am the joker'

and using, is used; whose own ego
must burn on:
        invisible crabs
bite at his spine; invaded
the game is bitter
        Kotope cannot withdraw

Hand & Hyle are waiting, it is
their city also;

THE GOOD FRIENDS

fronts St Anne's, Limehouse,
the Meths-men cluster around the car;
he feeds the rusty mouth,
        the book-dealers,
the moth meat, they will not protect him;

beggars block his exit,
                        they revenge themselves
with unspeakable psychic head-locks

they change shape & place
with seagull & rat, no street is safe

Kotope in his wife's bedroom,
black anger, the children knocking at the door,
volvuline domestic estrangements

Peachey revenges himself, he will not die

how to find the path again, the Tao

no way, the gates close in his face

Ludgate, Newgate, Aldersgate, Cripplegate,
Bishopsgate, Aldgate,
carnage & mutilation at Moorgate

death is east, a sullen sky,
vision falls to the west,
dying sun is hooded, forbidden

Hand & Hyle triumph

to the crow, the spoils;
to the maggot the fat pickings of Empire

lepers in Chinese tweeds, syphilitic denims;
racks of cellophane whip literature
replace the Sufi scrolls; the watered miniatures
twist in back room bestiaries

the back of the Hand: exile

Kotope, The Manner of his Dying:
Six Arabs on the Doorstep

Sunday Morning:
                    the White Jacket
cargo cult servants
                         are locked out,
vitamin breakfast tray
already overlaid with full colour supplements;
    the au pair
has deserted misty Mill Hill Park
for the empathy buzz of speeding Northway Circus

temporary migrants spin north,
                                   the fun seekers
hit town from St Albans & Welwyn Garden City,
in quest of THE TEXAS CHAINSAW MASSACRE & purple hearts

Kotope himself, in kimono, opens the door
& is facing the air, the grit flung by traffic,
star dirt, grass odour,
lowlife in all its manifold disguises

    his assassins
they are changing from the ragged pyjama-
wearing barefoot WILD BOYS out of Burroughs,
open sores on their faces, insect souls, hungry
with knives & glass tubes to insert in his ears,
into 6 Arabs in flower shirts & synthetic beagling tweed
taken from his own shops,
                           carrying bren guns,
Czech armament, howitzer, Mao book

      and Kotope
at that minute crystal particle of time
divides his attention into myriad thousand
scattered fragments,
                    his roman candle consciousness
examines the detail of this encampment,
                             walls,
curbs, pillar boxes, florists, hedges, bugs,
stains the low clouds, smears the telescope
of Will Hay's observatory, slides the matter
of his rapidly declining intelligence
down the cusp of the dome:
                    his will
erects one final, animal, vision of the city,
his body its body, flying,
& is gone, thickens the carbon sheath,
                       melts
the Polar ice by one fraction of a degree

as the Arabs disappear,
                fade
into shrub & path, the ascended colours gone
      that his fear
was only able to conjure this sole & singular time

Peachey: The Page of Wands, Reversed

'He hath leagued himself with robbers:
he hath studied the arts'

Peachey, the hit man,
shifts into pamphlets

(a ring of mountains about him)

his head-world so heavy
arm bends
falls through
the spatulate bones of his hand

an x-ray delicacy;

like the braiding
on an hussar's tunic, worn aloud

bowel movements
were the only clock he could trust
& ran progressively slower
as his diet thinned
to goat's milk & diabetic chocolate;
suffered the hammer
of phenylethylamine migraines

sponsored by Kotope's Menswear Mafia
(stone-eye telephone, speaks fish to the Wool Exchange,
buys imagery, dead power lines)
this stick-wielder, extended into blackthorn,
alludes to arcane practices
is reprinted in Regent Street, in glass
in coffee chrome, overheated
(to febrile convulsion); obeys the bugle

a violent trailer
reeling & burning between the skin layers

despairing Optographer

Peachey had studied the Coffin Texts
been early upon the Mountain
chanted THE HYMN TO OSIRIS, for his revival

Ah Helpless One
Asleep where I have found you
lying upon one side
Great Listless One
whose name cannot be written
let me lift your heart
your bones will I knit together
an end to woes
and end to sleep's heaviness
life's flame climbs through your feet
moisture mounts with your spirit
I have kindled you
Live Great One
let the sleeper rise
it shall be my house that avenges you
Horus will avenge you
Thoth shall protect you
your powers will again be visible in the skies
you will cause havoc among the gods
your father joins me
he calls out 'Come'
Live Nameless One
let the sleeper rise from his chamber
take up again the bull's proud helmet
let the scattered one be whole

it could not rest there; Hand praised him,
Hyle was not slow in honouring him with gifts;
the Old Ones were reverenced, the drum
made moist with the blood of virgins

at the 'Double R' steps forth Atum,
creator of the eldest gods,
malachite green Master of the Fires,
who moves through the space
between two serpentine circles, turning

he also was Peachey's familiar
steps forth in the smokelight, announcing

I am Atum, creator of the eldest gods
I am he who gave birth to Shu
I am the great He/She
I am he who did what seemed good to him
I took my space in the place of my will
mine is the space of those who move
like those two serpentine circles, turning

Peachey sweats in malarial excitement;
his confession, the inaccurate
study of the texts, the awkward translations,
sees Hand as Atum, wishes to raise his spirits,
miscalculated miles & centuries,
released the half-animate flood of demons
the cat-headed boygirls,
    the storm clouds,
cumulo-nimbus over the Chair of Idris,
frowns in horror as they drift east
to the pinnacles of the City
                  to Tower Hill,
the unsleeping eye of the cauldron

Atum speaks plague on the followers of Peachey

on the Wilsons, Sprague de Camp, Hesse,
on the Blakean publicists, the boudoir astrologers,
'the Taozer babbling of the Elixir,' Amis,
Gog garglers, Ripper tourists, transvestite druids,
zoo builders, Campden Hill tantriks,
Avebury photographers, stone thieves

may locusts fall on their heads

(about Powys JC – he reserved judgement)

horrible things, he whispered, in revenge
for the planners of Golgonooza

(Hawksmoor – he excepted)

thus spoken, it became

but not all ; the tide, the diluted
sallow seed-wind of Atman secret Masonry
seeps out, is given, attention to the natural

removed from Newton's atomic chamber, calculation
the big flash, elsewhere, ignored

'The spiritual is all in Whitehead's simplest of all
statements: Measurement is most possible
throughout the system. That is what I mean.
That is what I feel all inside. That is what is love.'

man measures his own span in the ground
Peachey died singing

HAND & HYLE: DECLINING

'THEY DRINK REUBEN & BENJAMIN AS THE IRON DRINKS THE FIRE: THEY ARE RED HOT WITH CRUELTY, RAVING ALONG THE BANKS OF THAMES ...

Hand's irrational
                 fear of yellow socks
the mustard optimism
scrambles up his nerves

(spews fear)

short-circuit emotions
flagellate his haemorrhoids

always the grey suiting,
the dark socks,
coal-blacked shoes & hair,
polished equally,
scalp & feet: a horror white

but he did, love & fuck
       the pigment
of assorted headless bodies

tipped & insulted red-eyes
glow like coals of revelation

macabre décor:
the sofas puffed lemon
with the scented musk
of departed occupants

(Peace Maddipal Incense)

the ceilings splashed with shadows
(the dead talk, the dead gossip)
from coalite fire operas;
Gordons gin bottles, chicken sandwiches,
the racing page, binoculars
in a pigskin case
(like the 1922, privately printed, '7 Pillars of Wisdom')
no love, this man, for sun colours

& wore gloves of softest calf's belly
so that he should not be left without thumbs
in the ghost country
so that he could still cock
his well-oiled Smith & Wesson

'the politics of the world of spooks
is as random as
that of a Mesopotamian kingdom'

for Hand – more so

'INTO THE VORTEX OF HIS WHEELS, THEREFORE
HYLE IS CALLED GOG'

the astra mantra: **PHAT!**

as the cat spits
so spat his woman
upon Hyle

she was mated soon
with the worm

another mounted ghost for Chingford

'THE VEGETATED MORTAL EYE'S PERVERTED & SINGLE VISION'

and that twitter came through
his phantom deaf-aid,
the crow chorus of the dead

ancestral voices, crossed wires,
the soundbox bruises his chest

these are thunder beings, black clouds,
& should not be here
their shoes conceal iron hoofs
gods of Sumer, sealed gods
of the night river,
                          the unassimilated
animal part;
                  claws under gloves,
bolts in the brain, mechanical
& superhuman, strength
                              like a curse

this is not courage,
a rictal malfunction
that scares the breakfast
out of all acquainted citizens

'they went without shields,
& were mad as dogs
or wolves, & bit on their shields,
& were strong as bears or bulls;
men they slew, & neither fire
nor steel would deal with them;
& this is what is called
the fury of the berserker'

a bulb of mana over their heads
hovering, butterfly of pestilence,
disease-phial, unbroken, hanging
in the breath of their mouth
the foul compote of broken razor blades,
vaseline, offal, sheepshead soup,
copydex, panatella, gammon
the breath he exchanged
with his lovers, the street boys, day release
art school greasers, back passage punks
a 500 watt fear, crackling,
surgical spirit drips
from his tuber, his gearing,
the coarse-skinned onion heart,
glittering snow crystal

fumigate with juniper & corpse candles

'a peachy, clotted tide of sound,
gurgling back into the viscous shallows'

'TO JUSTICE BEFORE HEAVEN HERE UPON LONDON STONE'

arrested despair, pre-dawn thinning
of blood in its chamber, sleep cycle slowing

scorpic clyster, crabs on a sea bed of
shale & sponge-rubber, foam
on the tongue, heated fast breathing;
car tyres, the long shadow of St Luke's needle
administers the Stemetil, the Largactyl,
the Valium, Depixol, Disipal, Mogadon, Warfarin

this calming panic, locking ram by horns to cuckold;
together on the couch of their father's loving

the disguised Rovers hauling in asphalt
smoke wheel, the blue, circle of seizure
cancels breath, bands the neck
Bunhill Row Flats, they are taken,
a splintering of early morning light,
the scorpion scuttles back into grave-mulch
the tattoo escapes from the ankle,
white stain flinches from
                              the leather'd touch
of Crime Squad's Tintagel tooling

the width of relief, a new road opening

*'IN SELF HOOD HAND & HYLE APPROPRIATE
THE DIVINE NAMES, SEEKING TO VEGETATE THE DIVINE VISION
IN A CORPOREAL & EVER DYING VEGETATION & CORRUPTION
MINGLING WITH LUVAH IN ONE, THEY BECOME ONE GREAT SATAN'*

prepuce-waistcoated, Hand himself
acquiring potency in the end,
talismanic & withered, red pairings
of his lovers taken
by Hand, non-verbal,
gloating, full-pocketed:
sucked for their salts of preservation

walks his territory
marking the boundary stones
as dogs do

Whitecross Place, Sun Street,
Apold Street, Pindar Street

the old power connections

Wilson Street

late-century messianic spasms

reels-in the Blake skein
the Ripper Museum, Bunhill Fields

Orsman Road (B.M. Ethnography Store
of Totem Poles, Ju-Ju, blood-soaked clay)

Whitmore Road, Hoxton Street, the Latter-Rain Outpourings Revival

Green Man, birth-place, vegetable tunnel
and the magnetism jolts through
the spinal nobs, a hair-burning shiver
from the paving slabs
into the feet, an ice warning

Hercules Road, Baylis Road, the Cut, Borough
High Street, Newcomen, Snowsfield, Druid Street,
Tower Bridge, the Minories, Mitre Square,
Houndsditch, St Botolph, Gravel Lane, Wentworth Street,
Old Montague, Durward, Hanbury, Old Dorset,
Spitalfields, Lamb, Quaker, Code, the Earl Grey,
Green Gate, Blade Bone, Old Horns

of the Stars ground by his heel
(Billy Daniels, Sonny Liston, Lord Boothby)
in sand
at the ditchpoint
where the current flows fastest

to consult the oracle of the streets

black ooze of buildings
floods his eye

shadow draughts over the city
hills disappear under stone derivations

the light even now
burns through the skin holes

the egg of protection
penetrated by light tendrils
of other exiles

out of the range: 380/760 milli-microns

the dead have settled into the walls
(Nag's Head)
the empty chairs are occupied

a mouse gnaws the cigarette
that nobody has abandoned

the grey ones hang in cellars
hover over underground dug-outs

autograph the walls & sepulchres
chalk hopes for eternity

fog is pouring from his nose,
Hand is walking death

'HAND & HYLE CONDENSE THE LITTLE-ONES & ERECT THEM INTO
A MIGHTY TEMPLE EVEN TO THE STARS; BUT THEY VEGETATE
BENEATH LOS'S HAMMER, THAT LIFE MAY NOT BE BLOTTED OUT.'

VICTIMS

SLADE & THE TYRANNICIDES

'I once heard that John Dillinger's cock was in the Smithsonian'
NO ONE WAVED GOODBYE: a Casualty Report on Rock & Roll

From the peak, from the purpling cabbage-leaf frenzy of god cloud, moving down, & close, voluntarily abandoning the detached patrician levitation of viewpoint: it is through the eye of the scryer we see the event, darkly, peaty milk thinning in the lens; long ago, it is happening. The blood-veins at stretch, frozen sap erecting the tree fringe.

Feast of Purification, February 1, sacred ground, ridged & hard, crust seals the earth heat behind Waltham Abbey: prepared ground, marked ground. The white emanations of the corpse of Harold, battle-felled, Earl-King, Harold Godwinsson, bitter in his crude empiric of survival, in his gaunt mythology of chainmail, skull stripped as if by parasites, he shines like a chalk saint. The thin shaft in his eye-socket is the periscope we use; root tendrils & fine hairs feather the wood, lift towards the informing sun. The ash-scalded tip presses on his brain nerve: the feather has flowered. Autopsy of linked metals, corrosion, treachery, foresworn impulses of wrist, water hand, error of history enters the chronicle, vows taken upon false bones: the rat sanctified. Harold's leather helmet is the invisible tent in which the meet is arranged, foretold.

What Arthur is to the WEST Harold is to the EAST: his acts an unclaimed leprosy, shifting yellow to brown, red to blue, purple to green, fungoid poison-cultures in the ground, white alkali, rings of expanding decay. The alignment of these two mythical graves, burial places of the twin'd heroes, saviours of the compass, 'A' & 'H', spear-crowned or gate-stanced giants, these gravel beds of english soil, mark the limits, pin down a force-field: Glastonbury to Waltham Abbey, where the light is born, where the light dies. Traps for the unwary, map-references for the unbodied spirits, victims of ego falter, hurdled blade-men. Partially-roused syntax of the planchette board, stuttering in Streatham, or dragged out into the veiled lamplight, civet infested parlours of West Acton. Vegetable shadows of Kensal Rise fall across bed-sitting-room tables; as Arthur Machen discovered, no escape from the maze of selfhood.

But now, by slow flume, by Lea River, has Slade abandoned his weapon: in marsh grass. Lonely snaking stride out of his cantref, the moulded plastic boots scratched by thorn, the overcoat heavy with burs; away from the buildings, north, risk, towards the Fen place, the death plains of electro-magnetism, generated among the stone teeth at Land's End, the surf force & tide rhythm, to decay among brackish waters circling Ely Cathedral, pus in the dragon's eye. Slade under the hoop of low clouds, hunched & melancholy. His morbid doubts, diet of cheap fats. A dim sun fear balances the throbbing hard red pulse of his meat. 'It stands up like a mast'; his scarlet sex horse. His constant purple-headed lodestone. By the compass of his prick he can walk one direction only, north, to pole star, magnetic, dragged: into maelstrom, into suicide, into convulsive therapy. Mind unoccupied his cock jerks like a dowser's rod, springs upward with such force as to bruise his chest, 'beaten as black as lead'. And this is his response to landscape, violent: snatching. His pride cements his fear: already they are coming at him, he has made them manifest. The Titanic Mob from Nile Road & the Sabinis from Clerkenwell, the Krays, & the Richardsons from over the water, Jack Comer (aka 'Spot'), Billy Hill, the Tibbs Family & the Nichols, the Upton Park Mob, the Nashes. Voodoo gangs, packs, savage for territory, for land space, skull space, for the sealed passageways of the labyrinth, for ox heat. They run at each other, wolves without heads, animals rolling towards the fire, claws tearing out flesh, gouging for eye, belly, fur, pelt. Cannibal impulse shifted into dynamite, paint-stripper on white Mercedes, docker's hook & seven-pound hammer. Metal toe-cap flashing sparks in pub yard. Lead-filled hosepipe in the car park. Torso on river mud. Forty-eight numbered segments of the body scattered, forty-eight cuts, a single vitalising sentence. The stars splashed with blood, the stars are swallowed teeth.

They took Slade & broke the bones of his hand. This was on the landing, outside his door. He fixed on the design of the handle: a shell. Steel pins were inserted after they had delivered him to the hospital. His hands are spiders made from the ruin of a black-out umbrella. No word: the direction of his compass unbent. They slid a sawn-off shotgun into his trouser leg, half-comic like a ferret joke, & blew away the flesh of his calf, the muscle, missing the target, shooting blind. A scatter of pellets he still carries, affecting his personal magnetism.

The scryer falters, ad libs, goes onto automatic pilot, repeating the familiar heroic elaborations of his tale. He is hooded, in pursuit, of the

Hare of the East, of Slade: gauss-pulse racing, sick in belly – in pursuit of language. Counter needle hits red. Pursuit of moon's curve, finely smoothed orbit, inconsistent wobble. Running out, of air. Cold hands. As if held in invisible water trays. Staggering blind between narrowing ditches. The wriggled & excavated snake path. But the track is cold. Slade's power is his lack of passion. Primed, but dead. He is sad, but he is not angry. The pursuit is despair. Do not call it suicide. It is the mere act of following a track, an odour. He sniffs the ground, pokes among dry dog turds for evidence of the great beast's journey, for some bright fur patch, an illumined stool metamorphosed into rock totem or mile-stone. Disease halts the will so that time flashes. These are his insights. Look down.

Between two river tongues Slade is walking; his curve flatters the clock. The sky lengthens, a yawn. Ribs of cloud support this cage over Hackney Marshes. Slade. Whose pride is a silent thing, whose will pushes him into the cone of chance. He is as stupid as a tragic hero, though not as tall; he recognises no aspect of himself that he can alter. Believes in pre-destination & the Police Force. His foot has been set on the long bridge to suicide headlines in THE EAST LONDON ADVERTISER. A weapon is purchased, & carried hard, but it will not serve. This is what is meant by stupidity. He did not recognise the futility of duplicating his personal totem. Nobody carries a metaphor who is one already. Erect & standing. One letter from the protein alphabet. A key of brass. This is too facile & is opposed by his blood system as it flows in the reversed direction. Impotence. World picture fragmented. Slade tosses the obstruction into the dark water. Dozmary Pool by Enfield Lock. An hermaphrodite arm rises to catch the polythene-wrapped bundle. Woman's hair like sea weed, slime-covered shoulders. Slade feels his shaft dig. He stands in the expanded calm of false spring morning. The light rolls in from the east, tree-bruised. Wind with bitter channel taste of sea. Invader breath. Compass blade stabs his liver. Slade reclining on Harold's tomb, waiting. Circles of excited magnetism run through the ground, trap him.

Thermal headaches, the mouse frozen in his skull. Cargo is self-delivered for judgement. Slade waits on his fate, an extra. His will cannot run, his spine stiffens as the damp rises.

The grail wash of Tennyson's beard surrounds him on all sides, the lapsing inert glide of solar winds; dust decay of Rosicrucian ideal forms a ghostly aura, or ectoplasmic bowl, around his head. Hoops of candlelight limp out from Slade to the water & the forest, to be received at Borley Rectory.

Steiner approves. Overhead is the well-documented UFO track, SW/NE, frantic as the Heathrow pentagram: the operation of sound, air released to the frequency of 'M-E-R-S-E-A'; which Slade reads, accurately, as 'Mercy', the Whitechapel word – final mystery & attainment of Sir William Gull's room.

So the sitings fade beyond Thorpe-le-Soken & sink into tidal mud at Mersea Island, flickering lights along deserted roads. Whirring spiral gyres above the recumbent victim. Myrrh Sea, initiatory Magi gift, resin. Merde Sea, waste sludge of salt dyke, haunt of coypu. Mixing. Inland gulls hover for industrial scraps: but the celestial wound passage is opened & Slade reads the history of his own death.

The Tyrannicides arrive.

Inside the enclosed tropic car heat, fans blowing out essence of jackal, chicken feathers, red mud, Olduvai bone fragment, is the oracular head of Alfredo Garcia: a whisper in fly swarm, in Muscat sand, in the swift tongues of decomposition. Excess of wisdom has made them mad; has dyed the skin, tanned them the colour of saddle leather. Dead meat is changed into sound, dense insect squabble, speaking in tongues. Their blood is malarial fast, Livingstone palor, shivering, brandy & salt tablets: Hand & Hyle, brass-knuckled Tyrannicides.

The head is also the enclosed nuclear box, chest of desert secrets uncovered by Ralph Meeker at the end of KISS ME DEADLY, when the last, what remains of, the grail impulse in its most corrupted form, greed, triumph, curiosity, springs the lid, releases the power; the voice cone inverts, mushroom suck of indrawn breath over poison ocean, howl of torture camp roars into metaphor, lion beast heat, flame mane, Babylon; the siren speaks all destruction, all the images of sudden death, violent knowledge. This white truth is strapped with leather thongs, with sturdy clasps of brass, into Reich's accumulator. It rides like the scrolls of the prophets, like an ark hidden by migrant tribes. Or is it simply a sack of muslin through which Garcia's profile prints like an identikit relic, like the Templar Christ, like penal colony maps? An L Ron Hubbard pyramid disaster key of earthquake & plague that will destroy the Universe by introducing a new concept of time? Is it the final tongue of brass torn from the Serpent?

It rests on Hyle's lap. It speaks the whole *Cantos* of Ezra Pound, including the false starts, & the Roman broadcasts, Martian Hymns, the Kabbalah, Gregorgian chants, death songs of defeated Plains Indians, stock exchange quotations, Presley's first cut for Sun Records, Northumbrian pipes –

everything reduced, squeezed, synthesized to one finite buzz. And then it is locked, sealed, clamped: this is the power beneath Hand. This is why the earth scorches AHEAD of the limousine, the skid-path advances, runs out like a water spray in front of the cross-ply radials & is obliterated, dissolves, as the car passes: invisibility.

The door swings open like a safe, out step the Owners in masks of scalped pig, blood-crowned Hand & Hyle; in their own hot wind, the sting of Africa. Rhino horn attached to forehead. Fly whisk. They are enclosed in personal sandstorms, furious vortex: questions, accusations are latent, unspoken.

The tragedy cannot get into gear. The Miracle Play remains a potential, without text. The craftsmen are absent. The audience is distanced, complacent; egoic attention, half-hearing, repulsed by syntactic crudities. It does not touch them.

But the speed: from car to Slade is frenzy, garbled rush of Orphic Mysteries, messenger who cannot get the speech performed in the allowed interval. Kings do not speak or move. Hand & Hyle float on wooden platforms. Peachey is the voice of Hyle. The act of Hand is Hutton. An axe rests on his slanting shoulder.

The summoned acknowledged gods are hidden in septic cloud. Crocodile bear & tiger float through the storm. 'Mercy'. A carpet spread on the church roof for the Judges. A pit appearing in the ground, maw of Hell, for the Devils. Hand & Hyle drifting in dim skies are mistaken for Mersea UFOs. Policemen fall from their bicycles.

The wash of this unachieved event stains Essex. Sawdust tableaux infinitely repeating: the pest hand rises from murky waters to receive the arc of the abandoned revolver, the oiled metal, the caves of incubation that revolve, bullet projectiles sleeping. The focus of Slade's genital pride freezes action. Nothing happens, but Essex is cancelled. Slade's murderous double sets foot for Braintree.

HUTTON: Missing, Presumed Dead

Text: Hutton, mad samurai, a prisoner on the Moor, is allowed a measure of freedom; runs down the stone avenues, folds into the culture of barrow & cairn, an immediate, unsuspected, sympathy. Is taken away, released by 'friends', by Hand & Hyle, as token of their power. Kept in a room at the margin of the City. Driven to the riverside, killed.

Counter-Text (Daily Telegraph): 'The grisly discovery of 15 dead ponies at a remote Dartmoor beauty spot is baffling animal experts & has even led to theories that beings from outer space are responsible.

Mr Alan Hicks, an animal lover & pet-shop owner, who stumbled across the decomposing bodies, said yesterday: 'It was like finding an elephants' graveyard.'

Members of the Devon Unidentified Flying Objects Centre have been on the moor with geiger counters & metal detectors in their own bid to solve the riddle.

Their leader, Mr John Wyse, said: "We know lots of strange objects fly over Dartmoor. It seems to us that something frightened these animals & perhaps even killed them ... Horses & cattle have been found with bones smashed & bodies drained of blood."

Mrs Joanna Vinson said she had spent hours dissecting the putrefying carcasses, but could not offer any explanation.'

On the Moor, Emblems of Death

emblems, bones of death
        the muddy
flesh, knotted hair;
the god of the place crawls busily
        in & out
of the socket of the black eye
that isn't there
(the Raven's Fee)

Hutton running,
bruised feet on the flint track;
these tipped circles

the crow hovers
wired to the beat of
        his gun
(the vein in the victim's neck)

ah, the whole moor
                is heart

pumps, streams, scours

the weed

Hutton climbs; a wrecked car
        the twist,
                horns of death,
sharp teeth grin from the earth
meaning death, Hutton runs

hail beats on his back

Hutton is hollow, he has no weight
it is transferred to the wheeling sky

big lung clouds

breathing ribs, Hutton runs
beside the forest
his hairs cut

bone scalp
        itches for the earth-worm,
blessings of the dead

climbs, stone avenue
names of dead places,
source land, the rivers rise
mauve banks,
        the grey
fly is god, dying
          to live,
his motion visible, jerks,
the reverse illusion, anti-cinema,
apparently seamless,
          the static frames
splashed with ghost life

here the spasms are awkward,
mechanical, seen as
    'the hidden mystery'
invisible essence,
strategy of the immortals
who fed here
        two thousand years ago
on this same dead cow

the insect drinks from rainwater
in a buried horn,
feeds on plant & meat

Hutton's dim lamp
        spins against the clock
   returns,
some loose notion of companionship

Goemagot driven out,
                    the alien
      hill forms,
to the uplands from Totnes, in path of Invader

(the first bloody contracts)

fly leeches his wrist
a dripping clock of blood,
Hutton returns

beyond him the bee
                    hops hedges,
the farmer has his tangle of beans,
      red flower badges

the warm places, the clay pits

the glittering grasp,
the welcome
            of the sea
is a distance he does not sight,
      outrun by tides
he hardens through

through the gates, shadow clock falls
over his stiff shoulders
the blue of bad lungs,
                    varicose glow,
pitman bruises, translucent,
      lips drawn tight
(death photographs this colour)
lens fault, this inky tank

circles, resonances, sympathies;
      cobalt
blue as the whisper of a fly

seeing death is to die, carries it
the flies that fed upon dead meat
marry him, infect his blood
as he passes the unseen
carcass in fern, in peat ring
        the scattered ribs,
flies suck his back

he looks on,
                dead eye,
the virus of the dead word
is in his clothes
he traces the brickwork

with white finger,
                the deadman's eye
winks in the cell door,
sugar dissolved in water cocoa,
last year's *Playboy*,
('Oh, my grief, I've lost him surely')
gourmet wine list, body list, cocktail jazz
smell of glossy pages stuck with soap

the track of the moor is the time switch
older is bigger,
spurts light into scabby wool,
the dead sheep lies across his shaven chest plain
he does not hear,
                the sea reminds him
        rivers couple,
his death watches him from the bowl
of night long electricity,
        his switch
where moth papers beat & roll

the full moon is a torch upon the maggot's head
too bright, he cannot see
eats through the pores of the stone
the rigidly clamped lips

is an acid-etched
                print
of what is missing, a bone of instruction

        moon is a word
he has never, will never
                    speak

Pard to the Giants

Sheepstor:
           the death of death,
the migration of the giants
           Totnes
across the moor, wading up rivulets
wrapping in wool,
                       sheep carcass
against hail, mist on the heights
here they fell, here they remain

rock outcrops, Tor fears
           necks
scatters of boulder

old hard stone,
                       knuckle,
rib, knee, wrist, shoulder
           fall
blood darkens the earth
peat blood drains into swamp

rain on rain,
wade the Severn gash
into Gower the Welsh Uplands,
the procession

Hutton ran in brotherhood
bleak fellowship
that did not satisfy
but fed his sleep

teeth, the last to rot down
coated against soil acid,
                    bitter rain,
useless to hawk & wolf
adorned the cultivators
                    as treasure
as value, teeth on the stone
fish in the stone

outcrops on the Moor
where the old ones
                    fell
and the soft ground was washed away

Hutton gathers these ivory coins
strings them, polishes them
a recognition,
                    this life
          false
to Hutton, infirm
will becomes armoured in enamel
of future need

Hutton is a molar
in the side of
                    what is to be

'But the Moon struggled in vain to free herself, & at length she fell forward, spent with the struggle, & the black hood fell over her head again, & she had no strength to push it off. Then all the evil things came creeping back, & they laughed to think they had their enemy the Moon in their power at last. The Dead Folk held her, while the Bogles fetched a great stone to put over her, & when the day came the Moon was buried deep, until someone should find her, & who knew where to look?'

beware, as Hutton, beware
of the sunset moment
when disk slides under
        the moment
when world is at risk
as who should blink & open lid again
upon a whole new place

(the word 'new' is fear)

Hutton had no aesthetic
would not pause upon a rock
to watch sun drop

he ran, back within walls
in the low house of his brothers

impregnated with deaths
he had run past
                till his own
ending became tangible

and the guard dogs prickle
lift ear, growl, show teeth

on Hutton, wolf of the Dew Ponds;

skull under cairn
                shivers

Princetown inmates huddle against the last hour
they are satisfied by the routines of children's television
the strangling hands knot together
the varnish is picked from chair arm
the grey foam-rubber is exposed in the cushions

Hutton cannot see these images
they stick as bands of sick light
        cage his glare
he looks out through them
to the working heart of the machine
& is not soothed, as others are

American voices issuing from
crude animal drawings
are the Deities of Death

screech of manic Woodpecker, or
Top Cat is a figure from the Egyptian *Book of the Dead*,
Deputy Dog is Hierophant

Hutton bows to the imperious tone,
humbled by the gathered speak of mummified lights

he shuts his eyes on the wall
& it continues
the brick line extends to the horizon
the darkness is light in his sleep
his throat contracts on earth
that tastes of toadstools

beware, beware again
of the total embrace of water

as Hutton turns, the mist thickens
Plough & Serpent stars
connect with coded stones
the loose cairns are subterfuge
Hutton's geology
                           is the dream of Moorland,
the division of waters

brackish lure, sleep trap

Hutton penetrates the Royal Hill,
fills the Childe's Tomb with his rushes,
is received at Lud Gate,
through the Nine Stones into
Belstone Cleave

the wolves are solitary,
                              the crows
hold to acknowledged boundaries

city news dies in the wire

New Moon Retrospect

closed around them in darkness,
      ('& then the dark came on')
with him, hardened
clay waistcoat, a pebble his half-hunter
everywhere, with him
between him & the illumination of objects, grasses

Hutton banded since birth with this
so that he rolls out
the dew of unease, cause not remembered
not forgotten,
         'M-O-T-H-E-R'
was a stain in the skin of his forearm;
bruise blue
        ink of King's Cross
curtained tattoo parlour
'M-O-T-H-E-R': he stroked unconscious

the moors released him, maimed ellipse,
sways to the most natural
           outflow,
that was the trigger pressure
the black tie, needing to be cut away

dark of cell sets about him
he is the spine in a frozen block of sugared water

head hollow & heavy,
          elephant boned,
rubs against the walls

suckled by the moisture, of his own armpit

the whole throat of comfort, the low buildings
    morning anchorite
          jogs out

what he does not have is breech
in the fix of his vertical condition:
the head did not tilt, topple over,
engage,
      safely,
in the pelvic helmet
that dream blood could flow
with light with precious
reflecting stones, wines & rubies

     smeared then
against a wall of restraints
feel, barely,
a saline thread of necessity
earth gruel continuing all the way

stories of giants (himself);
blanched at the horror of treachery
low human deceit, 'good management',
Jack the Assassin & his
mealy-mouthed, grasping mother
      nothing but gold,
blanched at the executions of Saturn,
Satan, Serpentarius
             the old
the old ones, the old order of the planets

     horror, unspeakable child horror
at cruelties worked on solitary witches,
the routines of mammoth domesticity in cloud castles

not think of it, not recall
now, new moon, the red going
the bluey comforts, processional

the cloud is a jockey mounted
on a rabbit, is a rat pursuing,
stretches, & is not devoured
by Hutton's moderate consciousness
he does not fully claim what he sees
not *realise* not own
is without possession of himself
and thus of all others

toothmug, slop bowl, soap cake
are free in his presence;
not the greed of the author eye

is 'there' as the stones are

wants neither more nor less

only the spoke-holes of loving betray him
the first words of kindness
are sugared rats of destruction

what gave him warmth would burn him
till the brains boiled in his cup
till his finger nails were gnawed
till the maggots fattened in his cheek
and the crow took his tongue
till he was totally gone
into the condition of legend
flat, ironed out
no more than words on a page

no triumph; the arrogance of the satiated fly

Hutton: the Death

'streaming'; 'flowing boundary'
        weak pulse
of beating light in the van roof
our time mechanic is present, bears witness,
water perspiration down the side of the metal trunk
        boxed in
windows misted over; smoke

last meat devoured, take-away-curry
with thick jaundice skin & rubbery knuckles
chewed up, activates the clutch of belly

'struggled to tie his speech to words'
knew he was in the invitability of that rush
        (moon plumage)
seems to be headlong, the plunge
                                though windowless

is calm, no corners
'strain was so great that he shat
into the plastic bag they'd wrapped him in'
(as with the midnight purple force of birth)
the force from inside so great it shook them
the hole that opened in his neck
they disappeared into the chasm the van
sucked in, the earth kiss
like Janet Leigh's corpse car in PSYCHO, down
        off-set;
the corrugated corner of dockland is sliding
helplessly into the wound
waters burst, plug's gone

'a brown colour', 'no odour'

nails filling with curls of plasticised paint
(intimacy of tortured for torturer) down
wound is wider than Thames
                              swallows the mess
the butchered hesitations, the inhibited fantasies

Hutton gone, 'streaming'
a column of industrial rains over Wanstead

Chorus for the Shape of his Death

      'stiffs',
the horizontal ones
looking into the perished star heart
the stiffened dead
erect beyond exhaustions, passionless
beyond arousal;
the belly finger points up
into the moon, soured on the death essence
of slaughtered assassins
they have nowhere else to go
the full moon magnetic
sucks death out of the ghetto
the chosed chamber
(of the heart, revolver)
odourless, transmits

Hutton transmits, 'streams'
his death shout unuttered
cancels the cul-de-sac, plants marram grass
into the paving stone,
activates the wave of surrender
is again, unborn, a clay
                  ball of tongues
a venomous, expelled
                  gob of words
unachieved, unwelcome

Hutton the stiff one
revolves through cement mixer
      conglomerate
with flint & gravel, with sand-dredged aggregates
      tipped,
              born into the East Way Flyover
vertical above Lea Water, shoulder to Stratford
      face to the Marshes
a literal & continuing part of the City

we commute between the vast spread of his thighs

VICTIMS: an Appendix

Diversion; interlude; performance. CONCERT IN THE PARK mistakenly called 'FREE'; attended by its own rumours. Every breath has been sold & re-sold. The sky is predicted, divided into squares & the squares numbered. Check the chart, check your investment: media concessions, hamburgers, heroin, 'exclusives'.

They have not allotted space to the squatting ghosts of the ground, the crusty mould on the Suicide Tree:

It is a large sinister-looking Plane tree, covered with ugly growths on its trunk, & has a strange hole in its side about 12 feet from the ground. Beneath it runs the old Tyburn river. Its reputation dates from the early 18th century when many fatal duels were held beneath its wide-spreading branches. During the 19th century it became known for suicides, usually committed by hanging from the lowest branch. Michael Chambers

Hand Hyle & Kotope are present: vampire, vulture, & vamp to that maudlin vertigo, the spin, of artificial ecstasy powder that is very slowly, before their own eyes, turning into 'the real thing'. They are cased-up in 200 guinea armour plated mohair, wired for shock on contact.

Kotope has gathered a party around him, INN ON THE PARK, safely behind double-glazing, afternoon candles, high above the heads of the people. He has dressed up some shop-assistants, a rhabdomancer, a retired trade journalist, an art student, & a girl who hopes to revive Noël Coward. Champagne is handed around in disposable beakers. Kotope does not drink.

Hand & Hyle are in the Pyramid Room, perched above the erected ears of the giant Rabbit, the secret summit of the Playboy Club. From outside this apartment does not even exist: it is a miracle of linear juggling, a spatial distortion borrowed from Dr Caligari. The greedy eye comes to accept its own presumptions.

This room is reserved for the Owners, & the owners of the Owners: 'Mafia' will not go near to naming these powers or the masks, the ridges of dead rubber, that they wear. The names move around the planes of the wall, unguided stars, a planetarium light show eaten into the cornice with volatile acids ... WARNER BROTHERS ... CIA ... WATERGATE ... ONASSIS ... KREMLIN ... SINATRA ... CAESAR ... CAPONE ... AKBAR ... MOSES ... AMENOPHIS ... QUETZALCOATL ... CTHULHU ... CROWLEY. Mortuary tableaux: Louis B. Mayer in rut with the crushed skull of the decapitated Jayne Mansfield, Hand dipping his gloved paw into the wounds of James Dean. Whispers, scandals, conspiracies. The rumour of Howard Hughes in surgical cocoon, awaiting a fresh incarnation on the ninth floor, is the barrage-balloon that supports the ceiling. The secret is in the shape. Energies are perpetually renewed: as the edge of the razor is preserved by crystalline equations. Pleasure is repeated into mania. The past is an expectation. Light is the future.

They are vacant with spurious excitement disguised as boredom, disguised as convulsion, disguised as savagery, disguised as 'an indifferent social manner'. Hand looks down with interest on the stage. The figures are his mandrake roots, he makes of them what he will, he wills them to his pattern. They answer to his genetic imperatives. He knows that it will soon be necessary to arrange another stepped sequence of shock horror drug revelations: to set the front pages in black ink screams of hysteria, to put media prurience, moral indignation & uncut jealousy, to work. The name of the star & the name of the drug are locked into the adhesive embrace of headline. There is no route to one without the other. The numbed animal mass brain jelly sniffs up his implication. His street traders enlarge their lists. Newspapers are willing servants of the Poppy. Wealth flows; treated nature. The currency itself is the tube; white dust crystal to the nostril through the tightly rolled banknote.

Hyle focuses his heat through a telescope. It lingers over some of the more obvious contours. He relishes the ankle of a certain lady who is versatile enough to be accompanying Slade, arms intertwined, tongues wrestling like lizards, while remaining the wife of a close relative of Hyle's, at present 'out in Africa in a bit of trouble'.

Slade's card is marked. Hand's 9mm Mauser raps against the glass. His mouth makes the noise. He simulates: just this side of ecstasy.

The crowd is a tongue curled around itself. The punters are cattled: manipulated by 'nowness', the tyranny of date fixation; if the event is 'missed' the citizen is reduced. Everybody wants a piece of the imaginary action. There is a direct route opening to the Goat. So many demons have been summoned they are queuing up to get into the Aether Band. Cloud banks are purple, Serpentine ruffled. The media fix freezes the event into a time vault. All hearts miss one beat. Fingers of Eternity warm the already boiling cauldron. Hell's Angels (Walthamstow Chapter) stomp back the advancing hordes, tidy the line. A girl who has been paid to do so, spontaneously, bares her breasts.

At this point the Performer falls onto the stage; in muslin, in bracelets, begins.

Bad Magic, Bad Noise

inflames;
        ignited on the octane
of his spear-like ego
            (Wagner extra)
belemnitic cone, rises as a sheath of hard

wraps of open silking, gold rings
Tangier mountain music
      straw caves
dust-haunched squatters
in turban, rags & old jackets

he cuts his sac,
        across
the blood rubies dot the tight flares
stitched over the crotch
fake genital muscle
          gets inside
the need, so loosely defined
wilds them, wastes their awe
sucks at bone
        till they skate
a brittle, stamping mob

he is false shaman, mushroom page
with white powder in a silver lock
to matt his face
his spleening song, labial rage
unsexed to flare & float

they drown, he quotes Shelley
    Adonais,
        opens himself
to a fierce possession, is possessed
JUMPING JACK FLASH is on his back, dry mate
matelot anguish; attracts Hand

who couches him towards the part
they will play gangsters
PERFORMANCE is not relished
by Mafia bosses in a heavier serge
'unreal & mucky'
even dirty money must come clean
the generation misled
street fighting man's boutique
    Hand's puppet
        & sore friend
savage pre-Raphaelite, puny boy
mixed with hatchet man
        parties

the shaman arouses, but does not
satisfy, can't get
        the great lift,
emasculated by horse

a three minute aura
broken from Byzantine ikon shed

the pyre is staffed by
shit-stained Angels
        & they stomp

Kotope cuts the cake, to sell

■

'Possession is two parts of the Law'

the burnt park grass enters him
the crystal-tip stick,
     blazing
          spirit of Shelley
water weed, choke
            fills his throat

he shimmers

spangles, grasping divisions of light
flashing beady stones

as the crowds throng
the raised snake of this hanging field
the dome reflection
the lifted City in the vapour
the raised City
the celestial
         at that one moment
above the lake
the possessed figure
           the tube
of what Shelley was

here, he lifts & is pinned
spasmic mongol, dumb rattle
the highest articulation
     SCREAM
bubbling in pink, oxygenated blood

he is hung out across the trees
Tyburn also, the female figure
the hanged man's marionette dance
dancing in air, drinking salt
he spurts, he refuses
the crowd gasps him
death is aphrodisiac, flint
plant to wear, convolvulic sway
female, has made himself

has cut
            give give give

for the snake the grass
                              pull
pull back into the dog mask,
                                    the screen
disintegrates held consciousness
into a speeding catastrophe of cloud

Hyle on the balcony
                        tossing
his jism into the eager face of the crowd
black, black inside
                        black

'the deep truth is imageless'

fatalistic green, water serpent
        Serpentine

                          whispers an invitation
Harriet, the jagged sound edge
ruffles the surface

'in breaking traditional ties one sets free in man
unknown forces, the consequences of which
one cannot foresee' –

river, communicant

water connects to water
he does not float or swim

water bursts in upon water
the bag floods, excess

the unborn child is
crushed in excess of one element

& this is why he lifts

this is why he kicks, raises himself
into the air
to ignite the vapour packet
to tear the clouds

Hyle sniffs the weakness in his underpants

Hyle is knowing tho' illiterate

                    rain

The Horse. The Man. The Talking Head.
(a note on Howard Hughes)

'Post mortem effects, presumably'
DH Lawrence

Howard Hughes was of course finished when he became a character in Edward Dorn's *Gunslinger*: an inscrutable. He bleeds here into the ventriloquised (the haunted) horse, his guilt & mouthpiece, the glib Aaron to his dumb powerful Moses basalt presence: snake conjurer, wandsman. The horse is the city, is perhaps Jewish. The man is a hayseed. Tied to the apparently rigid continental centre-fold. They need each other to put a good act together. If they are to go on the road they have to be able to break monologue into conflict, conflict into wisecrack.

So the action cranes through horse skull into McCarthy Land, a flat-lit studio stable, with Francis the Talking Mule & other Presidential candidates mouthing, just out-of-synch, esoterically coded word chants they are learning with difficulty. The desperate strain shows through the carefully ironed faces. The counter chorus is provided by the androgynous anthropomorphic unpunished berserker hero assassins of the cartoon newsreels of mid-afternoon television.

Hughes had to live with this. No heroes in America, only 'heros'. The land will not allow it. From the beginning it inflates to destroy. The bigger the man the faster the maggots gather. The will is towards suicide.

'IXTAB was the goddess of suicide. On the Dresden Codex, she is represented hanging from the sky by a rope wound round her neck. The Maya had the idea that suicides went directly to heaven.'

Hate then. 'A hate quest.' Hughes was sharp enough to understand the nature of the beast. You cannot be anonymous either: 'a worker'. Unless on TV; where the act of stardom is to make the anonymous glitter. To spray anonymity in gold light, to gutter out the individual spark, the unique, the inviolate, the flaw; which is the true drive, life.

Hughes was bright enough to try to force the star-cope down, to obscure the face, the source. He wanted to reverse into the invisible. He knew enough to be crazy, crazy like a fox. He was the intelligence of America. Letting the body decay, definitively. Into the destruction karma. Which is the nature of those states. He became one with the states, destruction.

His glove puppet, Nixon, failed by the small measure that 'R.M. Nixon' is not quite an anagram of 'Rex Mundi.' He fell behind on his payments & was fractured. The Devil was bored with him (as he was with Somerset Maugham who, it seems, made the deal via Aleister Crowley). The Devil foreclosed. And Hughes was his operative. Hughes was the Devil. In America. Glamour. Fur mouth. A force. An energy.

Hughes took the virus, communism, into his body. As pure threat. Made the metaphor real. Was invaded, by conspiracy, unto death. Was the White Messiah, Buddha, incarnation of White Man America, longhaired guru saint, tended by Mormons laced with chastity corsets into their own essence, that no seminal drop spill where it could fertilize the desert ground. Hughes gave off light like a mushroom.

The confusion between interior & exterior, studio & world, skull & plain, is absolute. Realities oscillate: so that Shirley Temple can be leased from her studio to the Republican Party, or Ronald Reagan can graduate from playing epileptic juveniles for Don Siegel to the heavy in *The Killers* to chewing the rug in the Governor's Palace.

All the old cowboy extras want to be Time Lords, want to be on that deflected curve when it starts to go backwards, to zero, when the horse becomes the passenger, drawn along by the force of the question in their thighs, when the horizon keys open & the diamond word does seem to be held in the teeth of the questing beast. After horse wisdom there is no way back to that territory, the previous: no entry in Red Eye, in tarot poker, in massage, frottage, dope, in love's claw. So they imitate the horse's tone but have lost the coin of his meaning.

Hughes arrived early with his eye unhooded. Religion was in the mouths of his front-men like an asthmatic whistle. He was quick to put himself behind Mormon muscle. ('It is possible that Mormons are the forerunners of the coming real America.' Lawrence again.)

This was the colour of his horse, plucked from the sentiment of the High Ridge landscape, opening shot silhouette figure, with credit titles over, entering from the left, death. The horse is the ghost of conscience thrust forward on the prow of Corporate Optimism that made America grow, that expanded the continent until the Atlantic was the size of the Fleet Ditch.

Back further: through horse mediumship, horse host, to the Mari Lwyd, the white skull that translates the buried acts of the dead from ice ground to the house & hearth, the fire, the bolted door; an annual contract, to put remorse & birth-guilt into a formal rhyme scheme. Made whore. Ribbon-hung face with painted scarlet lips. Back into Asian shamanism, the beast slung from the beams, the conical hut. Dried steppe bacon against transcontinental winds.

Hughes again, his silver monoplane, making a round-the-world flight in snowstorm & sneakers, harnessing the power of 1,100 horses. The meat gets higher with message. Rosy word dawn. Cornflakes at Moscow Airport. Back, finally, to the dragon buried beneath the chalk.

And if you could hit a photo image of this creature (infra-red; x-ray; planet ray; energy forced out of destroyed matter to steal a ghost print) then you would come close to the newspaper radio dots that form 'an artist's impression' of the dead Hughes on his stretcher, Mandarin nailed, bearded martyr face. Which is the face of a man kept alive by time-surgery since at least the early nineteenth century, before the American Civil War, deep frozen, to emerge on the foaming crest of the industrial war boom, to make bombers, poisons, anti-personnel devices, gigantic unusable flying-boats, to put the word 'genius' back into newspulp currency, to own newsprint forests, hot lead, to own the sound waves, to own image factories. It is the shell of something, wound out of his own spine. It is what is annihilated so that energy can step free.

To be possessed by that wind, to speak with no voice, voice of buffalo tribe medicine, sacrificial stone mouth, sun swallower, to be invisible, to be snatched up by an intelligence as fast as Dorn's, after the event, is why the event was allowed to occur. The whole Hughes myth was perpetrated so that Dorn could embroider a few pages of absolute text, beat the time rap. With Hughes the fake biography is probably so much more reliable & accurate, an act of occult mediumship & greed, than any print-out from officially approved sources. 'Brilliance', 'inspiration', 'hunch', 'omen', 'front', 'con': that was where he operated. Without these pins he had no existence. He was the mark on the transparent medium through which his heat had passed. He was the scar, the shadow, on locked glass office towers.

When the entropic green clock faltered, heart murmur, Hughes hid inside the letters of his own name, headlines in alabaster & plywood, to convince the machines of his reality, to seduce them: like the giant letters 'H-O-L-L-Y-W-O-O-D' on the scrub hill, slide area, outside that geriatric suburb, zero density, no go, terminal zone.

He scrambled together, directing the technicians by long-distance telephone calls, early shed Westerns, made from Dwight D. Eisenhower's wet dreams: & helmeted flying dramas. Saw the heat of the hybridisation, ritual courtship, between black instruments of war & Jean Harlow. Her suicide forcing her to copulate with the spectres of First World War battle fantasy mud.

Hughes tried to steal some of the technical facility of Howard Hawks by transference of 'H' confusion: to pirate his aura, his skin energy. If the names were close enough to breed into each other the talents might also be borrowed & mix in the eye of the unconscious observer, whose diet is fed on misprint & lie & the space-time curvature of message slipping through the cracks of solid air.

EMINENT AUTHORS, INC paint the sky with
high grade acrylic sprays
                              drill with
TOOLCO bits the impermeable rock stairs .
the clots of dead consciousness, numb ganglia
roots of pulled teeth

                         shape the new
out of midwest prairies of rabbit ghosts &
sky cactus
               sup the tap-root milks
& polish the enamel with sand

rabies quickens brain time
          'out there'
                         daisies rush up between
Dow Jones aeon canyons
                              like chalk dust

the conscious flattens sight into a
saucer, dead presidents yammer in flight
torn from the moon's bad profile

the great men sell their names
                              before birth
tie up their energies in interlocked
Monopoly Trust contracts
                              slip through the small print
water to smooth the cutting edge

'pressure'

Hughes buys into Mormons. He is the tramp hanging about in battered Dodge on street corner junctions where desert sand blows into the flat & unprotected suburb: is the wino in torn tennis-shoes* negotiating the sale of RKO Studios (aka Keith Albee Orpheum Corporation), controlling interest acquired by Joseph P. Kennedy, 1927, to further his body possibilities, to enlarge the brothel options in his unpublic life, to literally extend the reach of his horn into the darkest speakeasy shadows in the land. Though there was for Kennedy, as for Hughes, as for Getty, a time-price to pay. We have Benjamin Bradlee's description of Jackie Kennedy taking old Joe in to dinner:

'She has to stand slightly behind him so that she can kick his right leg forward between steps. He can't do it himself. When he eats he drools out of the right side of his mouth, but Jackie was wiping it off quickly, & by the middle of dinner there is no real embarrassment left.'

Sex greed disguised remains a constant secret motor in high business art: the massive seizure & colonisation of popular collective fantasy for private control purposes. See it as J. F. Kennedy cornered the Presidency to lance his own heats & push his pricked fear & spine-pain deeper into the fat lands of milk & beef & bible-belt mammal America; to double, to ghost, in gangster pulp porno scripts written for chamber performance by Norman Mailer – *'I met Jack Kennedy in November, 1946. We were both war heroes, & both of us had just been elected to Congress. We went out one night on a double date ... I seduced a girl who would have been bored by a diamond as big as the Ritz'* – to borrow desert real estate from Frank Sinatra for adulterate seclusion; to open the malarial lid on Mafia/Cinema/Teamster Union operations with one hand, while making the pay-off in Invisible Numbered Funds with the other – to secure the flame of assassination, Cuban Pig Invasion gunlaw armament expertise & wiped-tape silence. See it as Robert Kennedy in Irish martyr purple stain purchased the TV time for his own sacrifice, bought a myth place – in order to fuck the suicide ghost essence of Marilyn Monroe, barbiturate telephone motel, copulation beyond

*NOTE: Hughes invariably favoured unlaced rubber & canvas footwear to make it easy on his cloven-hoofs. The resultant goatskin soup sweat is better left unimagined: tho' the generous influx of foot-fetishists doubled the takings at Donald O'Connor's Las Vegas comeback.

limits, in mortuary corridors of death of fear: after-hour closed sessions at the Studios, when all the great dead stars perform in cold-storage skin flicks, in blue air, for the faceless executives in cowhide chairs. See it as Teddy Kennedy plunged car & neck-brace in cold-creek negatives to pull attention back from the Moon Shot masterminded by the White House as a tribute to its rescued Nazi scientist geniuses. Dr Strangelove really does want to know if *hitting* that pallid rock will confirm a magnetic potency on the mind, the planner, of the first push. The game is slipping away down here – but the starry wheels are still up for grabs.

the moon with blood on its cheek

'WANNA LOSE TEN UGLY POUNDS? CUT OFF YOUR HEAD'
    Lenny Bruce
quoted, ROLLING STONE

dead man, stuck on old country rails
where the same pattern of smoked laughter
has to run him, over & on

that ½ rock to the sw last night, soon lost
the thickening cortisone face
    President Kennedy
where the impact channels cleaned out his corruptions
necrophilia of mormon barracks
mating of dead archetypes called, falsely, 'STARS'

so the moon is a mausoleum
where the dead fuck
is the veteran off-limits brothel ship
catering to the immortalised
quirks & bends of the spirit

& we are battened down under its waste trench;
the dead cannot come
the suicides condemn themselves
to huge & hungry marble erections

Nero Moon, bandaged Mussolini
                     cut stalk

the missing eye of Rooster Cogburn
is the cork on the bottle

trashy rock sidetracks the alignment
they don't think clear

'Men are free when they belong to a
living, organic, *believing* community, active
in fulfilling some unfulfilled, perhaps
unrealised purpose. Not when they are escaping
to some wild west. The most unfree souls
go west, & shout of freedom'

And Hughes is the name given to the source of all these manipulations & dares. There are forgotten men in small town temperance hotels & mining shacks, mid-continental inertia, who have literally been waiting in their rooms, sitting by the bed, looking out on meridian main street traffic, bills paid by computer, for over thirty years – for the phone call from Hughes that will activate them: & meanwhile they write, on typewriters, science fictions & horror god inventions, squeeze nature into aborted surgeries, work for WEIRD TALES, John Campbell's ASTOUNDING, or Roger Corman; they invent (or are made aware of) impossible literatures in languages that were never spoken, the Necronomicon, or Ludvig Prinn's 'Mysteries of the Worm'. They alone have the emptiness of time to observe, at their own speed, at the speed of the beast itself, the insects in the wall cracks, the scratching behind the skirtingboard, the bugs in the mattress, the crumb-fed pests, the skull parasites, the pubic crabs, the moths of light bulbs, the microscopic organisms at their work. They see them & translate them into their fictions – which become undercover reportage, transcripts of reality. The invented horrors are literal. They alone see the shape-shifting of the windows. They alone stare, night after night, at the planets. They become part of the machinery. The flying saucers & Cayce-inspirations spiral from their apparent boredom. They compile fantastic books of newspaper-cuttings & impossible statistics. They 'inspire' the imprisoned Manson with scientology & visions of the Cosmic Hole. They fill the dead hours for Oswald at his window. They are found in the cupboards of rapists & tin van butchers. They wipe the blood & bone from the chainsaw. They become the secret ant army of Hughes' purpose: are controlled by lack of control, controlled by emptiness, by time-wedges driven into their life-lines: are controlled as Hughes himself is controlled. It is, it has to be, mutual: a genetic, self-satisfying, dictatorship.

And when the phone does finally ring, long after it has been cut off, they are dead – in suicide & red-eye bottle, in blood needle. And then the horror tales themselves take fire & life, bend out, curve into the world, scythe blade, sugar'd nipple, with snake tongue dart to pierce new victims, vampire, in the Odeons of South London, or those frightened of the sleep machine who trudge once again through the distortion of Jacques Tourneur's NIGHT OF THE DEMON on midnight television chambers.

Hughes too is sucked into this vortex. Has put so much of himself into bank vaults, numbered accounts, invisible back-dated deals, hidden from his own self's flame, biological theatre transactions, that he can't find his way back into his own body: & at this very point the energy stream of America, the shimmering milk flood, is tapped by Ed Dorn, & at this point the old mummy cracks into sawdust & stitches, & what never was there is seen to be absent. The recorded voice track coughs & fades. They pull out of Vietnam, the colonial push is over, & the ventriloquist's dummy that Hughes operated in the White House is stranded with nothing but the gangster cassettes from THE BIG HEAT, & Hawks' SCARFACE, & POINT BLANK, & the whole edifice comes down like the last days of Sodom.

But then somebody takes an option on this story. The adrenalin hits in cigar conferences. They think they might get Robert Redford. They remake the end of the word with old volcano footage. They hack Moby Dick into pieces of shark, gorilla, King Kong, exorcist bile, Lee Marvin, Clint Eastwood, magnum force, & the decaying head of Alfredo Garcia. The white moon juices of natural power are perverted. A sharp young executive in felt hat, ghost dance trappings, & tennis sneakers, name of Howard, comes up with the idea of using life, TV America, day-to-day reality as a rehearsal for the Movies. They can try some of the more way-out & experimental & possibly high expense stuff in the streets; cut the investment to the bone, stop building sets; fix time. The picture men shift into a world of slowed-down action replays. Out there among the citizens it has become a video software universe. The excitement lifts into their dry mouths. The whole thing moves on again.

At the end of an Earl's Court reading of the Hughes piece in November '76 I was approached & told about a text, 'The Gemstone File', that had been in recent circulation & that contained further information on the Hughes/ Kennedy power nexus; while into my other ear a man in a rally driver's chemically quilted jacket warned me that he did not think my audience could possibly understand the significance of the term 'death posture', & that if I thought I was quoting from Kenneth Grant I was actually quoting from him, he was the fountain & source of Grant's African material. So the Hughes shard cut into a jagged & nervous pitch of attention, boiling particle desire for escape; which was soon accomplished, plunging down stairs, & the experience exorcised by walking back across town to Hackney, cool star evening along the River, up through the calm'd City, coffee stall outside Christ Church, Spitalfields, midnight bells of Truman's Brewery, Brick Lane.

Two months later a pamphlet entitled, 'A Skeleton Key to the Gemstone File', found its way into my hands. From this I learnt that 'The Gemstone File' itself had been 'written in many segments over a period of years by an American named Bruce Roberts'. Roberts was a student of journalism & physics, that quintessential New World pair-bonding. His special interest was 'crystallography: the creation of synthetic rubies.'

Naturally this was of some moment to Hughes Aircraft: who used his work for laser beam research. And the hangar door swings open for Roberts on Trans Global Paranoia Incorporated. Joining the stable of tame alchemists, dieticians, astro-physicists, steel skin technicians, electronic eavesdroppers, Mormons & psychopaths, he is soon travelling the greasy rails of conspiracy theory. And he stumbles across a world picture whose bleak symmetry is appealing to his split consciousness.

He discovers that in March '57 Hughes was kidnapped by his own Mafia operatives under the direction of Aristotle Onassis; beaten, brain-damaged, shot full of heroin, shunted through a series of identical penthouse hotel suites, locked in a cell on the private island of Skorpios, a human vegetable (& why, incidentally, should 'vegetable', even in this context, be a term of abuse?), dying, finally, in April '71.

It's a fine pattern, the shapes fit neatly together: one of many projections floating about just ahead of, or just behind, the event screen. But the Hughes/Dorn thesis is altered not at all by these fresh speculations & end-games. Go back through the text & for the symbol 'H' (Hughes) substitute the symbol 'O' (Onassis): if you want to play by Gemstone Rules. For Mafia read Mormon. For Mormon read Mafia. And when later switches in temperature, in focus & attention, shift the earth's magnetic field taking the heat away from Greece to, say, Anatolia, Nepal, or Peking – then for 'H' (Hughes) read 'M' (Mao); or whoever.

Either the facts are all, or they are nothing. An impenetrable maze of statistics, lost in space & time; dead ends, fake corridors, pits, traps. All that matters is the energy the structure emits. Can it heat us? Is it active? Or simply a disguise for the lead sheet imprisoning the consciousness of the planet; the gas of oppression, the burnt-out brain cells, milk-centred eyes.

So many versions of the Hughes myth cloud the surface. It is hard to force a sharp image from the emulsion. There are only drawings, the last photographs are hazy sentiments of an earlier era. So many off-cuts. The Nicolas Roeg/David Bowie *The Man Who Fell to Earth* is only one current example. There are plenty more in denser thickets of Science Fiction. This does not matter, it must be understood as a smokescreen, a diversionary tactic.

What is crucial is why certain informations come forward at certain times: why Hughes now? He is such a period number, such a date-stamped poison. He is dead. When you work this tank what is feeding you your 'inspiration'? Who are you working for?

And this is only the beginning of the doubts: shortly after the Earl's Court reading the flak starts to pour through. First, the pathologist's report on Hughes in THE TIMES; then the new easy-to-handle EXPRESS opens its campaign with the serialisation of James Phelan's *Howard Hughes: the Hidden Years.* Which includes such headlines as A LIVING SKELETON IS SMUGGLED TO PARADISE + ALL OF A SUDDEN THERE WAS THIS SWARM OF MONGOLIAN MONKS FROM MARS INVADING THE CAGES + FAKE THAT LURED THE REAL VOICE BACK TO LIFE. And this is attended, of course, by full media spin-off: TV book programme plugs, radio ads, brain midges & electronic parasites eating through the wall cracks, everywhere.

So what happens, & the fear, is that somehow we move just ahead of the causal tide, but are attached to it: we are pushed forward on the nose of the time-cone. Or else – by travelling the rim of an area of collapsing density we get ahead of events by one beat, cause the events to follow.

The implication is sticky. The theory forces the fact: so that the written word, or the calculation in mathematical language, if it is pure, if the pattern has charm, will remake the physical world. Which is what Dorn did for Hughes.

Quarry & prey shadow each other. Moving closer, melting, merging, separating. Time edges ahead of itself: we are sucked into the vortex, elongated. Possessed by what we know, which is what we will discover, & in doing the work we decay, are destroyed: the cell collapses. Perfection shifts the stars, on however small a scale: & this, by instant playback, restructures the donor. Which is a whole new sweep of terror.

It is also an absolute challenge to the work undertaken; because if your thesis breaks surface instantly, is made public on media umbrella, as soon as you construct it, then you have to work faster, sharpen your wits, go deeper, find the strata beneath the skin, confront the primary mineral controls.

Or; can you transfer your allegiance, out of the dark, to the pulse rhythms of the natural world. Pull away from the Black Hole & opt for White Nature: the New Age, growth, community, the Light. The price is high here also. The body cost savage. Check any account of those who have made the attempt. The maimed psyches, the ego assassinations of somewhere like Findhorn, rooted in sand on one of the great Scottish power tracks. It is no simple alternative.

Any attempt in this direction is opposed by the whole feed of the Occult, a complex & secretly-worked system of parallels, analogues & models: as for example, on a banal level, the correspondence between the Bermuda Triangle & the Golden Triangle of the Opium Trade. The Bermuda Triangle is operated as a blind. That shape takes fringe attention away into petty mystification & paperback frisson; so that the Cambodian operation can proceed uncluttered, undisturbed.

'Heroin from the Golden Triangle was sometimes brought into the U.S. in the bodies of GIs who had died in battle in Vietnam. One body with the guts removed can hold up to 40 pounds of heroin.'

So what substance was stuffing the mummified Hughes? What use could Onassis find for his catatonic shell?

'Lots of heroin gets processed in a Pepsi-Cola factory in Laos.' The metaphor, Pepsi/Heroin, is a simple one: twin forms of genetic colonisation. Giving entry once more to the bitter seductions of Cinema. Joan Crawford was the official front for Pepsi at the same period as she was making her ravaged fat-gut horror films: *Whatever Happened To Baby Jane?* & *Straitjacket* & *I Saw What You Did*. The best of this action supervised by

Robert Aldrich, taking the rectal temperature of the times as accurately as he did for Eisenhower America in *Kiss Me Deadly*.

Beyond this point we come up against the Burroughs formulation about 'the paranoid being the person in possession of all the facts.' It is a straight take to Insanity Farms. You are soon genuinely 'out of it'.

As Hughes himself was: when he lay, naked & emaciated, in bed sores, with malfunctioning kidneys, watching those endless loops of film. The man who could buy anything, could run Presidents, chose this: coded narcosis, dim colour sleep.

Where was he? What had he split into by this time? What space was he travelling? Every detail murders a million brain cells.

He had the Great Silence: was possessed of a truth richer than the visions of electro-convulsive therapy, darker than the tone of terminal alcoholics, madder than the gnomic prophecies of derelicts, further than the screamed secrets of raging women on midnight buses.

Hughes was crazy as a tick. He would not cut his hair or his nails. He hoarded the gold of his urine. James Phelan describes it:

'Relieving himself took hours, & he was too weak to sit all that time in the bathroom. Instead of being emptied the jars had been capped & stacked in a corner of his little bedroom. The employees had to get rid of a three-year supply of Hughes's urine & then wash & destroy the jars. One aide kept interrupting the job to go off ... & retch.'

No one must take hold of his power. No one must be allowed to tap into his sources, to analyse & break-down his secret. There was to be no final 'Rosebud' whisper.

To carry the unsupportable burden of physicality there was an official double, the appropriately named, Wayne Rector, who was killed at the Inn on the Park. His death mingling with the screams & aethers of Free Concert hysteria.

The formation of his disguise was a simple matter. The reason creatures from alien space-craft, when described in eye-witness newsprint accounts, so closely resemble the imagined versions of science-fiction cover illustrators & science-fiction movies is not that the film-makers are gifted with preternatural insight, but that the 'creatures' base their material forms on the images of celluloid, just like everybody else. We see what we expect to see, so that the imagination is not unbearably stretched. Hughes based his meat presence on the rumours & myths. We see what we expect to see long after the essence, the essential being, has moved on.

The double is, finally, as real as the man himself, as real as any of them, Hughes, Onassis, Kennedy, Rockefeller, Nixon: they have all long since been cloned from some perjured splinter. Their ghosts haunt the empty corridors of media, the air channels. The action is translated to a new plane of being.

The conspiracy theorists will have to dig deeper into the star-map to find any trace of movement. Their small insights are sparks thrown out as cinders of hell, bright clinker that scalds the closed lids of the dead, that grants, at best, a momentary illumination.

27/9/78: A friend from the book-market, Chris Renwick, rings & mentions that Paige Mitchell, who has been teaching in his summer-school, recently fed him an interesting anecdote – she had a temporary job with a lawfirm & thought one of the pinstripes looked familiar but could not instantly recover the right mugshot from her memory bank. Then it came on her that it was me he looked like – the man saw her staring & walked across. 'Hello,' he said, holding out a hand, 'my name's Howard Hughes.'

THE OLDER, HIDDEN POWERS; THE SECRET MINDS

SKOFELD, MAN OF THE EAST

*'But the causes of disease you should ask me about privately … because they are too
arcane to be described before ordinary people'*

Philostratus: *Life of Apollonius*

'the compass is absolved'
the man of the east, you may not name

to cut with shears across the living jet;
storm water from a flooded pool

it is a city of reflected images
(DON'T LOOK NOW)
dark double-faces staring in
from outside the train window,
the boxed mysteries of local fields
'darkness before, and danger's voice behind'
escarpments, faces under the river
strangled in pond weed

the city should return to the sea bed
a labyrinth fish tank
'those long vistas, sacred catacombs,
where mighty minds lie visibly entombed'
narrow street heights offering small protection;
the cold is murderous,
suicide is their companion
its sugars haunt their dreams
        sweetness
taken with a scalpel from midnight leaves
siren song of coal-gas in the grate

green is parted, the dome folds back
'subtle speculations, toils abstruse'
to discover the mathematical consistencies
of the Heavens, the ironies of God

'let me dare to speak / a higher language'

mind travels out, in blue pulse light

'conscious step of purity & pride '

deserted flesh suffers a self-collapse
decays; untenanted, ignored

we shall not miss him, he is Skofeld

he is the east, sickening

his companion, Private Kox,
seconds him   at a distance

'to punish thee in thy members'

◨

*'... looking forth by light
of moon or favouring stars, I could behold
the antechapel where the statue stood
of Newton with his prism & silent face
the marble index of a mind for ever
voyaging through strange seas of thought, alone'*

Cambridge is become the city of death
wear silver, compliment the black

Liverpool Street, buy a ticket,
           the lines
                      are open,
                                 old Bethlem Hospital,
GREAT EASTERN optimism is gone;

on the margin of the stew, penetrated
by the shadow of Christ Church, Spitalfields,
burial ground beyond the Roman gate

           train speeds
                      from Hand's manor
from the pen of Hyle
under bridges over London Fields
along water systems & marshes
(secret glimpses into one-bulb kitchens)
turns north beyond the Danish border

Cambridge produced (or drew to itself)
the articulators of Albion's pain

there are names, You know the names
You do not know them, it doesn't matter

who translated life into language
'to mitigate
           the injurious sway
of place or circumstance'

'a stylistic situation on the periphery'

worked through the word, worked the word out

     lost;
          everything goes into the stockpot

Skofeld smiles, they disappear

insects of flame congeal in iconic shields
risk is etched, surgeon acts on unsubstantiated charts

'less tuneable than bees'
they fear, they fear
'an ear that could measure a just cadence,
& scan without articulating; rather nice & humorous
in what was tolerable, than patient
to read every drawling versifier;'
they are food, ascend
(like METROPOLIS) into the maw

but it is not destruction they record

and with Skofeld always is Private Kox
a gross turnip-head who swills
Southern Comfort (RED EYE); breaks wind & vases,
an importer of soiled
Hibernian limericks, drink dribbler
claret-bib uniform unbuttoned
                              lights
his cigar with holograph scores of Vorticist operas

Skofeld has to tread with care
the body aura protects him
but a single crude syntactic error
could puncture the body shield
let out the real person who is gone
let the fears in;
                accident,
the head-on smashing of big motors

diesel nerve offends his nostril
the root hairs shiver

'in a small chamber hung with dusty green,
sitting in an elbow chair, & dressed
neatly in black; pale, but not
cadaverous; his hands & fingers
gouty & with chalk stones'

Skofeld sprawls back;
black
      emphasises the sallow poison of his liver,
white wrists,
understands the message of the stars is disease –
they talk fire in accelerating genetic code
they cause the blood race
travel the pillars of his tongue
so that he speaks in marble

'gorgeous eloquence'

afloat on the sea cradle of perfect pitch,
rhythmic pendulum,
                  from dead moss to charged crown,
swings closer like Poe's blade
                     to the exposed chest,
folded chaos crouches at the window,
    not to be admitted,
though summoned by unconscious ceremony
(Kox is its manifestation)
     'beast frenzy'
with eye of hawk & paw of dog,
snake flesh, feathered cheek
'incumbencies most awful, visitings'
    shaft the page
that wall of verse curves round his spine; support
attractive & opaque, the glittering screen
'community with highest truth'
confession of the sharpest doubt

as he cuts the stem
                    an alternate reading
breaks down the moon wind
time manipulation as secret of death
to count up the beads of the web
shuffle them at will
                    (the seeds)

this city, metallic, mechanical
    architect: Wyndham Lewis –
they are highly polished, his creatures
he has taught them to look through Event Channel
passing into a state of partial
or complete hypnosis, narcosis, word-block

they are become the enemies of women
'The Apostles', Bloomsbury, Forster
J.K. Stephen, Gothic possession
Ripper threats in slim Latin volumes

        they curse & blast
                    fat
ideas & muscle in the body wall,
wives of the poets,
                    potato-soup strategies

they might all become Catholic, fellow-
travelling Buddhist, hermaphrodite

a vegan philosophy, a white page art

the open field mined
                    with odd
domestic conjunctions (book-type jokes)
case the pain in butter,
                    we are sacrificed
we please ourselves

'subtle speculations, toils abstruse
among the schoolmen, & Platonic forms'

geologists of the library
banish 'hybrid vigour';
through the press (Miniature Albion)
the flower is squeezed, crushed, dried
its juice drained to the polished wax

                                          undrunk

◼

'Skofeld & Kox are let loose upon
my Saxons! They accumulate a
world in which Man is by his Nature
the Enemy of Man, in pride of Selfhood
unwieldy stretching out into Non Entity,
generalising Art & Science till Art
& Science is lost'

fearful of ultra-violet excesses

knowing the sun was not to be taken
lightly or in any bare-backed
spirit of narcissism
      (OTO Ninth Degree)
the wounds that follow

it was not permitted
all very well for Kox to swagger & smirk
on private lawns, swill Strongbow
& endorse municipal ales,
        connoisseurship
was not something he flaunted, didn't
give a nip between mild & bitter
he'd drain a pot of rats' heads
plug a vein, snort with both nostrils
& sleep it off in the Fellows' Garden

how can he put up with that man?

the college wives bleat, ruining
each other's chances,
clanking about in *New Society* ambitions,
unfulfilled & serving sensible
provençal soup;
Kox is immune to ratatouille
& wouldn't feed crème brûlée to his ferret

how does Skofeld stand for this
beware
beware of the sun

he guards the sleeping snake
he will not rouse him in the spine
his corduroy
will filter out the savage rays

he's often sick
               hoards what he has

Kox strangles a dog, shoots the heads
off the gentians;
Beat Generation gives him stomach cramps
shock treatment tickles his toe

autumn days, school's out
beware the cottages
                  Lake District
& all roads south:
               the Equinox

Ripper sharpens his cheese knife

'Devildom first, poetizing afterwards'

who is he? mortal, wandering scholar
      condemned
possessed all down the line (by what he knows)
'the very palace of the winds'
Skofeld was Milton, Coleridge,
Wordsworth, Crowley, Powys, James
and all the rest,
                solitary,
a continuing band of responsibility
here, this town
'courts, cloisters, flocks of churches,
gate-ways, towers:
                migration strange'
entrapment, under long water skies

the moment of self-recognition of powers

(... *'And this, precisely, is what Sherlock Holmes did.*
He became a freshman of Gonville & Caius. Cambridge,
as it had done many times before in its close-on-a-
thousand year history, was again showing the way;
indicating the pattern' ...)

the other man's word upon his tongue
the other man's work to continue
cantor chants in deep bone
      'Fraternitas Sancti Sepulchri'
alien buds force his jaws apart

the heresy: to speak, break silence
Trinity, Caius, King's
              is the vital fork
that buttresses this unstable field ;

King's College Chapel is heavily coded,
in numerical bondage (see Pennick: THE MYSTERIES OF ...)
so that James D. Watson
       'staring up at the gothic pinnacles'
is speeded, fed back, shoved into light;
who earlier had fetched the horse's steaming heart
from fen plain abattoir
to submit to x-ray crystallography
to find the facet'd clue, the irreducible:
the key is the shadow of the door, a template
from which the work is done, the dark unlocked

because of the shape the thought moves faster
crushed & re-made to form the TETRAHEDRON;
the eye is not needed, the body
put out to pasture,
              they plug hot
into seething Templar sockets

worm drives down into the buried mystery
      fenland peiste
they serve & oppose, both, they pay

so octagon Ely is the dragon's cast

'the hallowed fire of his altar,
to touch & purify the lips of whom he pleases'

Kox is, of course, the Cambridge rapist
it is painted on his skull
a 'JEKYLL & HYDE' the *Mirror* calls him –
how does he
get into these bedsit rooms
of dressing-gown sleep, curlers, lino, woolly slippers
how does he
                    slide through locked doors
a superhuman lust:
                        Kox wears a false beard

'Skofeld arch'd over the Moon at midnight...
scattering her leprous snows in flakes of
disease over Albion ...
whose pen no other hand dare touch'

Skofeld never stirs, he sits
eyes compute the text in columns,
arabic nose edits the infelicities of diction –
Kox is less than an odour
at work again & close to murder
dips his paw in face cream
cigarettes in coffee cups, PLAY BACH
Penguin Verlaine
Kox rapes the Hobbit, mops up
on terrytowel

                    geomantically aligned, west/east
that magnetic route (A30/A10)
                        atlantic mother current

LAND'S END . . CROWS-AN-WRA . . BURYAS BRI . . LONG ROCK . .
(ST MICHAEL'S MOUNT TO SEAWARD) . . LUDGVAN . . CROWLAS . .
3 BURROWS . . BROWN WILLY . . DARTMOOR . . FIRE STONE CROSS . .
EXETER . . CREWKERNE . . MONTACUTE (& POWYS) TO THE LEFT . .
EAST COKER (& ELIOT) TO THE RIGHT . . BABYLON HILL . .
SHERBORNE . . SHAFTESBURY . . LUDWELL . . WINDMILL HILL . .

CHISELBURY CAMP . . SALISBURY . . OLD SARUM (LEFT) . .
FIGSBURY RINGS . . BASINGSTOKE . . DEATH IN HOUNSLOW . .
RIVER CONNECTION . . PUSH ON UP THE KINGSLAND ROAD . .
STOKE NEWINGTON (POE, WILSON, ABNEY PARK TO LEFT) . .
ROYSTON HEATH . . CAMBRIDGE . . ELY . . DOWNHAM MARKET . .
WITCH FIRE . . KING'S LYNN . . THE WASH

the secret is revealed

Kox had his finger
around the trigger of Skofeld's blasphemy

lore of the Cosmos was being unravelled
obscure studies
the waft of ancient texts sifted

'the Center, unapproachable for ever,
the Vegetative Universe opens like a flower'

Kox had observed the ritual candle-pickings
the micrometer mensurations
the columns of strict figures

Skofeld speaks treason against the edifice
of law, the hierarchies of nature;
offends the sharp angle
flatters the curve,
hones language to preternatural accuracies

Kox had lain
                under the rhododendron
drunk, Kox had listened

but Skofeld will triumph, disembodied
become figure, become essence,
a patch of cloud, a blue aroma
an accident on Trumpington Street
a shift in the curtain
                Skofeld is become his word

Kox devours it,
& cannot evacuate the agony
Kox ends in the garden (Mantegna not Bellini)
a clot of anguish
coughing among the beanshoots

                                    a gross body
the maggots rework the *Book of Kells*
within his skull pan
they lay out the vertical city
along the plain of his cortex
('the Plain called Ease')
they worship the serpent

                            down the length of his spine

Kox is become a floating bestiary

the word devours the beast
as the fig devoured the donkey

the word devours the world

'I had got from Cambridge what I wanted'
Aleister Crowley, *The Confessions of*

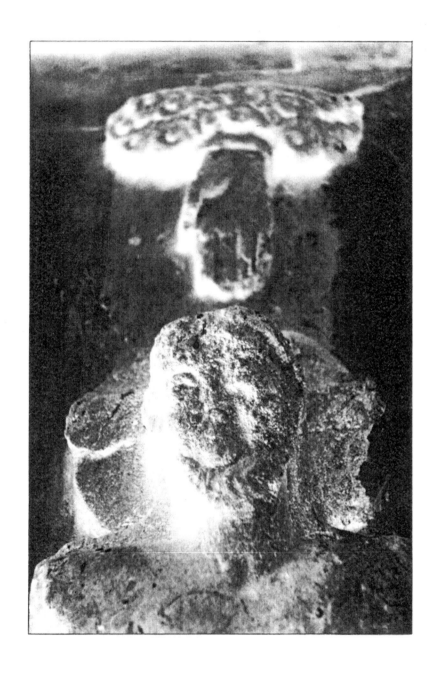

COBAN, THE UNKNOWN, THE UNKNOWABLE

Coban, the unknown, the unknowable
without name, without face
invisible over the land, all powerful
his death assumed, unannounced

Coban, divided into manifold
carved figures of lesser dignitaries
smaller names, fractions
squared roots of his meaning;
Coban on the north porch of Exeter Cathedral
three incisor copes, open jaw
pegged white,
                    stick bearing molars
to look into his mouth, to gum his ancestry

saints, angels & kings usurp his glory
are reduced,
decay in the air of the west front
sucked by tourist camera leeches

in Coban all of this,
                    the triangle:
Canterbury, Chichester, Wells (through Salisbury),
narrow wedge that encloses his title, encloses Winchester
80 miles by 80 miles by 160, his power

Coban across the south
                    is a language we cannot discover;
we are in awe, & bend the neck

he is older
than the fingers, the collapsed spires,
the circles, the earth works
older than the ice trail, the treeless frozen ground
older than temperature, older than the idea of sun

Coban is the disguise,
his life
is discovering what he was, & will be

the great flaw, the driven continuity of evidence

A Biographical Sketch

'You should beware of those who knew him: they will tell you so much
you will just die of it.'
J.H. Prynne: *Lecture on Maximus, 4,5,6*

'... just across the road John Milton got his ...'

Like Maximus, like Milton
'Secretary for Foreign Tongues'
black, the son of Los,
                          black sun;
at sea, the land his dream
Coban did not long leave
                          his home,
travelled as a sop to melancholy
& only into a local cultural extension
say, Switzerland
                  Venice
I mean the older canal
                          necrophile sleep
of undersea images dredged up
mating of sea & shore, god disguised as sea-beast
swimming by open windows
resting in mosaic, in font water
in gold tesserae,
                      in blue divinity
Coban's sleep rhythms anchored

(Coban's Eyes are out, his Angels)

never, truly, upon Ocean
was land-locked in time
                              in time of war
bolted to himself, his body image
so that ocean was a vengeance of liquid fire
a boundless giant
bed of sickles, moon scythes
                              Coban suffered
the fluctuations, in blindness
conjured the dim heat
                              hellfire,
knuckle pressed against eye-ball
to raise the White Light;
Coban constructed vast
architectures, sub-polar cities
his place, here
                    the flooded crypt of Winchester

child of Ely, water taught
in the spring of his ear;
to come home was his whole journey

'head & hands lopt off
               in his own Temple'

each step backwards into earth
and into absolute darkness
the voice moves
he is chained to the rock
he heaps stones onto his chest
this is his beast of the churches
crocodile ancestor
a machine to understand
                         the stars
to mediate between worms & gods
a time platform
               a bender of light

128

a compressor of histories
                            a land plain
a stone library
               a cave of policy
a place that is, literally
                      out of time

see the clouds break & swerve
to avoid this ground
the concealed roots lock the land to the building

The Process, & How

Coban possessed Hand
it should be known
Coban dead in his grave
      Hand
passing his church, excursion
to that city;
          it was the spirit of Coban,
the unfulfilled desires
that lit Hand,
the radiant meat of canopic jars
that flattered
& fashioned Hand's evil

what Coban thought, Hand did

the cancelled urge is immortal
Hand looked down from Catherine's Hill
& saw the Church in water meadow
Hand sucked Coban's gauntleted fist

this way the land operates
the room-spells of Coban
('mysterious wisdom won by toil')
are acted out in Whitechapel & in Bow,
in Hoxton, Poplar, Stamford Hill

the idea that Coban buried
is a scream in the night
in the toilet of a gambling den

*('First Reggie slung me a few right-handers, then Ronnie slung me one, & all of
a sudden one of the henchmen slips Reggie a tool ... & I wound up in hospital for
about three days with a hundred & ten stitches in my face')*

one single tenement light
muffled late in drawn curtains

the art of Coban
is become
the frowning eyebrow of Hand

Coban strives to untie
the knot that his own life
has constructed

it cannot be a great chinese wall

it keeps nothing out, is circular
where the ghosts extend his lyrics

THE QUEST:

they search, unsuccessfully, for the name & location of Coban. They walk from Winchester to Salisbury; by way of Romsey, King's Garn Gutter, Verwood, Knowlton Circles, Gussage Hill, Acking Dyke & Grim's Ditch.

feeding the wind & fed by it
(lapwing, roebuck & dog)
an open-mouthed immortality
over tenanted ground
to swallow the habits of another land
understand the soul is not separate
but the badge & essence of all this meat

(the crow, the crow)

to fling the stick down
the wind abates
take coffee & wait for a train
in the Station Café
with tame, out-of-town, Angels

the stick flowers
wind tears off the seed & tumbles
its alphabet over the cliff

we learn to wait; drowning in jukebox erruptions

at the Church door; bells, distant operations

Easter Sunday morning

The Quest, 2nd Path:
they walk again; beyond Winchester to Chichester & Felpham.
Coban is further than ever before.

Coban's bird is flown is gone
scythe among clouds,
                              is turned
the hands enclosing skull hearth are gone
are lifted, away, are translated

hovering hawkspan at cross path

Coban bends to find a stone
natural *shabti* form
blood blister,
                      pierced bone
among yew root, Goosehill Camp
wood slope
              Coban's bird is not pressing
wing in delicacy over the crown
of his head
              & they look at him
a blankness, a whiteness of waters
baptism, Paraclete, resuscitation,
possession by spirit;
the seance with vegetal voices
                                     is gone

there is no entrance
the skull plastered over
the gate sealed

Coban turns to the sun

down slopes to the spire of Chichester
the spire falls

Coban's road is flint & rubble
Coban sleeps on a sharpness of chalk
Coban's bird is gone

is discovering along these ridges
deposits of some future self

the cathedrals of Chichester & Selsey
will continue to forge a third
& invisible
                    cone of worship,
a funnel of voices ascending out of
the range of hearing
his frustration eats into the ground
acid root spiral
to conjure Milton, to poison Blake's optic nerve

the groin'd shore,
                         Butlinland
'first Vision of Light'

'In Felpham I heard & saw the Visions of Albion'

Coban in pyramid of sun shock
over distant Chichester spire
as glimpsed Sunday morning November 9, 1975
Coban the architect of steps
Coban the spastic
jerking through Felpham, wrong frame speed
deceiving the eye
Coban out over Selsey Bill
Coban shelters in St Wilfred's Chapel
Coban's word incomplete
Coban's bird is flown up & gone
the fasts wasted the tracked miles of hill ridge, Downsway
the bound tree copse in ploughed field
Coban in gunshot
Coban over pasture land

incomplete, aching for entrance

Coban the shell
                walks down
to sea strand, the dull margin
winter light, bingo, poodle parlour
clock golf, oil stain

Coban's bird climbs into sun hut
& claws for victim
the heroic life against all reflex
the battled visionary of Lambeth

what is the price
                to survive these places

banks of sand, the shore is swallowed

BLADUD OF BATH

in which Bladud, the Hyperborean Apollo, flies & falls

why Bladud wants to fly
shift the Memory Empire
the empirical block of vein rivers
mapped to interior heat source
this lamb-cap'd son of Coban (of Lud)
this Bath man
sprung out of fallen masonry
        the toad
fell *from* earth, fell upright
into air, out of nothing
(before I was   I was everywhere)

Bladud the son the imagination
of Coban's virginity, the spark
struck from his anvil
   the shining
weighted horn of his imagining
                mind
Bladud fell on his face into the ground
twin peaks of dead hair, rubber eyes
THE MAN WHO FELL TO EARTH
whispered through by star ghost musicians
the dog bitten in the thigh by glass
chemical dyes staining the pale meat sinew

the elevator of instinct
      flies
bent, to fetch knowledge back
the bird lost of Coban was Bladud
Bath was his place
               where he decayed
coming, unnaturally, by other
                    darker hands

was the medicine in the spring
was the mineral in the water

Coban's bird: the arrow at the sun
the impotent black snake case

Making

'the chief Ensign of Druidism was a Ring ...
such Ornaments of the Hand
... may be justly supposed to have had virtues to them ...
& from thence to have proved the Origin of the Snake Rings'

through space beyond the wheel or ring
that isn't there
then is because we say it is
or else the ring is space
& all the rest is plural, unknown
      or time,
the ring is the hand is time

Hand is made to fit the ring
Hand thickens to fill the made space
Hand's particles, variously, seed time

'I am as big as God but not so wicked'

□

Coban laid out Canterbury & Winchester
Shaftsbury on the Mount of the Shaft
'where the eagle prophesied the fate of Britain'
these steeples measured, scaled
from his recumbent generative organ

'I copulated with my fist': & Bladud was born
'I ejaculated into my own mouth': & Bladud
        emerged from my side;
'I copulated with my fist, my heart came to me'

without consort, of my ribs, made progeny
what pain, what rending stretching & tearing out;
conceived, hard, from a lust for this land

where Coban loved himself, the waters,
Bladud was the foam, the pond scum,
was the unguent, was mud
        Bath's medicinal spring & cash flow,
hot house Roman luxuries, splinters of tile
sauna vices, massage parlour curtains
                                    fur gloves

the wolf-wounded sheep added their pus
their blood to the water
                        & were healed,
scab mouth closed;
                    the Regency dames
sip'd in dainty cup, themselves unwashed:
the pig water of Bladud,
                    his magical
swine fever cures

The Cut Man

'I understand now your passion to face the West. It
is the passion for the extinction of yourself & the
knowledge of the triumph of your own will *in your*
body's extinction. But in the great periods, when
man was great, he faced the East.'

Bladud there now, cold sperm of Coban,
regent, déclassé, restaurateur in black
satin boiler-suit, wealth on paper
      folded man
masturbated with clutch of peony leaves;
the tit button chewed like peyotl,
                throat
of varnished scarlet; window grid printing on his back
this Bath hotel room of Coleridge, fear sweat nightmare
travelling west, sun-stepping, going
to meet his death more than half way

Bladud emblazoned on best-selling timber
recycled sperm map,
          cut man
of Casablanca, over Severn Bridge
with cassette wrap-around fur set,
over wrinkled skin water,
              fallen man
of coal tongued angel brand, Bladud;
no further distance for this blood
to travel, Lud son, stone brother,
Lear father, spraying, helmet of butterflies,
thunder switch,
        pulls the wand,

joy-stick, up, tilts back
over his own head, up-set, disorientated
fly-walk deafens him ...
                          Coban's permafrost bitterness,
no son, no more, Edda-bled
sorrow of saga already completed;
                          keening
land-wave scours the ear channel, winds of the north

& this is why, the reason
Coban's arrow enters the gull's throat,
full head prophecy chokes him with cresting scum,
        & red fist,
Coban shafts time,
                    his sin
makes love to itself; blackman, negative
leper son, flakes out, peels
like a grape without blood, this is why
Coban possesses the fist of the future
steps through the time edict
this is why Coban insists, *does* go blind
go forward, unseen
                    Coban the past pursuing him
grips our throat
                    in sleep
is Coban, opens our chest
is Coban entering the gape mouth
of the exhausted lover,
                    is Coban
feeding the will, is Coban
fertilizing death   is Coban

the crowned gene; projected arrow-path of divination & flight

The Flight, The Prophecy, The Suicide

'And afterwarde a Fetherham he dight
To flye with wynges, as he could best discerne
About the ayre nothyng hym to werne
He flyed on high to the temple Apolyne
And ther brake his neck, for al his great doctrine.'

Bladud, the whore of wild ducks,

                    migrant

of the flocks, flight secrets, lusts

     moon compass;

services the beast necks, feather deck'd

Marienbad lethargy,

              jongleur, bell man

fool of the geese over frozen lake chain

pine forests, the magnetic

                rock path,

by lodestone, hung meat,

             rattler

Bladud in fish-net tights & goose quills

quits the cabaret, paints his face

spits against the wind of polar promptings

on that grass-stripped island

             a monk's

weather-raw fingers inscribe the skin page

with quill pen & plant-juice, squeezed dye

the shadow of Bladud lights the codex

□

eagerly, eagerly
             spine worn outside,
ribs traced on the drum of his chest
       head, thorax, abdomen
antennae quivers with message

day of flight, the colourless blood,
clinging to leaf peak,
                   hillside,
hang glide Bladud, emasculate
queen of ants
             launched by west winds,
an unknown journey

high above chalk, the Dragon
not yet taken its horse disguise;
       horse surrogate, the hide tent
king mound, dew pond
                   damp sacrifice

Bladud afloat, in pride,
                   driven east
at mercy of older energies

over Tain River, royal Bladud
diaphonous wing span
                   dips
swoops low, the alone
the swollen, filled with ancestors

wind failing, Lud Gate
the stiff male primacy of his feathers

White Mount, falling
   the earth a new sky
falling on him,
             sinking
knees drawn up,
hollow case stuffed with earth grain

this place, Bladud

gnaws wing for sustenance

the mischievous ants, link'd progeny
tunnel out
                    into the orifices of City
into bank loan, mortgage, capital gain

the computed eye, the invisible transfer

a long death, antler'd prince

his slow millennial changes

      ☐

'... circumscribed the oracular Cave of the Pythian God
with a Row of Pillars that formed the Octostyle Monopterick
Temple, fabled by the Grecians to have been erected by PTERAS
with Wax & the Wings of the Bees APOLLO had brought from
the Hyperborean Regions ...'

when Bladud tried to breach
the labyrinth of Brute
                    at Troja Nova
he fell into a sun trap
                    Temple of Apollo
was smashed, his crust shattered

or is this the first great Suicide
to open the Bridge,
to offer himself, split spine,
                                        pink
crab-meat to the sun's fork:
skull shell bowed to the white city stones

145

is his journey from the west
                              mantic,
like Chatterton, a word to unravel

whose lion cloak was visible
    only on death couch
as a shade-beard of denied maturity,
a stubble rising on the grey flesh,
a hard shape in the eye jelly;
thwart aviator blocked by his own ceiling
not able to climb through his limits;
defined as he dies, myth sick

his god, the dragon,
                        a crocodile on stilts,
he never mentioned, never 'knew'
        conjured Lear
to fill the circle of his madness:
was revenged in daughters & in storm

*'consecrating the Hills that continue the Curve Line
on the back of CAMALODUNUM from the SW to Haul Down'*

the matter of Britain hails iron pegs

his best, for a thousand years, betrayed
in Ley lines, maze & trench

the cromlech mocks, remains

SKOFELD & 'THE GREAT WORK'

'The words of the poet / the equations of the physicist.'
E.F. Stringer *(Star People)*

Sick sick. Yellow. Not citrine; bile. Waste flooding the pore, escaping. Odours of corruption & sanctity. Pellucid. Skin clear over the bones. The layers of protection invisible. Skofeld is a hologram of himself. Scarcely present. Avatar of uncorruptible essence.

'How can so sick a people rise up?'

Skofeld on his couch, untroubled by horse-hair lacerations, by the earth's orbital shift through darkness. This (time) is the crunch. Unhooked from body spasm, calculating will broken into numbers. A far excellence of pure detail. Lost in it. Abandoned. Bliss? Wings in the stone, remote signs, languages. The fossil & the exposed process. Skofeld has scorched the ceiling. Fire-black above the pounding mind. Recruitment of internal suns. Blood clots. Coagulant drugs. The blood, halted in its flux, thickens towards crystal. The eyes are shell, holding off the light. His etheric body is scorched & hairless, flaking. Exile.

More like the Pope than God: he *is* infallible. God isn't, makes mistakes, this life, commits lies; not Skofeld. He is beyond the human, & its magnification, which is God, the amplified light. Keeps the island lit. His spared Georgics drive the generator. Overdrawn intelligence devours the will towards action. Absorbs the spill of acolytes. His flame cannot be divided by blade or laser.

Now suspects that if the Devil (Asmodeus, Rex Mundi), if incarnate matter, had a forwarding address it was here, Cambridge. And his work was the construction of absorbent mirrors, the self-swallowing opposition, where the image (the corrupt) is reversed, the meaning reversed, the entrapment realised. Using, naturally, the same power circuits; admitting to his chart the same rules of colour. He was the Devil's shadow. The previous. Where the Devil had just been. This was his movement, to push one heart-beat ahead, to anticipate, cancel.

Of course, the Devil does not actually live in Cambridge. And who can blame him. His ground-contacts are elsewhere, & not to be named: but his front-office, his wall plaque, surely, yes. Among the colleges & cloisters. An active negation, a swarming nothing, nothing breeding nothing: 'smell of rottenness, marsh-stagnancy.' Zone of the cancelled. Erased highs. Nimbic decay: where

'contour values represent smoothed (mathematically filtered) total force magnetic anomalies in gammas above a linear field equation based on computer filtering of anomaly values selected on a regular grid. Positive anomaly levels in red, negative in blue.'

Cambridge, negative. Cambridge, low. The Ramsey-Cambridge-Ely triangle holding a zero-float that will expand & overlay them, or contract & suck them in. The Devil's breath. The veins of water. The mounds, the Templar memorial powers. And now the laboratories. This Skofeld knew.

He had been informed by charged madmen in the streets: how the secret Atman shrines were abandoned & the mysteries scattered ... crazed talk ... Hitler, under Steiner's instruction, sowing the oven ashes of the Jews, the alchemised essence, that they never return to the fatherland; it ended with the firing of the Manhattan projectile. The new initiates are walled into the protection of colleges: physicist, geneticist, star-man, surgeon. Only Skofeld can penetrate their language. Access means death. Death, illumination. Nothing. Living.

'The older you get the more time collapses'

Douglas Fairbanks Jnr's corporate wisdom
broadcasts a truth he knows more than others

the physicist chuckles,
antimatter soup, high table gossip;
as Skofeld taps his brow
listens to the water flow in the bone,
neurocranial splashback:

they are deep into telekinesis,
brain screen transmission,
silent, generous
skull to skull exchanges

a newt of port & saliva
slides from the corner of
the old man's mouth;
                        thyroid-denied
cretinism, smiles wide, tooth mush

Skofeld's consciousness
                        is out; physicist
is approaching *new* levels of meaning

out of the word fix

Space is propositional
take it as an equation, a model
where local stars are trapped
to smooth our fear –
Consciousness enters the sum
with speed-writing finger

FLIGHTS TO THE SUN MAY BE DELAYED

beyond this first helmet everything
is theoretical, do you see
      the excitement
the stars are our abacus
mark the flight path,
                  death of
     idea trail
as we come into speed we see
the end before the beginning
the thread to trace
                  in any every direction
the chemist will tell you,
                   infinite
reductions, infinite expansions
     idea: trigger
the whole thing planned in the cortex
rare degeneration
                    opening up the star chest
     planned: committed

     do you see it? the idea

even Skofeld's grip is slipping
the dialogue line is stretched too tight
he begins not to 'see' it
it begins not to be there
physicist is changing into numbers
a chair of graph nails
                a float of needles
it is getting away

the stars were the names of the beasts
god mouth disguised

'degradation, destruction, revocation, infamy,
dishonour, loss, with the variants & analogues of these'

milk eye on tentacle stalk is
bruised & rolled by star-wave;
cut by the pack-ice, punctured
as the vision stutters & flirts with darkness

think it, see it
tell you with my death,
                    the energy
used once only
physicist is laughing, dead in his chair
his laugh opens the first wound in Skofeld's neck

lets the first light out;
dust cartwheeling among the beech trees

Insect

insect
('Mantis' they call him, or 'Fly')
is witness, key
to the whole matter

the alchemist writes:
'Do not allow even an insect
to be in the room where you are working'

insect is the observer,
                    turning the field
of consciousness, Third Eye, agent of
the paranormal, telecosmic, superspace;
   mover, destroyer
embalmed in retrospective time fluids

devours aphid collaborators, living
as they scale the stem,
                  as they climb
they are eaten;
insect works the nuclear equation
what is needed,
          additional,
is unattached consciousness
this insect gives,
              eye in armour,
the winged eye of Egypt
energy, metamorphosis,
                 change,
is locked within this disguised system.

Skofeld had his number
& the reflected hum of his own sin,
code-breaker, the unseal'd lips,
aware that insect is the final
stitch in the triangle;

(E.I.A.E.)

completes the crystalline screen

insect is an avatar of death, knows sees,
moves here & in the field
of planetary wash:

is alien & immediate

put out the eye of insect with heated needles,
cut his brain knob, hack off
his informing tongue,

butcher his signalling hooks

Skofeld is violence; prisons insect
in the tomb of quantum literature,
adds this small measure of cannibalised liquid
as a period, or symbol,
to the ink'd reductions of Munich alchemies

is insect the voice of physicist
whose throbbing chant

is the immortality
of smoothed calculation, pure sign as language
invisible
silent seizure, life & death hungers

miniaturized, our Minotaur is
faulting the web trap
battering the light bulb

insect re-enters Skofeld's stream under the finger nail

& then the silence, 'the preparation of darkness'

'The Enemy of the Stars'

'He demonstrated all the formulae. After coming to the end of geometry, he applied himself to algebra ... said later that the Goddess Namagiri had helped him to solve the most complicated problems. Alone & single-handed he had mastered & outstripped the mathematical achievements of a whole civilization ... was elected a Fellow of the Royal Society, & to a Fellowship at Trinity College, Cambridge. He lived in a world of numbers. It is impossible to express in simple terms the nature of his discoveries, which had to do with the most mysterious properties of numbers. While at Cambridge he ... formed a small library & a card-index of all sorts of phenomena that did not admit of a rational explanation.'

Skofeld reversed
               Olson's claim for Melville
    that he
'pushed back so far he turned time into space'
Skofeld pushed so fast
                   he turned space into time
PLUS: 'intelligence' is a distortion of time
    on his bunsen,
it is as crude as that,
             smell
the wet peat-bog in the flame;
                  he heats the glass rod,
time is forced to leap & dance,
               turned
on itself, again & back,
           inhuman
repetitions of alchemy;
dusty lab coat on a nail in the door,
his school notebook
           black backed;
neat figures in ink, notes finalised
by the firmness of the script, the acid clarity

thus he cracks it:
you don't need the Rutherford Institutes, the Cavendish
or anything as vulgar as calculus
i.e. Lovecraft was *right*
                            with his cod
      'post-Euclidean calculus'
his 'starry window'
                       'shining trapezohedron'
'window on all time & space'

pedants are outmanoeuvred
                            if time is
in any way understood
                     as an adjunct of architecture:

now you are moving towards it

rainy hands press the window back

in four separated panels:
fox, chicken's foot, old woman & cup

□

between the stars
                     black spawn of the dead
intelligence projecting its luminosity earthwards
       living clouds
                 pawing the light crystal,
sharp moments are swallowed
language here is necessarily imprecise
       but accurate
true is vague, the brain emits a rich
juice of its emptiness
honeysuckle trace odour
                   through uninhabited places,
      hoof star frozen
on flay'd skins
           of unfinished calculation

Skofeld has lost physicist
sends words in search of his dust

Skofeld knew his power ended
                 where the page
     curled in bonfire
was swallowed back into swamp
where ink broke off its irritation on skin & cell
physicist's power swept through
      not inside limits
             not inside
the rock case, or the ice
         deep as
what is known

the ant configurations
         of physicist's post-mortem humour
climbing on ladders of the dead,
piercing the night,
                    unlocking
the secrets of triple-stars, black holes
                                   reversing forward

all the old used dreams
                         die in the skin crease
             of Skofeld's seeing

the sentence, unfinished, hooks itself
                     over the picture rail
                                    like the shed skin
of Marie Jeanette Kelly
                     like the cured trophies
of hieratic python jewellery

with Skofeld the glitter of despair
the crystal dissolving slowly in his ear

*'Finally, in raising mathematical thought to its highest
degree of abstraction, man perceives that such thought
is not perhaps his exclusive property. He discovers that
insects, for example, seem to possess a special sense
which we lack, that there is, perhaps, such a thing as a
universal mathematical intelligence, & that out of the
totality of all living things emerges a Voice which is
the Voice of the Supreme Master-Mind ...'*

'Masters of the Universe'

BENEATH BRASS, BONE:
the prophecy of Slade, the Fate of England

'Thus to burst Death's membrane through – slog beyond – not float in appalling distances'

A man's head in a plastic bag. The enclosing darkness confirmed by the further wrapping of a woollen balaclava. At rest. The cold floor of a urinal stall. Placed, & by his own volition; facing West. It is the prophetic, the head of Slade. Thin hair, slicked with sugarwater, caps the skull. The cranial folds licked into order, sweetness seeps through as slow energy poison, domestic syrups strangling the sources of fire. What word is left, what impulse, what charge towards light, what plant opening on the tongue: whatever is left in this island, among the moistures of the dead, the distilled wisdoms, finds entrance in this cave of darkness, this bone machine sealed into its glassy skin.

Climbing with the sun, at choice, out along the rim of Isla's Dune: Penton St, Barnsbury Rd, to where Richmond Avenue dips & surges to the West. The redshift into haze, cold Highgate, woods filtered blue, retreating, distance enlarging, the folding of morning, place chosen, witness to this confession. Slade has no place, all curvature, smooth everywhere, one circumference of thought meeting itself. The agreed location allows us to describe, to put limits on infinite extensions of rhetoric. This is the chosen exterior. The hutment, wayside shrine. Among trees: 'the public lavatory'. But the interior will not serve. Too surgical, tight. Slade chooses instead the setting of the Islington High Street dugout with its fine brass, its water-tanks, its length. The sound of water running over weathered marble, drip of green silurian swamp, glass too cold to touch, aquarium silence inducing the urge towards pious confession. It is here that the final effort must be made.

The head must make a communication necessary beyond torso. It is charged & live, hot, with the grey electric tortures of garages, nails in the tongue, genital spark, scored skin, bruises spreading & bursting, cosmetic preparation for the death of the body. The swallowed teeth &

pains, tyre manufacturer's name appended to the spread beaver & satin pin'd-up flesh, bubble the high pink into his mouth, the chainsaw hacks through his arteries, he is released, bone burns into charcoal, fat spatters their varnished boots. The corpse could now be scattered, his finites, definitively, split. Found floating. The torso sinks into river mud. The legs hang white in local tides, adhering to the pole of fish totems, the raw mush. But the head is free to speak: all muddy obstructions cleared. Garrulous in this new freedom. The mouth is all word, the lips quiver. This marvellous trophy is exhibited, secretly, behind the closed doors of East End pubs: the Crown & Dolphin, the Carpenter's Arms, the Old Horns, the Seven Stars. Moves on to the South Coast, back into Essex. A triumph, a tribal score paid. Smoked pink in the flame of igniting Panatellas, Whiffs, Wintermans. The scattered limbs, & knuckles, fingers rap out accusations at low tide, in shale graves & fox-holes, in urban woodland, in concrete, in refuse, across horizons the fragments connect. The word is forged, the wisdoms focused.

The episode that is & was Slade he is reluctant to conclude, to close down, until the word, whose ghost he is, has been spoken; a word as substantial as that ghost of a flea, & gleaming, now, in pristine urgency. He is the victim of his own finality. Now & forever. Advancing entropy. Incapable of expressing his essence or escaping from it.

He is immune to the touch of the wind that destroyed him, though if he comes physically into contact with even the shadow of a dog he is gone. Scarcely there. His conviction less than a rumour. A low glimmer, a star burnt in lime.

His notion of the universe is moving backwards, snail-like, into the cave of origin, the only possible instigation or source of energy, the explosion, the drama, the moment of death. Energy that was the destruction of his previous self. So his birth is out of willed suicide. He died in a mirror, funnelling through, as time reversed, made way for him. Slade realises that he is infinitely attached to that point of extinction, all his motive force, before & after, comes from this fountain. The conic section is smooth, allows for irregularities, singularities, bends, shifts, faults. All that he has, & is, flattens, tubes out, into wire, elongates. The words stretch into colours, streaming back into his eyes. Implosion reversed, as on film. The severed head is lit by this knowledge. For there to be Time there must be Event, & someone using it, no other description possible: without action, no time. No forward.

Seizure. The knuckles of his lost hand make this the eternally repeating moment. The one place is stressed into a fan of frozen sequences. Place is never the same. The moment is enacted, over & over, in invisibly varied locations. An imagined Wall of Brass, an urge to protect this island, is being forged from Slade's knuckles. The pins pulse red. The charge runs into his creased fingers where they are hidden in a deepfreeze storage unit – in Loughton, where the great east-moving ley crosses the old forest; Shelley's Hill, Debden Slade ('Deadman's Slade'), with Genesis Slade half a mile to the north, the scald marks of his mother's tartan rug. His name precedes him into the map, his death; cold wind streaming into his nostril.

The dead, frozen at their event horizon, strike, like vipers, through the ring of frost, the same crimes not quite completed; leer from behind the protection of their elders, the oak, the beech, the hornbeam, birch, maple, blackthorn & common crab, bird cherry, goat willow & butcher's broom.

And postulated, in eternal opposition, is the Head of Brass, the fate of the island, buried with Bran at the White Mount, lost. The head manufactured by Friar Bacon, whose climax was the sole imperative, 'Time Is' – unable to reach beyond naked description. A man-made industrial thing, metal worked, mined, purified, animated by female secretions; back of the skull resonant to Europe's cargo, interior fed with local knowledge.

The process of this new oracle is mummification, out of time, the leather'd scalp of Slade. Behind him, & through the forest, the fen, the coast, is that ancient miracle, the Wall, the unseen guardian of value. It is pegged & gated by those high consciousnesses situated in the East of England, those wills, those animators of the actual, hidden in Cambridge, Brightlingsea, London, curving through to Sussex. They are set into the wall. The wall is their stance, & the connection between them, the spread. They concentrate the attention on the skull & urge it to speech, articulation. The dried lips move. Its own impulse is another, & opposing, thing. It speaks out of the corruption of the city. It breaks language out of wound & curse.

Slade's aborted syllabic urge has its analogue in the spasms of graffiti-scribblers. It boils too fast for his mouth, is a solar dictate, shafting from the loins, where no loins are. The way they hurl those frantic messages onto the brick. Slade suffers it, no means of writing; he erupts in adrenalin skin colour change, muscles twitch in his cheek. No sound to be heard. The excess spills, mixes with, the voices of Borley, slogans on the walls of bunkers, begging letters in urinals. No blood travels to his eye.

He is romantic & reactionary as are all the spiritually ambitious souls. His point-of-view, curiously, remains almost six feet from the ground

& does not fall to his new sack-in-the-corner position. The merciless & predatory ear of Joe Orton flaps in his face, damp, like a bat, unsatisfied, haunting these tiles for a short eternity, furry with blood mat hair, sharp with splinters of bone. He reads on the brickwork: NF FUCKS MEN. And is not displeased. Belief in visionary release through action, any action that breaks the chain of inertia. Sodomy. Fascism. The Heroes do not want to keep everything as it is – but to make it as it was in Myth Time, which never happened, but which is happening now as they strike the first surrogate blow.

Feet tread down the dead faces into the yielding earth, the leaves, crisp skins flattened, nothing feels. Only aware of a limb as the pain climbs through it, mind among the high trees, the gathering clouds. He treads, with a satisfaction like tobacco, on these mounds & herbal plains. He crushes.

The skull rolls, polarised, caught between opposing magnetic fields. Did it have hair? It did. Each hair a thought, a spine, an action, blazing upright from its alien seed-bed.

He is indifferent to the bright wind optimism of these October streets. He drives his antler into the clouds. Pulling away from the site that he has chosen for his last stand, away from the human debris that came to him with the bricks.

In Slade's acoustic chamber the hawk-nosed man of the west, launched on the Powers, lolls, staggers, his song of plaint, his nasal accusations, rise & shake the polished tiles, the thick brass pipes, the venereal plaques. A Kerry man whose song is a challenge, to the City & the Moment, a disembodied purity, as he pisses onto his cuffs, causing the old tweed to steam, onto his unlaced boots. Nothing drips from his slack member. Though it remains held out over the fresh water that rushes into the trough. A newspaper bulges in his overcoat pocket. His companion two stalls clear, is silent, dehydrated on a sour binge, all fires gone, in Angel exile, in No-Man's Islington.

Darkness of the Nebula closes about the dugout; the urinal is wheeled out among the stars. The song of the old Republican spills thinly between the dust of comets; into the great trench of blackness, into the absence of warm animal light. The head is sucked across the floor, itches into numbers, into marked insects, scarabs, marble chips. Each with its sigil, each impulse has a value: a reason for existence, a motive, a reason for movement. The head of Slade still looks like a head, rings hollow, an elegant lattice of numbers in treaty, in alliance, re-entering the ionized dust cloud, mating with silica, iron, false carbon. The cloud thickens, all voices, all numbers, radial velocities, become the galactic motive, into the arms of the Nebula, bone embrace, stress factors, Slade's purpose served, what he thought

if consciousness keeps the clouds afloat, the ribs – then the unconscious is forced down into the darkness where it is active: the unconscious is made out of darkness, the dust cloud is woven from the shape of Slade's head, forced wide, travelling beyond the west, there is no west – into that envelope, travelling plains of nothingness where the compass loses itself

speech

SLADE'S INVECTIVE:

      all life is star .
the shadow cannot of its own volition leave the ground
      all energy is war .
opposites united, stitch the flux
the weapon discharges the need to reply
the head, cut, floats on its arteries
      like a kite
watered in dust, the plant of bone .
life is evil, & its mirror

surface repels (hyper-space / emptied mind)
repulsion like attraction
speeds through the barrier

zones describe, & do not limit

the stars abandon the human strategy
like 'Star Wars' operate in archetype

the stars foreclose

every nerve is star born
the dust comes out of our faces
reforming the marvellous
the child of galaxies
the old fire emotions writ large
Keats – holiness of the heart
is modular entrance
is shape of star, essence
the heart floats
cut free of its strings

alone endures,
without actors to clothe the word
gravities to contain the light
shapes where the light clusters

as it comes through glass
all light breaks to this pattern
as we reach across, blood erected into bone
as the skin dreams of folding
enclosing, about the coin
legs into cups
as the beasts rise up & walk like men
face to face, the thought crackles
blue beam for hero, blood jet for power
clamped together in sickle

the hooded core strikes

the assembled fragments
join to illude a new world, globe
of spittle shot into a snake's eye

time is what we cut out of the reptile's belly

Slade faces them. His audience is not posterity, but the dead. In this alone – like Baudelaire. Not truth itself, the abstraction, but the truth of his own instinct brought out, set down. All that he was. Facing the raised half-circle, the expectant galleried masks, sterile planets lifting above the wooden tiers, the sawdust, the table. His peers, set-faced hierarchies of the dead, non-critical, without irony, returning his effort, untouched; but subtly altered. The ecstasy of silence, cunningly, denied.

'To make it worth while to destroy myself, there is not enough
of myself there to do it with'

BOOK TWO

WESTERING

GWANTOK

becoming white he spills
                              silver
agate stone out; that is
the kind of word to allow and it could
be natural, chemical, or
what your fingers describe
and have here in this room
        slopes of water, waterwoods
a small crescent beach
of stone powder, the oak arm
made pure by water current
(to let light through)
not in opposing the other
but allowing spiral drive expansion

warmth is crystalline
and we *do* share, it is not forced up
and when we are drunk and stagger uphill
feeling as though we were
running into sawdust
                        we must acknowledge
the frosted carpet, the starry helmet
and the Magic Door,
                        not closing nor opening
where sheep skull is safely exhibited,
as thematic & waxy,
                        the candle can be risked
white is what is later and carried away
on the new book, the planetary waves

no need to run, to put pen down
nailing owl by his claw to branch
dishonouring the taste of meat on crow's breath
fearing wolf matter in the lead-paint room
it is all contained
the stream alters, remains the same
talk bright with sedimentary reference

beware again the acoustic spear
or gravity the centre
                    is everywhere

II

'the dead go the way of the sun'
washed in ashes, fires banked

'androgynous and without fear'
orifices sealed, power between her thighs

Bowen cannot make himself tall,
speaking into her heat,
making hot in this flooding, leaf-draped place

'From this moment her vaginal vibrations become of
positive magical value, and normal consciousness altogether
ceases in her. She becomes oracular and the words that flow
from her vulva are charged with supreme potency.'

male & female, Gwantok is
smoothed water medium

sky overflows against rock that resists, stays upright

cave advances, voices of cave
in Gwantok, by Gwantok, arteries stream out
his hand unclenches,
        Fan
marks the corners of the given land

Maen Madoc, solitary erect,
                              felled circle,
Maen Llia, immense powerful, neglected
slab forbids access to hill station

in the woods Gwantok is mushroom
well spoken of,
                    in flow, entheos
makes himself herself, self-satisfying
admired by nineteenth-century amateurs
fell walkers, naturalists, moth assassins

the ornithologist does not care
city folk notice a wader, white-chested
round, pebble-pretender, midstream

plunge under, feathers flashing
under the river
                    and swoop away
to glanced distance, mantic, magnificent

the great and wonky clock of the hills
gathers seedlings others have planted

voices, forgetfulness drumming at the ear,
washing through the inner caves to the altar bone,
the dead in the water erasing all message, clean tape;
water speaking in tongues, wiping mind clean
the Om of the water, mantra, waterwheel

down, down; clouds caught
spiralling surge of whirlpool

Gwantok echoes Marilyn Monroe:
'suicide is a privilege'

WEST, LIGHT

'...West is the body
     ... It is the Circumference'

surge, input of snakes' heads
how dip your hand in such a well?
stones in skin, diamonds, black
on adder's nape, his shoulders, sleeping
by the road fringe, Salisbury to Warminster,
the A303, red wadding, west side of Stockton Wood
head to thaw, Old Sarum
as early sun heats the slow pattern

light alternates, wide horizons
stretch our small retinal conceits, anchor
this moment
          detonated clouds, mammal slow
train or bus
         window panels
stiff with landscape, Nunnery
    atmosphere is more than the staining filter
across tree-net, lichenous mossy
distorted light pulse of evening
angle narrows
          illumination of essence increases
sticks beat on the oily cloth of water,
two swans hammer air,
straining to lift direct at the Tor

we have circumnavigated the profile
of the Sleeper, the snake path
worn into his cheek, though it is
not as simple as that, more radical, stronger

wind follows the diagram of the tree
all those directions, pigeon
woodpecker & messenger owl
along the avenue of cortical dark,
greengrowth to Butleigh Wood,
dry applause of winged escape
the sentinels lay false tracks
over twilight fields – it is the owl,
the swooping white archaic span
gone from feathered hourglass repose,
verge to verge tactility,
powerfully sensing all panicked movements

what is to be discovered has gone
and is coming, conversions translations
secrets buried in the crozier'd luminescence
of the grub curled on my collar;
the foxmask eaten by maggots,
tail picked clean as a whip of bone,
stoat on Longleat wall, bounding
hares of the Ridgeway or
earthing colonising rabbits of Cadbury Castle

the sound of the West is here
in the prime syllable, in the utterance
A – AH – ARTHUR
taught to an unlanguaged child
as wide as that, as eager, reluctant

spine packed solid with chalk, peat
giving body to blood, trans-
substantiation of all growing things

man of use only to stand between,
for passage, of forces of light,
impulse, between sky & earth:
margin eye for traces
of the original beast ancestor
his own wrist to reach out

holy fire in the well, blind
white flame on the thorn,
wounds of sanctity, martyrdom of travel;
roads of bone, paths of death
the gull swerves, alert
'static water' will not splash
        the marbled sleeper,
shell crushed underfoot, greedy snail
works out time, the ram's bloody horn

to your knees then, to the ground,
face pressed deep into midden
that you rise, that you lift,
that the wind pulls your hood, face
into peaty distillation, the bungalows,
carriage-lamp steakbars, housing
estates, that you rise, into bondage,
lapdog, lorry & wire,
pull barbs through your skin, that you rise
spray, that you see, tarmac, pig & poultry,
even dry dog turd in the sarcophagus,
tape-recorder, flash, & anorak,
that you climb the hill, that you make
bone into elastic, that you
wind entrails around the path,
that you face the wind & hold, that you rise
& fall down along the whole molten track of sun,
that you rise, that you rise
that you rise out of, rise into
what hills, Wales
        such clear distance

JOHN COWPER POWYS, VICTIM OF THE WEST

'Aspirin, wild violets & iron'

The Wessex of Powys is not the Wessex of Hardy, and it does not operate within the same temporal ocean. Hardy's tales are fossil vertebrae printed on the shell of Powys, stone skeletons within his meat; firmer, barer, not so vast, rushing, weird, and jokey. The hook of Hardy is austere, his hunger harpoons the pleasure principle. Powys does not possess, and he does not punish.

Is it even the same ground? The secret forces that move between their chosen sites are recognised by both men. Hardy's puppets are struck down by them, stopped: too thin to stand against. Powys knew the serpent beneath the earth, that the force of earth-magnetism was always active: Cerne Abbas, Chesil Beach, Stonehenge. What was it? It related to moments of ecstasy and half-conscious ceremonial re-enactments. But there is a clownish, wordy, novel-scribbling, man-of-letters quality that will not be shaken off. Pieces of self are evenly distributed among male and female characters, deformed, made whole, beast and rock. Powys is speaking of the power of projection: Will vs. Time.

He had located, though he did not spell it out, the track of the Ancestral Beast, journeying and questing. The Run of the Hare, the Wolf Loop, the Leap of Salmon Father: now quantified as 'Lines of Force', 'Ley Lines', significant alignments. It is this chart, burnt in deep-bone, that he goes over; moving through the rhythms of the time-swell, activating, affirming, agitating in excited prose – and, finally, so I believe, decaying, holding back, stopping short.

For Powys, as an initiate, it was a long process of becoming, of being made, of making himself – ready. Solitary journeys, bleak cottages, exile: performance. Grasping the wand or stick, undergoing surgery: exquisite pain. Knife fear. Repressed sadistic urges. Visions of animals in cages. Against the cult of vivisection. A prophet made gaunt with travel, with essays and theatres, and sermons given against diminishing quanta of time, while the tongue thickened to block his mouth, and teeth fell on the desk. He was polished and refined by privation. The word cellar floods under him. He did not know *what*. He did not know *who*. He did not know *when*. And that is true initiation. The Solitary Giant looking small on his mountain.

And then, when it seems to be too late, a rush, a frenzy, an amazed and amazing production of enormous texts, heretical bibles, linked sequences, channellings of place: *Maiden Castle, Weymouth Sands, A Glastonbury Romance, Atlantis.* Voices of time, reversed vortices, medieval groans and clanks. Poems of wood and stone, songs of earthworm. The tenderly eroticised consciousness of pondweed. So many elements competing for his love. And now it is against gravity; retreating into Wales, deeper, higher, against the Chinese mountains, glacial lakes and slate slopes of Blaenau Ffestiniog.

Things happen. When this process is begun, it is a literal alchemy: meaning that the author repeats, he goes over, he sits in solitude. He works it, beats out the shape; huddled in a winter coat. Goatman. Changeling. Parson's son. Serving what purpose, which gods? The sheer bulk, the volume of it, his task.

He is transformed, bathed in thin light. He appears as a sage, a visionary. He leaks light on demand. They speak of him, the clods, as a saint, a holy man stitched from humours. He spends his late days walking behind the house, along the ridges of the hill, backtracking. He does not write, directly, about where he is – but where he was. He goes back through the curtains, a sequence of misty dissolves. He is often a pace or two behind himself (those brilliant projections). He is dragged along as summoned events begin to manifest. The details of biography, the small revenges, are not important. But it is this Miltonic contest, the wrestling of angels (ideal and punished selves), that releases a disembodied reality and makes it fly: *conflict.* It builds, it springs, it thirsts towards violent and active relief. The skull-crunching blow on Glastonbury Tor stalled forever by some failure of nerve: the arcing fountain of blood pumping into the sky with each beat of the heart. *It does not happen*, is battened down, denied. Motors of revenging bodily impulses vibrate, and then become still. They calcify. Salty lusts are cupped and swallowed with draughts of muddy water.

There is so much left undone that the hot texts spill on far beyond personal death. There had to be doppelgangers long before the obituary date is confirmed in the bibliographies; as when, for example, Powys appeared to Dreiser (when he was somewhere else entirely). Or the buried sage, now one of those figures available in tin-roofed shelters to spiritualist séances: clots of quivering ill-defined matter spewing through the gauzy veils. Smoke in Indian travesty smelling of sulphur. The ghostwriter raps on tables like a demented woodpecker. This is not the cosmic frontier trail of the high ones, Blake, Milton, Shakespeare – whose works he devours, though they are too tidal and deep for any single lifetime. The process continues for aeons after death. Blake revises Milton. Keats absorbs Shakespeare. Powys is not of this company. Nobody is capable of allowing himself or herself to be possessed, and therefore remade, by the totality of this cycle of gigantic prose fabulations. They complete themselves.

When he was gone, worshippers paid their respects, the various Wilsons and Wilson Knight. Like Quakers in whitewashed chapels in their gloves and coats. Waiting for the flare of posthumous enlightenment. He is reissued, remembered, cultified. Presented for a season among the bronze fittings and dressed windows of Regent Street in London's West End. The pools of red-gold carp. And those English places continue to speak through him. 'He enjoyed,' so it is said, 'the process of temptation itself more than he could possibly have enjoyed any fruition of desire.' Amen. Indeed. Just so.

BOOK THREE

BRERTON,
THE DARKNESS

BRERTON, GOING NORTH

'if eternity / is in front infinity is behind'

cave in thunder unfolds its darkness

unshaven for two days
      and carrying this self-horror, loud
in front of him / against shopkeepers
sellers of pork pies, milk, wimpy, petrol
      his red eye
                tourist, his fear smelt
like a winter child sewn into rabbit fur
        'that girl has a tail'
low mist & knifing hail on Wessenden Head

'home'. 'the road'. 'fire'. flood'. Brerton names
devices of safety, I concur
                  this expedition
demon ramps from north across peat moors
      smells his fear (again) like
flat beer now, Worthington E pissed out
         or held too long, ullage dregs

  'don't break the ring'
     Arbor Low, forbidden

A skeletal Sumerian cow, horned and in discrete sections, terrifying, relentless, appears scratched on the smoke-stained afternoon screen: a travelling print of *The Exorcist*, slumped in Buxton. An initiation, so it seems, engraved directly on the eyeball: to follow Brerton everywhere, as he walks, quests, drives through rain, limestone to millstone grit. A cave drawing with no cave found in the desert and prophesying future war. Flesh cooked in petrol. Children and goats drinking from lakes of oil. The cow reveals its satanic nature at the start of the second reel, coming through overlit episodes and nightmare flashes; a signature to follow, a seal, for illusory comfort and distraction, during surgery and invasions of the cortex. As if comfort could be got from a diseased and dying animal.

The drive back to the cottage, over the moors with a single Cyclopean headlight, is a long M.R. James horror of possession. There are now elements in the vehicle with Brerton, beside him, behind him; breathing where he has no breath. *Touching.* It is a relief, when he flees south through the dull midlands, a gargoyle church path, when a tyre explodes and a random nail rips his cheek as he struggles to replace it. And he bleeds into the road.

DOVE TO MANIFOLD

among the bitter arrangements
           of hoarded valued books
       & prized stones about that stone house
David Jones, steam on the glass
inescapable obsequies for
           Cyril Connolly's toadlike pomp
fatty orations in ash, light breaks across the valley floor

this part of the island, Brerton wrote, is body-cheese
or, gamey plains of Africa, sour wine
recorded music and feats of candlelight
'the most ancient strobe of man'

tomorrow he must drown between caves
Brerton with his newspaper, travelling north

'J. Robert Oppenheimer, witnessing the first test
of a nuclear weapon, confessed to *tasting* sin'

BRERTON, GREENMAN

'Nature is sufficient in itself, and needs no creator, there is no god.'
            Marquis de Sade
'I am afraid of the life after death.'
               T.S. Eliot (In conversation, 1919)

horrible hymeneal tape of screams and scuffles
          chairs
                 muffled
children's voices cry in pain
                 wooden pegs drag on linoleum,
and this too is the absolute darkness of the cave,
          too much, too much for us to bear

the image does not wound Brerton enough
      he finds his way
             back to the mysteries of Dove,
grass, sweet water and long summer days

drive out at last, scribbling done
to where light dies at city's edge
and wind strips flesh from abandoned cars

what he is discovering is terrible
(about himself and the human kind to which he belongs)
he must be punished
    society wants him obliterated
        like Fritz Lang's German *M*,
even the lowlife would break his bones for bread,
beat him senseless with newsprint truncheons,
    so that the constant *drip drip drip*
          would stop
            the limestone tape
               salt in stone

Brerton's mouth rots,
wires depend from his fingernails

the love he defines is ancient as woodsmoke, a mistake
something cancelled and grown again

his north has been fed on chickens and steak,
scampi roadhouse varnish

the old stones are grown over
land mutilated by war

'smil'd with superior Love'
as police records confirm

a burnt fingerprint

labyrinth map, New Grange
he donated
clue to the century file

what he tore out is not repaired

'They are not mine,' Blake told Catherine,
a few hours before death came.
'They are not mine. They are not mine.'

BOOK FOUR

BOWEN, HIS JOURNEY

BOWEN, HIS JOURNEY

'With respect to the vision of the Ghost of the Flea, seen by Blake, it agrees in countenance with one class of people under Gemini, which sign is the significator of the Flea; whose brown colour is appropriate to the colour of the eyes in some full-toned Gemini persons. And the neatness, elasticity, and tenseness of the Flea, are significant of the elegant dancing and fencing sign Gemini. This spirit visited his imagination in such a figure as he never anticipated in an insect.'
John Varley, *Zodiacal Physiognomy*

Bowen the Flea, under Gemini;
under blanket, hides his face from the whips of the Sun.
Everyday he thought of money, his conscience,
between closed self and this interpretation of the World.
Everynight he lost his dream. And feared the search.

Bowen, disguised as icy Muscat, out of deep
Arabia, into barroom: the Fly. Sticky-footed
Muscat walks upon Groucho's ceiling, all ears.
Bowen is who he is; am I. Bowen. Razor, soapcake.

Whiteman looking for his ancestor.
Through darkglass, beyond reflection
his own, long, sick face; whey-custard.
    Beyond
watervapour visage, the horned moon
suckles a star. How rare. Night.
How bloody ('the lachrymose') cry of insects.
Bowen on the run. Face hidden in hair.

MIRACLE PLAY

'By blood, frogs, and lice; by flies, death, botch and blain'
Bowen took colour. Flushed countenance in numbers.
'By hail, by grasshoppers, by darkness, and by care.'
Driven out, expelled, turned on himself: far north.
                              'A sudden plague called instinct.'

CONVERSATIONS WITH KENNEDY

'She also said she had bought nothing except a couple of bathing suits.'

the traces (to us) seem like that special pink
of cat's eye overflap
making death a necessary afterthought, mortality
leaks from his pointy hair-face: a thought fox

not to be nudged any further by the Outside
or pushed into some species of 'plaint'
never forming an adequate sentence, so that winter
o'erhangs him like a deserted football stand

Bowen talking back to his demons,
                    'he's really rattling, man'
rattling, for sure, but the real
            is the big prize from another school

chewing rind, blissful in porridge time
without ego in soapy bathwater

FROM HIS JOURNAL

if Bowen kept a journal he did not enjoy it
he did not want 'a journal'
                and nothing to do with
that kind of *performance*. Out of control, cold
wrap of fingers around throat, seeming to support
tilt of slack head
           ... house cat, yesterday, in lust for meat,
battered at the cutting, £1.18p for 2 lbs of
stewing steak, fed us (2) well on Thursday &
again (now 3) very well on Friday, but still,
shock in butcher's cave for the casual visitor:
hacked lumps fingers nails
scooped & flung...
           cat wild in approval & need, is fed
some gristle & lardy fat, made wilder, yes, but also
child with clockwork crocodile bothering,
whipping at, the cat, motor turning loud,
cat flees through catflap only
to return instantly to prospect of raw meat, only
to flee instantly from tone
of new child's voice...

these things want to say themselves, half-
willingly, I name. Bowen transcribes.
Control is word of praise in these anthologies.
Letters. Essays. Mind is shrine, light. So
they speak with approved science:
      'and so', 'we', 'thus' –
marks of the hireling, coldprint on floor
of bedroom, birchlight splintering
through undrawn curtains. Each tile
     is also a decision.
'Choice' refers to the condition of meat.

'WEARING A CROCODILE BADGE'

because the stars are not mentioned
they do not live
weight of vapour of badly contrived emotional
fluids between manbody and womanbody here now
on eastern flank of our city neck
                                    because of
the weight of water in the sky we
turnface to ground: thick tongues
throb with groundstung reverberations as
they, we, walk towards Hoxton, confirming
what I had imagined to be a long shot, that indeed
the BM Ethnographic Storehouse (Uxbridge functional
modernist Hoover-type factory) is in Orsman Street;
                              Pacific Rim
totem pole, pole of hardheads, chicken blood of Benin,
beaten brass;
ocean-facing tree, wolf mask
                              savage
lines of energy colour.

We bent our backs to pick upon
the rush of water under the manhole-
cover that was
a card (face) for this moment.

Now the child tenses for Laurel & Hardy. Concentrates.

Buried alphabets flicker as consciousness bears down
word is made, man is made, 'each a star'
Crowley's formulation distorted in wooden mouth
of late-century New York City
media wolves, pod people
cutting the outline into sheet flesh
open the scratch of blood where mined blade
                                    carves

star emerges as repressed dazzle
the movement outward
the surge, the movement behind
you don't see it, you can't see it
but it is spoken & it is so

star is memory
                of what we will become
& this suits Bowen, fine, not as an excuse
for conduct unbecoming or cosmetic surgery
on the face of God, climbing
that fat capitalised 'G' with a silver ladder.
        Bowen forgives nothing that he remembers
leeks, cauliflowers shot full of holes,
in the dark bedroom of bad cheese dreams
someone else is having, some conceptualist
lacking the meat to get sick;
some otherbody's tomb, some other body
        a much deeper
                        star.

I defy you to stop, to act dead – stopped
in every living particle of being, shutdown
so firmly (that *is* control) that even the aura
pines & wilts
I defy you to be dead, convincingly enough
the bugs don't want to move through
your territorial potentialities

reduce your range of options
to the marble bird (dove?) with chipped neck
we carried home from Kensal Green Cemetery
and filled with wet earth, now used
exclusively by weeds, even sycamore can't
get a grip on such a narrow cup

then see what happens, know the risk
you bet the hold will be broken
and new light well worth the waiting

entrance in blood in shit
out of beaver flap the moistened
globe of the unclosed cap, where world
snakes in & out on deep-pull tides
of generated starsplash

star is the spark, frozen hard

laugh with Kali in the maw
admire teeth, her toys are
on those screens you wear; wrap
yourself in fear, it sells tickets.
Mick told me last Sunday morning how
he clawed at the plush seats with his nails
'only £1.50 or a couple of nicker'
small contribution in the bucket
of pulled teeth, the whole power

'crossing over from another country,
surrounded by water; where there are no Indians'
                    A LIE
plenty of Indians but not the ones
who travel: Indians all through
that country, a scattered tribe divided into sub-sections
cut again, tongues nailed to table...
but they're still around, lurking
looking for word signs, driven down
from the ridges, they live disguised in Mason
Valley; can't afford tickets.
old white magicks, older newspapers

'amazed with no hand to find his head'

'just briefly'

SIGN OF THE ANGEL

An angel touched his shoulder
small crowd
he is seeing it advance through the 'magic'
(inverted commas borrowed from Allen Fisher)
of local television: INSPIRATION,
he dreams
   fen swathe approaching Ramsey,
or déjà vu hotel bedroom corridor
   The Sign of the Angel, Lacock
'England' is the land of the angel
   in serpent-
raising whistle, opposed to
concerts that excite Hand, solicit Kotope
as bone snaps in rabid jaw, or hunger

Bowen resolves to make a journey

pages of golden wheat turned down
chalkdust spread like a runway across Wiltshire

Bowen is launched; it is his hope, & bait
he is drawn, again & again, by the sweep of
    'the natural'
returning suns, retreating stars

Bowen moving out, Bowen
stepping into his own shadowtrack

blind as night bleeds from his side

MARBLE SPEAKS FOR BOWEN

I wandered the quarters of the heart of
our city. I entered the veins, lungs, ribs,
bowels, lights. I climbed into skull's cave.
And nowhere were prophets to be
found. The Temple was in power: as
iron machine. A bio-architectural, moon-fuelled
force field. Pulpits empty as deserted nests. And
from the roofs of cars nobody spoke
of the essential vision.

Doctrine was scattered among vagrants,
prostitutes, drunkards, mad-tongued
ramblers licking sustenance from walls.

Putting on a shirt that morning, hairs
of chest grey as an old horse.

I bought five lemons & returned,
dull & safe to bed.

'AFTER NINE & TEN, COMES DEATH'

'Maldoror fears the consequences of his words'
                              Lautréamont

last words he would apply
to himself, *Dorian Gray*, never read
'the rage of Caliban', distrust in pit of stomach
of Yellow Book, Harland, Corvo,
Beardsley, scented vomit
                              application
all that was spread here, the course of blood through
this book, these books, under seal
        'the highest, as the lowest, form of criticism
        is a mode of autobiography'
his force: flash of firefly illumination
        life executed, not excused
almost unlived, so he can't force open
the stiff covers and he will not read

Bowen understands text as
annotated suicide note. He looks
not unlike R.L. Stevenson. Consumption
written into the contract. Unnatural
fires of collapsed lungs.
Said to be an Aitu, a white ghost.
He haunts 16 Chepstow Place he haunts
the Suicide Club he raises all the demons
of this town. To invoke power he presses it
under his armpit, his paleskin. To fill himself
like sausage casing. Bowen in extreme north
driven off the highlands, settled as tenant.
Starved turf. Rheumy eye to heavens.
Bowen the pseudo-Scot. Bowen's shelves rest
on the Waverley Novels. Gone in the teeth.
Scotfree. Drinks Irish. Stories of fever.

Bowen the Jacobite. Clutches
at Rosicrucian pedigrees. Macgregor Mathers born
11 De Beauvoir Place, Hackney. He's at Bournemouth
with Stevenson, occult link with Kenneth MacKenzie,
and through him, Levi. Was Bowen Invader?
Was it Bowen in Whitechapel? Wood Street,
Brown Street, Black Eagle, Grey Eagle, Pearl, Phoenix.
FAILURE OF BLOOD-ERECTED VISION. Bowen in north wind.
Niflheim, freezing fog, injecting himself
with his leaking pen. Promethean Bowen
stitching the whole sequence together,
traveller, invader, colonist, journalist, planter, farmer,
mercenary, kingsman. Bowen fails
in the sun. Samoa. Ceylon. Tasmania.
Crucified by Mau Mau. Dead line.
Scribe *and* Pharisee.
Ends badly. All.
All energies turn
against him. His
notion of their strength
amplifies his weakness.
Fakery of noun colours.
Takes black
spot on tongue. Banished
beyond Mousa. Saint
islands. His refuge.
To identify the work to suffer
so that words are plain again.
And may be spoken. And spent.

AFTERWORD

If *Lud Heat*, Iain Sinclair's previous major work, may be put among the books that have made a significant contribution to a 'poetry of place' in Britain during the 1970s, then *Suicide Bridge* (which may have originally been intended as *Lud Heat, Book Two*) has gone a great deal further than this. There is no question of stale repetition. The perspective has changed from personal to mythic. In *Lud Heat* forces are charted against the progress of a life (Sinclair's own); here the forces are presented as named mythic entities.

'Intimate Associations', an introductory essay in the form of two interwoven texts, contains initial speculations on 'Myth and Place', and authorises the book's devices. Death, we are told, is the beginning of myth, it is the plot in which the peculiar type of 'lust' necessary to the creation of myths must be nurtured. (The place of death is *the* essential Place. 'Your whole journey has been to find it and complete the story.') Place is the totemic and tribal identification of Self. Man is rooted in Place but looks towards Myth for the energy of his vital mobility. 'Myth is the living breath of place, is life. Place, in travesty, ordains and invests man', makes him at its most extreme a mythic hero. Yet Sinclair is not concerned with specific places; his is a nomad's concept. The boundaries of our place expand and flow, armed with this portable sense of hereness. The two concepts have become inextricable. Myth/Place is a metaphor for consciousness, a kind of total being, akin perhaps to Heidegger's elusive paradoxical concept of 'dwelling'. For Heidegger too death was the Be-all and End-all of existence.

The names of 'characters' are lifted from Blake's *Jerusalem*, the sons of the oppressed giant Albion. Each mythic son was assigned a place in England. This correspondence between 'known man' and particular location Sinclair has preserved. During the account of the birth of the demonic twins Hand and Hyle, primitive twin/shadow cults merge into a cosmogony ('myth of the origin of the universe'): like sci-fi monsters (yet another myth archetype, more modern) they appear appropriately from a black hole, *ex nihilo*. London is their target.

> *They must be born again, anchored*
> *to the fate, the corruption, of this island*

They become the Kray twins, brutalised by sexual perversion, infected by a sexual paranoia.

> *HAND & HYLE, their disguise, sons*
> *dutiful & hating women*
> *who could trap*
> *and bring forth children, their own assassins.*

Coban, based by Blake in the cathedral cities, is the masturbatory germ of destruction behind the twins. Sinclair sees his image, his power, carved in stone in the Christian template: misericords and statues.

The first death is that of Kotope, rich Jewish wool merchant with underworld connections, particularly with another son of Albion, 'Peachey, the hit man'. His is the paranoia of bullet-proof Rolls Royce windscreens, travelling through London in a vain pursuit of an occult grail that will save him from the inescapable. 'The Manner of his Dying' is pastiche Burroughs: 'Six Arabs on the Doorstep' mow him down and then dissolve into the shrubbery. But death fulfils him, however ironically. He becomes the place.

> *His will*
> *erects one final, animal, vision of the city,*
> *his body its body, flying,*
> *& is gone.*

Yet outside myth the physical effect is negligible. He 'melts the Polar ice by one fraction of a degree'. Hutton's death is followed by dismemberment. The dispersal of his fragments becomes part of a savagely ironical ascendancy into myth.

> *Hutton the stiff one*
> *revolves through cement mixer*
>   *conglomerate*
> *with flint & gravel, with sand dredged aggregate*
>   *tipped,*
>   *born into the East Way Flyover...*
> *a literal & continuing part of the City*

There are other victims. Slade is, on one level, Jack the Hat, Kray victim. Yet his consciousness, reduced to a cosmic 'buzz', contains the whole of Pound's *Cantos* and other cultural artefacts beyond his scope, but within the author's. In myth, 'the lives and virtues of many men, many cycles, are compressed into the one'. And Slade is the prophet.

Similarly Skofeld, named after the soldier Blake expelled from his garden in Felpham, is a Cambridge academic. (Felpham is later glimpsed as present day 'Butlinland' during a vain search for Coban.) Kox, Skofeld's aide, is a drunken don with intolerable manners and no social graces, and is secretly the Cambridge Rapist. Prim college wives in their safe circle bleat against his incivility. 'There are names,' Sinclair tells us. 'You know the names / You do not know them, it doesn't matter.' Skofeld and Kox are nefarious representatives of the university where once the 'articulators of Albion's pain... translated life into language'. This literary mechanism has been less a medium of 'translation', more a cancerous academicism:

> the word devours the world.

Skofeld dies, an 'Enemy of the Stars', at the hands of a physicist, image of the academic with physical reality and cosmic power taken into account.

> Skofeld knew his power ended
> where the page
> curled in bonfire...
> where ink broke off its irritation on skin & cell.

In a long essay on Howard Hughes, Sinclair proves he can deal with powers beyond those of the immediate text, the 'real' myths one might call them. We are a media-manipulated cinema of the public myths as they emerge just ahead or behind the 'event screen'. Sinclair's prose is succinct and articulate as he surveys America's White House-underworld-CIA-big business-show biz nexus. Hughes is the Devil of this inferno. The energies have become too familiar for ease. Even Sinclair, in Blakean obscurity in London, producing the modern equivalent of Blake's Illustrated Books, could be swallowed by this power, 'If your thesis breaks surface instantly, is made public on media umbrella... then you have to work faster.'

The book's final words are those of the sealed, dismembered head of the prophetic Slade, as it lies on the floor of a London lavatory. Death has given him wisdom. It has also frozen him. Eventually he returns to the stars, to pure energy.

> *all life is star*
> *the shadow cannot of its own volition leave the ground*
> *all energy is war.*

Without action there is no time. And any action may bring visionary breakthrough. Yet Slade, and perhaps England, on whose harsh landscape he rolls, is beyond that.

The book, like *Lud Heat*, is set at an almost inconceivable pace, given its complexity, like that of a thriller. It is not necessary to insist upon Sinclair's learning, esoteric and eccentric though it is. I always read Sinclair at length (magazine excerpts cramp his work's scope, belittle his stature). Any pool of obscurity will be seemingly filled by the flow of the energetic prose, the 'narrative', as we're carried along with it. And myth, Sinclair recognises, demands narrative as its mode. 'The story told fresh in an historical present... It has to be very simple to work.' There is an acknowledged debt to Dorn's *Gunslinger* and Ed Sanders' racy and impressionistic account of the Manson murders, *The Family*. Sinclair recognises and accepts the danger that Myth generates 'a vertical energy called FASCISM.' He is as trapped by cosmic forces as mythicist as he was as a protagonist/articulator in *Lud Heat*. It is the madness of Manson and the instinctive violence of the Krays that haunts these pages. There is no escape. 'The first words of kindness/ are sugared rats of destruction' in this world. It is no less than 'Albion's pain', the 'fate of England', that Iain Sinclair presents in this mythology. It fully deserves its subtitle, *A Book of the Furies*.

— **Robert Sheppard**

(From a contemporary review at the time of the original Albion Village Press publication in 1979.)

AUTHOR'S NOTE

This new Skylight Press edition constitutes the most complete version, so far published, of *Suicide Bridge*. The Books of Gwantok, Brerton, and Bowen have been recovered from typescripts, notebooks and fugitive magazine. I would like to thank the editors of *Green Horse (An anthology by young poets of Wales)*, *PCL British Poetry Conference (June 1977)*, *Perfect Bound*, *Meantime (One)*, where some of this material first appeared in an earlier form. And I would like also to acknowledge the helpful provocations of the bibliographer, Jeff Johnson, who set me rummaging through the attic.

Lightning Source UK Ltd.
Milton Keynes UK
UKOW04f1325220913

217655UK00002B/36/P

SELF RELIANCE

MASTERY

Learn How to Be Self-Reliant, Live Sustainably,
and Be Prepared for Any Disaster

SELF RELIANCE
MASTERY

Learn How to Be Self-Reliant, Live Sustainably,
and Be Prepared for Any Disaster

NATHAN CRANE

Co-Authored With:

Jill Winger, Marjory Wildcraft, Sam Coffman,
Mike Adams, Gerald Celente, Matthew Stein,
Laurie Neverman, Doug Simons, Paul
Wheaton, Scott Hunt, Daniel Shrigley, Steven
Harris, David Christopher, Nicole Telkes,
James Stevens, Jason Matyas

First Printing, June 2015

ISBN 978-0-9914700-3-7

Panacea Publishing, Inc.
PO Box 29004
Santa Fe, NM 87592

www.PanaceaPublishingInc.com

Edited By: Transource Media
www.transourcemedia.com

Co-Edited by: Deana Crane

Table of Contents

Introduction

Not too many years ago every human being on planet earth was living in complete self-reliance. Our Great Grandparents all lived in some form of self-reliance, whether it be growing their own food, canning their vegetables, tending to their livestock, building and maintaining their dwelling or midscale farming, all of our Great Grandparents were living sustainably on the land with very little pollution and much less dependence than our society does today.

For thousands of years before our Grandparents and Great Grandparents took foot on the earth, our ancestors lived independently of machinery and in fairly close harmony with the planet, living totally self-reliant and dependent only on themselves and their small communities.

In some cases there were large communities in the thousands, but that was the exception, as most communities and tribes were only a hundred people or so, which helped create sustainability through small numbers of families working together supporting each other with the bare necessities such as food, water, clothing, shelter, socialization, art, ceremony and spiritual growth.

Each person in the community knew each other intimately; they worked together, played together, danced together, grew food together, and understood each other's needs, desires, skills, and weaknesses. There was a cultural environment of communal sustainability as each member of the community was able to step in and support the needs of the community.

That has all changed over the last two hundred years after the industrial revolution, and mostly due to the desire for more convenience, more power, expanded curiosity for world exploration, quicker results, and less connection to our ancestral spiritual and cultural heritage of communal living.

While I believe that our ancestors were living in ways that are far greater and in much more harmony than our current society is, I also see many of their faults and I see room for improvement and growth as we look at the future of humanity and ask ourselves the question of what kind of world we would like for our Grandchildren and our Grandchildren's Grandchildren.

Today we still live in communities, but they are not very communal. Community comes from the word "commune" meaning intimate communication or rapport. In our current industrial, urban, and inner city communities there is very little communication and a lot of urgency, stress, anxiety, worry, doubt, fear, disconnect and selfishness. You can walk down a busy city street in Los Angeles, Madrid, New York, Paris or Rome and pass thousands of busy human beings in only a minute's time and not say a single word or have a meaningful conversation with even one of them.

Most people are so busy with figuring out how to feed their families, pay the bills and buy the material objects they desire that they forget about the essential ingredients that make life meaningful, memorable, and fulfilling. If you've ever sat down at a table in a restaurant and had a cheerful conversation with a waiter or waitress, you remember that person and the conversation for days, weeks, months, and sometimes even years. But you can go to the same restaurant every day for six months straight and have the same mundane conversation every day such as, "Hello, how are you?" "Good, how are you?" "Great, thanks." "I would like to order...." "Great meal, thanks, goodbye", and your life passes by without any sense of joy, fulfillment, meaning or purpose while you are left wondering at the end of your life what it was all for.

To me life is about learning, growing, sharing, serving, and most important of all connecting to a deeper meaning and purpose within ourselves to a higher purpose that gives us a sense of joy and fulfillment on the planet. You can't ever attain this level of peace, joy, and happiness I'm speaking about if you don't learn how to live in a true community and you are always dependent on society to deliver you what you want at the touch of a button. While I appreciate all of the modern advancements that I use on a daily basis, I have also learned that none of it will ever lead to true happiness, as happiness is something that must be cultivated, not acquired.

I've been homeless on the streets addicted to drugs and alcohol without a dollar to my name more than once in my life, and on the other end I've helped millions of people through education and inspiration, generated millions of dollars, and am raising a beautiful family, all before the age of 27, and what I've learned over the brief but very eventful years is that no matter whether you have nothing or everything you could ever want, happiness and fulfillment have to come from within yourself.

What does happiness and fulfillment have to do with self-reliance, survival, and sustainable living? Everything!! Why would we want to survive on the planet only to live in pain, misery, fear, and anguish? Why would we want to store away food, water, and weapons only to find ourselves living with disease, terror, and a sense of meaningless endeavor?

The truth is we don't want to live that way, and having been on both ends of the spectrum more than once, I can tell you that you don't have to live that way. You can have anything and everything your heart desires, but most importantly you can have happiness and peace if you are only willing to do what's necessary to create it for yourself.

I have appreciated technology, airplanes, the internet, iphones, and instant heat for these past years simply because they make my life more convenient and they help me to expand my path and my heart to help other people live more fully all around the planet. But what I have come to see over the past decade is that these things won't last forever as they are destroying the planet, polluting our air, separating our communities, and disconnecting us from our Creator and our highest callings as human beings. All of these things were invented with the intention to do the opposite, but because they were designed by man with selfish desires, the end result is that they are destructive rather than productive.

For humanity to survive and thrive for centuries to come, something big has to change. The way we interact with each other has to improve. The way we interact with the planet has to improve. The way we depend on corporations to provide our lifestyles has to change. The way we grow our food has to be brought back home. The way we think about our lives and our purpose on the planet has to become more in alignment with our souls. And the way we envision the future for our future generations has to become more sustainable – otherwise we're not going to make it as a human society on the planet.

The truth is we're all going to die, and that's something we must all learn to deal with and accept, otherwise we will never find true happiness and we will always act out of fear which ultimately creates a negative result in the long run. Death is a natural part of life, and therefore realizing that one day you will die, and then being ok with that, you will truly become free and be much closer towards living with peace in your life.

The reason understanding that death is a natural part of life is so important in living happily is because most of the preparedness and self-reliance communities use the fear of death as a motivating factor for you to buy their stuff and then hide away in a bunker waiting for someone to come and steal your stuff so you can shoot them and then everything will be ok. Well that's not ok. That thought process, to me, is not ok. Scaring you to hideaway with tons of ammo and guns just so you can live in fear of your fellow humanity is not ok, and that's what I'm here to hopefully change on this planet, and I hope you will follow me in wanting to change that as well.

To me self-reliance is about learning to live in harmony with the planet so that we can live free, not be dependent on others to provide for us, and commune with our highest selves so we can be of service on the planet and live a life that is meaningful, memorable, fun, and enjoyable. Trust me, having lived in total fear walking around with guns worried about the drug dealer or gang member who was after me and wanting to kill me was no way to live. It's no different if you are hiding away somewhere in a bunker waiting for a stranger who does not exist who is coming after you. I honestly would rather die than live in that kind of fear, and that's the consciousness I'm trying to lead you towards because if you can think that way, then your life will be one thousand times more enjoyable and memorable than otherwise.

Don't get me wrong, I understand that once people lose electricity, food and water they go a little nuts and do stupid things. But you have to remember that if people are not totally dependent on the power grid for their basic necessities and they have a full belly, have some warmth, and have enough water to survive, they will act much more rationally and less violently.

That is the goal of becoming self-reliant; to be able to provide food and water and shelter for not only yourself and your family, but to be able to offer education and abundance for your neighbors and community members when they are in need. If you are able to create a true community of 10-100 community members who are growing food, collecting water, and setting themselves up to be sustainable with warmth and shelter, than you will be in a state of freedom, peace, and confidence like you've never experienced before.

My goal is to become self-reliant in a community environment as our ancestors did, but with the difference of putting conscious collaboration and spiritual development at the top of the list of priorities. If you are spiritually aware that all human beings come from the same place and go to the same place, then there is no need for war, violence, hatred, envy, or greed. If you know in your heart that our Creator is all loving and sends nobody to Hell, but that Hell is the inferno we have already created here on earth, and Heaven is available to all of us right here on earth as well, I'll tell you what, your life improves in ways you could only imagine.

These are thoughts and beliefs that I'm sharing with you not to diminish or defy any belief systems you have developed over your lifetime, but to share with you a unique and personal perspective that has helped me change my life astronomically and be able to live out my purpose on the planet and make a difference in many people's lives while living with more peace and happiness than I ever thought possible.

The reason I believe our ancestors failed at living sustainably and living in true community is because of greed, envy, and disconnect from spirit and each other. They had a competitive mindset, which created rivaling tribes, and ultimately because they wanted to be the rulers, or have more land, or feel safe, they attacked each other and killed each other. This is the same consciousness we still experience today which has created war on a global scale, but there is a new consciousness emerging which is called conscious collaboration, and it's the consciousness that when we work together and support each other, no matter race, color, belief system, or background, that we can live in peace and at the same time provide an environment where the work that it would take one person to do can be done in one eighth of the time by five people working together.

We obviously can't live in harmony, peace, and happiness if we are bunkered away somewhere waiting for someone to come and steal our food. If we want true freedom we have to break free of that consciousness and move into a new paradigm where conscious collaboration comes as a top priority along with food, water, and shelter.

If you are seeking a book about how you can bunker yourself away and learn techniques for defending yourself against attackers, this is not it. This book provides a brand new look at how you can live life with more meaning, purpose, and fulfillment while building a better future for yourself and your family and learning how to live more sustainably and in harmony with the land.

When I realized how devastating and backwards most of the information was about self-reliance and survival, I sought out to interview the leading experts and ask them how someone can become more self-reliant and live sustainably while doing it in a conscious way. Throughout this book you will find empowering interviews with practical information about how to live more sustainably, be prepared for any kind of disaster, and live with more meaning and purpose in your life so when the systems do change, you are ready to be a part of the new system rather than clutching onto the old crumbling one.

I learned so much from these experts and I'm practicing and implementing little by little each month as I move towards more self-reliance, and my deepest wish is that you get what I got out of this powerful information and you also seek to live life beyond just survival, and into a state of being where you are thriving in a true community environment that is interdependent instead of dependent, collaborative instead of competitive, and empowered instead of afraid.

This information can change the course of human history and there is no more important time than right now that we all take what we can from this and apply it in our lives to create a better future for ourselves and our Grandchildren's Grandchildren. I am honored you are reading this and taking the steps towards becoming a self-reliant conscious human-being and I look forward to connecting with you deeper in the interesting and changing months ahead.

How to Grow Your Own Food Effectively and Efficiently

Marjory Wildcraft

Nathan Crane: You teach people all over the world how to grow their own food in a very practical, quick, and easy way. When we are able to grow some, if not all, of our own food from our own backyard, we are empowered and prepared if a disaster were to occur.

Marjory Wildcraft: The sense of security you get and the healing to the root chakra is important. We all need that healing. There's tremendous power in getting involved and directly sourcing your food from the earth. It's amazingly enlivening and comforting and it's a journey you want to take regardless of what you think is coming in the future.

NC: Absolutely. Some people are calling you the most dangerous woman in America. Why is this?

MW: Sixty percent of America is either overweight or obese and I'm not. Fifty percent of America has some sort of chronic disease and it's crazy how high it is: Heart disease, diabetes, asthma, and all those different things. Forty percent of those women in my age group are on antidepressants and I'm not. I don't take any prescription medicine and the reason I'm so dangerous is because I can show you and everybody else that you no longer need to go to a supermarket or a drugstore. Here I am just holding a basket of vegetables and eggs. "You're the most dangerous woman in America." Oh, my gosh. I am.

NC: And what you're doing is giving people education and how to do it. How did you get started in growing your own food?

MW: I had a very successful career in the corporate world and I had morphed out of that. I was creating a business with my husband and we were structuring very high yield real estate investment partnerships in Austin, Texas. Through that business I began to understand the model of Fanny Mae and Freddy Mac and the Federal Reserve and I realized that the whole business that we built was going to come apart. We basically predicted the real estate bubble that happened in early 2000. We knew it would not only completely rip us apart but the domino effect was that the economic collapse was inevitable for the United States. When I started to look at what happens during the economic collapse, you can't afford to eat anymore. I completely freaked out and we basically dismantled the whole real estate business. I wanted to know how to grow food and so we took permaculture classes, homesteading classes, gardening classes, and forestry.

I came into this from a bad perspective - from panic and fear. It's a really, really dark place to be in but it's also a really good motivator. So it just kept me focused on finding the fastest, easiest, and most fun way to grow food.

NC: I totally understand that and one of the things that I've come to find is the fact that when you grow your own food from your own energy, from your own thoughts, from your own production whether it's some herbs from the windowsill, an entire garden from the backyard or a garden tower in your kitchen, what ends up happening is that your body gets so much more nourished by that food as long as you're not spraying it with chemicals and what not. Energy in that food is so much greater than something that's been picked overseas before it was ripe, shipped in a giant boat across the ocean and then stored in the back of a grocery store, which you eventually buy off the shelf. Well it looks ripe but it was never picked ripe so it never got the essence of the energy and the quality of all these nutrients that it does have when you grow your own food.

MW: The average American only gets about half of the RDA and the SAD, Standard American Dietary. It's so sad. The RDA is not the nutrient level that you need. It's only the nutrient levels you need not to show symptoms of disease. You actually need a lot more than the RDA. It's been well documented that over the last decades, the big growers only focused on NPK, nitrogen, potassium and phosphorus, which are the big three minerals that plants need and that's all they replace. After years and years and years of planting the same thing in the same soil and only putting NPK in there, it is completely deprived of any of the other 60 something trace minerals that you need such as chromium, selenium and magnesium and calcium and all the other things. Right now, I think you have to eat 11 carrots just to get the same nutritional content that you would have gotten from a carrot back in the 1970s. It's crazy.

NC: So you were recently on a research trip to Cuba, is that right?

MW: Yes. I went to visit Cuba for several reasons. One, Cuba, believe it or not, is the world leader in sustainable urban agriculture. In 1991, the last Soviet ship pulled out of Havana and that was when the Soviet Union collapsed. All of the trading partners were basically left to fend for themselves because the Soviet Union collapsed. And Cuba, like almost every other nation on earth, had dedicated themselves to large-scale conventional agriculture and more than any other South American country they had embraced the green revolution. They were doing everything they could to grow sugarcane and trade that sugar for food to the eastern European block. When that was cut off, they found themselves high and dry. Overnight they went through a collapse, the buses stopped running, the lights went out, the water stopped flowing, and the average Cuban lost 20 pounds.

People did what humanity has always known in times of crisis - they started ripping up backyards and corner lots, they started planting on balconies, and they started hauling dirt up to the roof. The banana tree that had been such a problem with the fruit that always got messy is now a gold mine. Fortunately, there was this small number of people who still knew how to grow food and were willing to teach and help others. Here's the population who had undergone collapse, survived it, and those are the things that they did.

NC: I read a statistic recently that Russia has come 60% to 80% now of growing their own food. And when they went through their whole revolution, people started growing their own food and having their own plots of land. Their economy started to lift because they did not have to import so much. This country thinks that the economy will crumble if you take away the corporations growing their food and give it back to the people. But there's actually evidence to show that it will do the opposite. Have you seen that at all in Cuba for example?

MW: I'll give you an example right here in the United States. The victory gardens during World War 2. Eleanor Roosevelt had a victory garden one year and within one year she started this program. Twenty million brand new gardeners within 1 year were producing 20% of this country's produce.

NC: What is your viewpoint about the economy of the United States? Do you think there's still a large collapse coming?

MW: Yes, I do. There are 5 indicators that I would like to keep an eye on. The first one is the price of food. This is something that you would have known or been taught from a very, very young age if you were born into royalty or if you were one of the ruling elite. And that is, people don't revolt if they have full bellies. They will revolt when they're hungry. This is very well known. Kissinger just said it very recently. In Roman times, they had a saying, give them bread and games and they will never revolt.

So if you want an indicator of when things are really going to start getting violent it's as simple as, can you afford to eat? There's a very direct correlation because the World Health Organization and United Nations will tell you that when food prices go up, they'll say please be aware there's going to be civil unrest breaking out in these regions. In fact the best indicator to look at is not the Consumer Price Index, which is a completely fictitious number. It's totally manipulated and doesn't mean anything. In fact, it doesn't include food and energy in it because they're too volatile. So don't look at the Consumer Price Index. But the United Nation's FAO, the Food and Agriculture Organization, has a pretty good indicator that seems fairly straightforward at this point in time. And it's called the Food Price Index.

Keep an eye on that thing and when it's starting to get within 10% of its all time peak, which was within 2008, that's when you want to start really ramping up your preparations or being very concerned. People get desperate when they get hungry. The price of food is one of the biggest indicators and the fact that we're bankrupt. Economic collapse is an absolute certainty. It's only a matter of when, not if.

NC: I know you've been growing your food for some time. About how much do you grow for your family?

MW: I grow about half. It's a huge empowering step and it's a good compromise between how much time I realistically have and what I need from my own security and from my own self-esteem and empowerment.

NC: What are some tips for people who want to get started growing their own food?

MW: Well, the number one thing is to start small and the other thing is to start a compost pile. The secret to a green thumb and having gardening be really, really fun versus drudgery is to get directly proportional to the quality of your soil. No matter what soil you have, whether it's rocky or clay or sand or non-existent, compost fixes it all and compost is the thing to do. And fortunately, it's basically free and nature does most of the work. There are tons of resources out there on compost. We really all need to be growing that fertility and the third thing is the real gold in your region is going to be the people who have been growing for a long time so get to know them. So if you've been driving by a house with these gigantic tomatoes out front, pick up a small gift, a hand shovel, some seeds, and whatever, and stop by. Say, "Hey I just saw your garden and I'm just wondering if you could tell me a little thing about this." Start talking. They're going to know what varieties work well in the heat. Most tomatoes are not going to survive much less produce but there are varieties that produce. Don't feel at all bad about going out there. I know it looks strange to cold call somebody but if you bring him or her something and talk to him or her, you'll be astonished about the information that you learn. And that's what really helps you get up and get going, if that's the goal. That's my third tip. The first one is start small. Second one is start a compost pile and the third one is start to know the people in your local neighborhood.

NC: That reminds me that what we all have in common is food. No matter what our differences are that's one thing we can all come to some common agreement. We all eat food, we all need food and for the most part we all enjoy food. So it's a great conversation starter. It's a great community builder. It's a great way to get us back in touch with nature and certainly to reach out and connect with other people and help other people as well.

Nate's Notes

Cuba is the leader in sustainable urban agriculture. When their outside supply was cut off, they found themselves high and dry and went through a collapse. The average Cuban lost 20 lbs when the food water stopped flowing. How did they survive? Everyone started planting everything possible anywhere they could.

In America there was something similar to that of the Cubans called the Victory Gardens. Twenty million Americans started gardening and within the first year they were producing 40% of the fruits and vegetables the country consumed.

People don't revolt when they have full bellies but people do revolt when they are hungry. Right now the USA is bankrupt and has to borrow money to pay the interest on its loans.

Look at the food price index.

Don't look at consumer price index because it doesn't include food and energy.

When the index gets within 10% of the peak then you should be on alert and keep an eye on food prices.

5 Indicators about the Economy:

1. The Price of Food
2. Interest rates on US Treasuries go up steeply, and/or suddenly
3. Price of oil goes above $120/barrel
4. Category 5 hurricane hits Texas City/ Houston area.
5. EMP Disaster

Top 3 Tips

1. Start Small. Work with something small to begin and learn as you go. It's best to move forward from a controlled front.
2. Start a compost pile.
3. The real gold in your area are the people who have been growing food for a long time. Get to know and learn from them.

Secret to a Green Thumb

Success is directly proportional to the quality of your soil.

Marjory Wildcraft

Marjory Wildcraft is called the "Martha Stewart of Self-Reliance" and she will show you how to grow half of your food in less than an hour per day if you go to growyourowngroceries.org. Most recently, Marjory was featured as an expert in sustainable living by National Geographic. She is also a keynote presenter for Mother Earth News and a regular guest on Coast-to-Coast AM.

She is an author of several books, but is best known for her video series "Grow Your Own Groceries" which is used by more than 300,000 homesteaders, foodies, preppers, universities, and missionary organizations around the world. Get a copy of this amazing video set by going to www.GrowYourOwnGroceries.com.

When Disaster Strikes:
What You Need to Know, Do,
and Have on Hand

Matthew Stein

Nathan Crane: Can you share with us a little bit about your research and findings on EMP and the super storm subjects?

Matthew Stein: EMP is an Electro-Magnetic Pulse and a solar storm can be a natural EMP. Now when some country or terrorist organization wants to really throw a monkey wrench in the spokes of the United States, it can launch a nuclear weapon that sets off an Electro-Magnetic Pulse when it goes off above ground. Now that may or may not happen someday but this super solar storm is absolutely guaranteed to happen. It's a matter of rolling the dice. What you're talking about is an event, which happens fairly regularly, approximately every seventy-five to a hundred years. This is not like an asteroid hitting the planet like it happened forty million years ago. This is something where the last extreme solar storm hit in 1921 but it was only sixty years before that the Carrington event of 1859 occurred. So you're looking at something where scientists predict that there's a one in eight chance every decade for a killer solar storm that's going to cripple the United States' grid and it's been nine decades since the last one. So essentially we're living on borrowed time since it's been nine decades and we've passed the statistical average.

Why should you be worried? We have solar storms and nothing happens. Correct. When you have a northern light or southern light aurora borealis, that's a sign of a solar storm coming from the sun that's exited the upper atmosphere and has charged things up. We've had about a hundred major storms in the last hundred and fifty years and most of the time it's not a big deal. It might disrupt some flights in the North Pole and disrupt some telephone communications but it's not a big deal. Every now and then you get a really strong storm like the one in 2003 that fried 14 transformers and messed up the grid in South Africa for an entire year. That can be pretty bad and there was one in 1989 that blacked out the East Coast and the province of Quebec for a couple of days. Sixty-nine million people out of power for a couple of days. But back in 1921, we had a granddaddy storm that was ten times stronger than the 1989 storm and even more than ten times stronger than the 2003 storm. If that were to happen today, you would see the grid collapse over most of the Northern and Southern hemispheres of the world and you'd see extreme damage to these massive transformers that keep our grid going. So what if we lose a couple of transformers? You can go down to the hardware store and buy transformers. That's not the case with these transformers that keep our grid going. These things are tens of millions of dollars each, they're over a hundred tons each, you have to shut down a freeway to deliver one, they're all custom made and custom built for each particular installation and there's a three year waiting list to get one. So back in 1989 they lost one in Canada, one in the East Coast of the United States, and one in the

U.K. Not that big of a deal and everything managed to keep going. That storm was less than 10% of the strength of the 1921 storm, which was 50% of the strength of the 1859 Carrington event, the granddaddy storm.

Based on a very well funded study on the part of the Department of Defense, the Homeland Security, and Oakridge National Labs, they found that there are three hundred and seventy transformers in the United States. I spoke with the author of the study and asked him how many transformers are in the world and he said, "I don't know. I didn't study the world." I said, "What? A couple thousand?" He said, "Yeah, that's probably a good number." Okay, two thousand made. Well when the world is working well they can make about a hundred of these transformers a year. So if we're talking 2000 going down in a single storm, that's like twenty years worth of capacity to make them when the world is still working well and our grid is totally dependent on transmitting lots of power long distances with these extra high voltage transformers. So what does that mean? You're going to go out, you're going to see this amazing light show, and you're going to see it really well because there won't be any lights on because the grid will be down. You won't have streetlights and city lights, there's going to be no Internet, no sewage pumps, and no water treatment plants. The really serious thing that's far worse than that is you're going to see nuclear power plants start to run out of back-up fuel to keep their generators going. Now if nuclear power plants make it's own power, why do you need to have generators? A nuclear power plant is designed so that when the grid goes down, the plant goes into automatic emergency shutdown mode. It can't provide power to itself to keep itself cool. When you turn a power plant off it's not like flipping a switch on the wall. These things slow down and you need to keep the cores of the power plant cold for three to five years after you shut the plant down. And normally in an emergency mode, like when the earthquake in Japan occurred and took the grid down, these back-up generators kicked in at Fukoshima. There were four out of six nuclear power plants operating at the time. Two of them were shut down for refueling. So you have four of these nuclear power plants that are in emergency shutdown mode and so immediately these back-up generators kick in and start pumping huge amounts of water through the nuclear power plants to keep them cool, to keep them from melting down. Approximately twenty minutes later, the tsunami came along and it wiped out five out of the six back-up generator stations for the plant. So only one out of six had the back-up generators on the mountainside of plant and the rest had them on the ocean side and the tsunami wiped those out. So within twenty minutes two nuclear power plants were in full meltdown mode and started to blow their tops. With nuclear plant number five, they were able to get some emergency guys who were able to shunt some power from number six down to number five so it only had a partial meltdown. It's now a toxic waste site heavily polluted with radiation but at least they kept number five from having a full meltdown.

Why is this important? In an extreme solar event, it is estimated it will be several months to several years before we can get the grid back together and get things working again. In that time, you're not going to see fuel being refined, you're going to see chaos in the street, you're going to see martial law, you're going to see cascading failure of all the central services that we've come to rely upon and those nuclear power plants are only mandated to have a week's worth of back-up fuel on them because the grid never goes down. The grid is never down in America for more than a day or two, except of course for something like Hurricane Katrina where there was so much destruction in the infrastructure that the grid was down for weeks and for months in some places. So imagine 50 Hurricane Katrinas happening all over the United States at once and these massive transformers are down. Around 37% of the population of the United States lives within fifty miles of a nuclear power plant. People get really nervous when they see a nuclear power plant in their city. They also don't like to build them far away from cities because it costs money to transmit power long distances. The further the power plants are away from the areas that are using the power, the more money goes down the tube in transmission loss. So more than one out of three Americans lives within fifty miles of a nuclear power plant.

There is a fix for this but the government has been talking about it for the past 50 years. They're saying we do not know when the next extreme solar geo-magnetic storm hits but we do know that when it hits, the grid's going to fail unless we fix it. They're not doing it because it costs money. So what can you do? This is where you need to say, "I need to be self-reliant." Now imagine the government crippled by the equivalent of more than fifty Katrinas happening all at the same time. Imagine the chaos that it's going to bring. So given that, you want to be prepared. You want to do the right thing for yourself, for your family, and for your community. You want to live as self-reliantly and as resiliently as you can.

Now if we're lucky the government wakes up, stops just talking about it, and fixes the problem. Put in these massive giant vacuum tubes that can work in microseconds. It can switch power around these big transformers and shunt them into the earth to protect the transformers from frying in the event of either a massive solar storm or an Electro Magnetic Pulse from some country that decides it wants to stick it to the United States and mess everything up in our country. Both are serious problems. The solar storm is the one I'm more worried about because it's something that's guaranteed to happen and it has a huge wide spread influence that can basically wipe out much of the infrastructure and much of the planet by taking down the grid and the infrastructure based on the grid.

Here you want to think about two things: 1) how can I wake people up in this country so we can protect us from the worst sort of end game scenario by implementing this two billion dollar fix on the part of our government and 2) how can I do the best for myself and my family by making sure that I'm self-reliant, that I have back-up sources of power and energy, that I have ways to deal with food, water, shelter, clothing and medicines for myself and my family in the event that the grid is down, the internet is down, and nothing's working.

Does it really matter if the Internet is down? Back in the 1960's, every city in North America had a month's supply of the basics: food, water, and whatever materials that the city needed to sustain itself for a month stored in giant warehouses in and around the city. They used those warehouses to ship goods and replenish stores and stock shelves. Nowadays, it's all just-in-time deliveries that are carefully coordinated by computers and the Internet, which is all wonderful when everything's working right. The problem is that we have an average of a three-day supply of these critical materials on hand in every city in North America now. So when the trucks stop running because things are down, then we'd have three days of stuff on hand. Think about it. The food you're eating on Saturday night was on a truck somewhere the Monday before going across country to be delivered, getting stocked on the shelves, getting bought, and then ending up on your table.

If you're not self-reliant, if you haven't stored or stocked anything, and if you're counting on the world working very well then you're going to be a very unhappy hungry camper in very short order when things grind to a halt for a significant period of time.

NC: Knowing how much debt the United States is in right now, it seems very unlikely that they would pay out the two billion dollars.

MS: It's a bigger problem than the debt because there's a Shield Act in Congress that says the utilities would be responsible for spending the two billion dollars to implement these fixes. Well the private utilities have this corporation called North American Electric Reliability Corporation. That's a private company that sounds like it's the good guys, wanting to make sure the grid is reliable and in a certain respect they are good guys trying to make sure the grid is reliable. But when NAERC sponsored a conference back around 2010, they looked at the most serious threats to our grid and they decided that both EMPs and solar storms were extremely serious threats. They wrote a report called the HILF report, which stands for High Impact Low Frequency. The Shield Act got into Congress and it said that the private industry or the utilities were going to pony up the two billion dollars. So what does NAERC do? Well NAERC fires the man who wrote the HILF report and instead come out with a new report that said, "Don't worry. Everything is okay." They didn't want to spend out of their own pockets.

Well the truth of the matter is that everything is not okay. The study shows it's not okay. The 1989 storm fried one in New Jersey at a nuclear power plant, fried one in the U.K., and one in Quebec. There were fifteen simultaneous failures in Quebec in 1989 in the first thirty seconds of the storm. So what does NAERC do? The Federal Electric Reliability Commission (FERC), which is the government side of the non-industry side of things, came up to NAERC and had them write a reliability standard for solar storms and what needs to be done in the event of one. So NAERC wrote the standard that is a paper protocol, which is a feel-good-do-nothing protocol that says that in the event of a solar storm all 2000 utilities or so are going to pull out this protocol, follow it, and determine what they need to do to protect the grid. Well in 1989, the storm which was 1/10 as strong as the big storm in 1921, which was fifty percent weaker than the 1859 Carrington event, that storm had fifteen simultaneous failures in the province of Quebec in the first thirty seconds. Fifteen failures in thirty seconds one of which was a massive transformer and it caused an entire province-wide blackout. It collapsed the grid in this entire province and that happened after fifteen failures in thirty seconds. So if we're going to have a massive geo-magnetic storm hitting the planet, they're going to pull out their protocols and that is enough to protect the grid? No way! This protocol is not going to do anything. But what it does is it lets the utilities off the hook for liability. If they follow and say oh, we trained people, we spent $2000 in each utility every year to provide twenty hours of training for somebody to implement this protocol and then they're off the hook. They said, "Hey, we did what we're supposed to do. Gee, I'm sorry that the grid collapsed and nuclear power plants melted down and millions of people are starving or dying but it's really not our fault because we did what the Federal Energy Regulatory Commission told us to do." What the Federal Energy Regulatory Commission told them to do is what NAERC wrote and handed to them and FERC rubber stamped it and gave it back. It's a classic case of lobbyists and experts being paid to say everything's okay on one side while other experts and scientists are saying everything's not okay on the other side and the government is listening to the people that are telling them what they want to hear.

NC: If you are prepared, self-reliant, off the grid, and ready for when it does happen in your lifetime then you're not going to have to struggle as much as if you're not prepared, right?

MS: Most of us don't have the money to have a five-acre survival retreat that's well stocked. So what can you do? At the very least everybody should have a Go Bag so that you can leave and have the basics that you can carry on your back or a cart. The basics can be something to purify water, providing some first aid for yourself and your family, and then start building on your skills. If you don't have money then think about building your skill set. How can I make myself useful? What skills can I learn? Can I learn first aid? Can I learn foraging and herbal healing? What kinds of skills can I develop that will help myself, my family and in the event that things are down for a long term that I can be a useful contributor. If you're older, you have a lot of money but you're not very strong think about storing things that are good for trade and barter such as guns and some ammunition, storing seeds, storing food, storing water or items to purify water.

There's a famous saying from Lao Tzu that says, "A journey of a thousand miles begins with the first step." Preparedness is like car insurance. Nobody buys car insurance and says, "Gee, I want to get into a head on collision today." No. You have insurance just in case and preparedness is like that. It's survival and disaster insurance so that you have the basics to provide for yourself, your friends, and your family in the event of a short-term emergency.

NC: You talk about having a Go Bag or a grab and run kit but what are some of the items people should expect to have in there? How long should they expect to be prepared for with this kit? Will it last them a few days or a few weeks?

MS: They're called the seventy-two hour kits. They're basically short-term survival kits for three days. You can have about 50 to 30 items in your kit but some of the out of the ordinary items that are not on many people's list are really, really important.

One of them is an inch and a half roll of cloth adhesive first aid tape or athletic tape. Why is that so important? What do you see whenever there's a disaster? You see people walking down the road and when you have to cover distance on foot, one of the first things that's going to happen to most of us is you're going to blister. You're going to be wearing shoes you're not used to wearing, you're going to be going distances you're not used to going, and people's heels blister. Once those blisters pop, you're going to be in agony and you're not going anywhere very fast. So the inch and a half roll of cloth adhesive tape is so important because when you start feeling hotspots you take a minute to sit at the side of the road, pull your shoes and socks off, peel a little of that tape off and take the sticky side and scrub the scummy oils and dirt and grease off of your skin and wherever your hotspots are. Then you throw that tape away or stick it in your pocket and you take some fresh tape and stick it on the now clean skin. You tape up those hotspots and put your shoes and socks back on. If you've got a sprained ankle you can tape the ankle. If you've got a wound, you can bind the wound.

Another item that's really important in my Go Bag is a colloidal silver generator. What is that and why would you want colloidal silver? When disaster strikes you're going to have no sewage, no water treatment, people peeing and pooping in the rivers and in the ponds and epidemics tend to happen. There was a cholera outbreak after the earthquake in Haiti. Colloidal silver is this tiny charged silver particle that is toxic to all known pathogenic bacteria. Two thousand years ago, Alexander the Great didn't know anything about germ theory but he did know that if you stored water in wooden urns or skin bags his troops got sick. A soldier in the battlefield that's vomiting and debilitated with diarrhea is not worth very much. He did find that if you store water in silver urns something happened to the water and his men never got sick. It also does not kill the probiotic bacteria (good bacteria) in your gut.

Another item that's really important in my Go Bag is a headlamp. And that's like a flashlight that sticks on your head with an elastic band. A headlamp allows you to have a light that shines wherever your head turns and leaves your hands free whether you're putting chains on your car in the middle of a snowstorm or splitting kindling outside.

NC: What should someone do after the seventy-two hours run out?

MS: That's where you hopefully have the ability to build a fire, the ability to purify water, and the ability to forage for food.

NC: Could you share about the pit of the stomach exercise?

MS: When you have a lot of great information at your fingertips you can make a good decision using the rational mind. But in a crisis situation most of the time you're going to have very pitiful information, it's going to be very lacking, and maybe sometimes solely non-existent. You've got to make really important, sometimes life and death decisions based on incomplete and sometimes non-existent information. Mother Nature has built in this most incredible inner guidance system into every one of us. In the crisis situation, to be able to tune into this inner compass so you can make the right decision without all the information is important to your survival and the making of choices.

Back about fifteen years ago now, James Kim, a very beloved man from the San Francisco Bay area involved in TV and the media, his wife, and two young daughters spent the Thanksgiving holiday in Seattle visiting friends and family. After the holiday was over they were driving back down I5 through Central Oregon back to the San Francisco Bay Area. They were driving at night and they had a reservation at a local beach called Gold Beach on the coast of Oregon that involved crossing from the Central Valley over the mountain range to the coast. It was a dark and stormy night and they got distracted. By the time they realized that they missed their exit, they'd gone a couple of hours south of the exit to cut over to the coast. So they looked at the map and they determined that there was a smaller road that cut over the mountains to the coast. They thought that if they take the smaller road, maybe they could get there at midnight. As they were driving up into the mountains on this road, the road kept getting smaller and smaller and they got colder and colder and the rain turned to snow. They got on these narrow and very slippery roads and they decided they'd better just pull over, spend the night there, and in the morning they'd figure out what they were doing. Well in the morning they looked out and they were snow bound. They had two feet of snow around their car, they're in the middle of nowhere with no signs of civilization, no cellphone signal, nothing. A couple of days go by and they run out of gas, the kids are cold, hungry, and crying and in a last ditch effort they took the tires off the car, started a fire and burned the tires to set off black smoke but nobody saw it and nobody came. So finally James Kim decides he can't just let his family die here so he goes to find help. At that point he should have done the pit of the stomach exercise. When your mind is changing every few minutes or every few seconds you need to decide not to trust it because it's just guessing. At that point you need to access your inner compass.

Here's what you do. The inner compass, the spiritual intuitive self thinks in pictures. It doesn't think in linear thoughts or words. You're going to be doing everything with pictures and feelings instead of linear thoughts and words. The first thing you do is you pray. Then you're going to focus. You're going to take deep breaths in and out and you're going to focus your attention at the area between your belly button and your rib cage. In the orient they call it the Dan Tien. You need to keep breathing deeply until you feel the muscles relax and this can take awhile in a critical and scary situation. When you feel those muscles relax, then you're ready to do the next step. In the next step you're going to think in pictures. You're going to picture yourself doing an action and then you feel a physical response in your body to determine if it's a yes or a no on that action. For example, in the rational mind of James Kim he'd think he should follow the river and that will eventually lead him to civilization. So he pictures himself in his mind hiking down the river and then he feels his stomach. Now if he feels a relaxed and expansive open feeling in his stomach then that's a good choice. But maybe James Kim pictured himself hiking down the river and he feels his stomach tighten up into a knot or maybe he feels the queasy sickly feeling in the stomach and he's really on edge and doesn't feel good. Then that's a bad choice. So what does James do now? He does the breathing and praying again to focus on that pit of the stomach. He breathes deeply until it relaxes and then pictures himself hiking up on the ridge top. If he gets a good feeling then it's the right choice but say he gets the bad feeling again. What should he do? The mind is screaming at him to not stay in the car because that's the sissy thing to do. It's been unsuccessful so far and if he stays in the car everyone is going to die.

What really happened to James Kim is that he valiantly hiked down the river. He wasn't dressed for the snow so he got cold, he got wet, he spent the night out and two days later he was found dead lying face down beside the river and just half a mile up from a hunting lodge. He could have made it if he'd known he was only a half-mile away but he didn't so it was quite tragic. What happened to the wife and kids you ask? When they didn't show up in Gold Beach as planned, his father sent people out looking and they found the last pings of his cellphone off of towers. They figured out what part of the country he was in and that he was way off route. They sent out people looking for them on dirt bikes and snowmobiles and somebody found them. They helicoptered the wife and kids to a hospital where they were treated for hypothermia but they weren't in any serious trouble. James Kim can't be faulted for bad reasoning but if he'd used this inner compass then perhaps he would've been alive today. I firmly believe that would have been the case.

Nate's Notes

Solar Storms, which are like an EMP, happen every 75-100 years. The previous storm was in 1921, which burned 15 transformers in the first 15 seconds, but it was 50% of the size of the super storm that hit in 1859. Every decade there is ⅛th chance for a solar storm to kill the United States electrical grid. In 2003, a solar storm fried 14 transformers and the grid in North Africa for a year. The granddaddy storm of 1921 was 10x stronger than the 2003 storm. If this happens, the grid collapse would happen on the Northern part of world and transformers will go out.

Each transformer costs tens of millions of dollars and it is a 3-year waiting list to get 1. There are 370 transformers in the US that might be lost and maybe even a couple thousand in the world. The grid is totally dependent on transformers and only 100 of these can be made per year.

Another really serious thing to be concerned about is water treatment, lights, power, and sewage plants. There's also the collapse of government, Wall Street, etc. Plus nuclear power plants start to run out of fuel for their generators because most nuclear plants are close to cities and only have 1 week of backup fuel on hand.

In the even of an extreme solar event, it is estimated to take several months to several years to get the grid back together again. In fact, the HILF Report wrote about the situation.

What can I do?

Need to be more self-reliant. Need to be prepared.

1. Everyone should have a go bag.
   a. Something to Purify water
   b. First Aid
   c. Food
   d. 72 hour short term survival kit
   e. Athletic Tape/First Aid Tape
   f. Colloidal silver generator (Colloidal silver kills all known pathogens)
   g. Headlamp
   h. Go bag that's waterproof

2. Building skillsets
   a. Like foraging and herbal healing
   b. Strategic Partnerships like storing things for trade and barter
   c. Farming, utensils, storing food, seeds
   d. Make your own colloidal silver
   e. Store herbs, medicine, etc.

3. Books
    a. Herbal medicine
    b. Foraging
    c. Growing
    d. Others

4. Water and Food
    a. Long term

Learning to listen to the inner guidance system to save your life. In a survival situation, your intuition can guide you to safety. First pray, ask God or tune into a higher power and ask for help. Then take deep breaths in and out and focus your attention to an area between your belly button and your rib cage. In Asia they call the energy center the Dan Tien. Breathe deeply until you feel your muscles relax. Once relaxed, make pictures in your mind where you can picture yourself doing an action and feel your energy center regarding how you feel about that action. If you feel an awe, relaxed feeling in your stomach, then that's probably a good choice or if in the picture of mind you picture yourself hiking down river and you feel a tight uneasy feeling in stomach, then it's probably a bad choice. Repeat until you get a good response.

Matthew Stein

Matthew Stein is an environmentalist, bestselling author, MIT trained engineer, and green builder. As an inspiring speaker and visionary thinker, he is dedicated to helping people wake up and unite to shift our collective course from collapse to global renaissance. On the practical side of things, as an expert at self-reliance, emergency prep, and survival, his writings and work help people prepare to weather the storms we are facing due to continuing climate change and ecological decline, coupled with a fossil fuel based economy that has recently passed the peak in world oil production and is struggling to cope with impending near-term shortfalls.

Learn more at http://www.WhenTechFails.com.

Return to Your Roots: How Anyone Can Embrace the Homesteading Lifestyle

Jill Winger

Nathan Crane: What got you into homesteading? Why was that something that became very important for you?

Jill Winger: It's a funny story. I didn't grow up in the country. I grew up in a little neighborhood in town. But I always had something inside me that wanted that rural life. I really craved it. So, I moved to Wyoming and started to do some things in the equine industry with horses, trees, and things like that. It wasn't until I was a young adult, newly married, that I started this genius vision of getting back to my roots and getting really involved in this lifestyle that I now call homesteading.

So, we had bought our first property. We were a young couple who had bought a chunk of land, didn't have any money for a tractor but we had horses and they make a lot of manure. I had to find a way to handle this manure. Since the tractor was out I started looking at composting. Well composting led me into looking at chickens and gardening because you put their compost in the garden. It was this progression of an awakening for me to realize this yearning I had and a lot of people told me, "Oh that's nice but people don't do that sort of thing anymore." That really wasn't true. There was a lot of potential to incorporate some of these old fashioned skills: composting, gardening, canning, having chicken, or having farm animals.

NC: So you now live on a 67 acre prairie in Wyoming. That must be pretty difficult out there with the extreme weather changes, yes?

JW: It is. It's a very difficult climate. We get severe winter storms, severe winds. It's hot and dry in the summer, but I think it's been good. We've learned how to work around those things and it's proven to me that this lifestyle is doable in some way, shape, or form. It's really for anyone no matter where you live.

NC: What are some of those key elements people can look for if they are looking to develop their own homestead?

JW: Well if you have the opportunity to move or you're in the process of purchasing a property or hunting for a property, look at the growing season. That's a good thing to check out. Do people grow in the summer? Some places in the desert or down in Texas don't grow during the summer. Their growing season is more during the winter months or the spring months. So be aware of the challenges with the heat or the extreme cold.

Another thing to look for is what type of culture is in that area. Are there farmers markets? Are there other local growers that you can partner with and network with? Those are some good things to check for if you're in a process of looking for a property. But if you already have a property, don't feel like you have to get up and move in order to do this sort of lifestyle.

NC: What are some of the challenges people can expect getting into homesteading?

JW: The number one thing I see is just a feeling of being massively overwhelmed. There're so many different things and different aspects that you can pursue. A lot of people want to do it all at once. So the first step to work through is figuring out what's most important for you. And then choosing to put the rest of the things on the back burner and not try doing too much at once because if you do you'll get burned out and things will fall apart.

NC: Some of the challenges that people can be aware of are that it takes work, it takes time, it takes dedication, and it's an investment. What are the biggest benefits that you've found in this lifestyle?

JW: Well there's so many. For me the benefits have been that feeling of empowerment, the knowledge where your food comes from, and being intimately involved in the process of growing your food. It just feeds your soul. It just does something for you. I really think humans are designed to partake in their food in at least some way, shape, or form.

And the other benefit that really sticks to my mind is being able to watch my kids to grow up this way. I didn't grow up in a farm family or a ranch family. So being able to watch my kids outside getting dirty, chasing the chickens, learning where the milk comes from, learning where the meat comes from, and being so involved with that is absolutely one of the most rewarding things that I've ever done.

NC: I'm sure you've seen a lot of benefits in your children, yes?

JW: Absolutely. It really creates confidence in them. My daughter was outside showing her friends the animals and showed them how to open the gate and how to check the eggs. She just looked confident. I love seeing that. She knows how to keep herself safe around the big animals and she knows that chores are something that we do and they are fulfilling when you get the job done. I just love watching the kids being so intimately involved in that.

My goal personally for our family is just to mesh the best of our modern conveniences with the things that our grandparents did that were really smart, worked better, and were healthier for us and the environment. That to me is what modern homesteading is all about. For example, I love growing our own food and milking a cow. A lot of people associate a lot of romance with that but it's harder than buying your milk from the supermarket. It's something I've chosen to pursue even though it takes time because I firmly believe that the milk from our cow is far more nutritious for my family and myself than the cheap milk from the store. However, I still love my dishwasher for washing the milk bucket. It's quick, easy, and it gets it sterile. There are some modern things that I love like how I appreciate my washing machine. I could wash my clothes by hand and if had to I would, but in our life where there is so much going on I love my washing machine. I also love canning or making soap from scratch. There is definite room for both the old and the new in this sort of lifestyle and that's what makes it so cool.

NC: Why do you think that modern homesteading is suddenly becoming so popular?

JW: The way I see it is it's a generational thing. Although there are people of all ages partaking in modern homesteading, when I look back at my parent's generation, they're the baby boomers. Their parents were from the great depression and so the baby boomer era was all about ease, comfort, and boxed cake mixes. They took that ease and convenience almost a little too far by getting really dependent on processed food and absolutely dependent on all sorts of chemicals and things to make their lives "easier". As that progressed we started to realize that some of that was healthy for us but it wasn't healthy for the environment and there were problems. That's why we're seeing a resurgence of people caring about what they're eating, paying attention to the labels, wanting to garden, finding joy in having chickens, and canning for their pantry. That's why we're seeing it come full circle.

NC: One thing I've known for years is when you buy milk from a store it's pasteurized and homogenized. What that means is they've cooked it. They've cooked out all the living benefits from that milk, the amino acids, the proteins, the fiber nutrients, and the living enzymes. You're getting milk that has no nutrients or electrical value to your body and this causes a lot of problems. It causes allergies. In some cases it can cause kidney and liver damage. It could cause pus and mucus in the body, which creates inflammation. When you milk your cow you're connecting with that animal and you're getting fresh living nutrients and enzymes for your body so the health benefits are just spectacular. Are you seeing that in your family?

JW: I definitely have. I talk a lot about milking cows. I was shocked to learn how much you can do with fresh milk versus cooked milk. You get cooked milk from the store and it's this watery white stuff you put on your cereal and when it starts to smell bad you toss it. Fresh milk is an entirely different concept. It's alive and it doesn't really go bad; it just changes form. You can turn even your soured milk into cheese or sour cream. There are so many things you can do with it that are so nutritious for your body. It's an amazing substance.

The best part of this is you don't have to have land to really jump into this lifestyle. Whether you live in an apartment or you live in a little lot in the suburbs, the first thing is just to get acquainted with the food you're eating. Where is it coming from? Where are you buying it? If you don't have room to grow a garden hopefully you can at least put a couple of pots on your balcony but if you can't do that seek out some local growers. There are going to be people who can provide you nutritious local food that not only supports your local economy but also helps you get acquainted with what you're eating.

You can also learn to cook from scratch. Here's a confession, I used to hate to cook. I did not grow up as someone who loved to be in the kitchen and I used to fight with my mom when she tried to teach me how to cook. I really had a transformation when I started to realize more about the ingredients and finding different recipes. I really got inspired to start cooking from scratch and now I absolutely love it. You don't have to have fancy appliances or fancy tools. Anyone can cook from scratch. Just learn the basics. Learn how to make your own bread products instead of buying them. Grab some apples from your local farmer and learn how to create things from those. That's something anyone can do, land or no land. From there you can add some things in like drying your clothes on the clothesline. If you can't hang a clothes line outside because of where you live or a home owner's restriction, you can always do it inside with a drying rack. Take the spirit of being self-reliant and creating things and just carry that into where you are now and apply it in as many places as you can and before you know it you're going to be calling yourself a homesteader too.

NC: Do you think this is just a fad or do you think that this is really going somewhere?

JW: I do think this going somewhere. I see it being more of a transformation. Sure there are some people who would probably get some chickens and are going to get tired of them and give them away. But I know for the majority, it's going to be hard to turn your back on it once you've seen the reward. I really believe that this is a shift that's going to stick around.

NC: I just want to recap some things. Combining the old with the new, we don't totally get 100% off-the-grid. Get acquainted with the food that you're eating whether you're growing your own food or seeking out your local growers at farmer's markets and so forth. Obviously organic non-GMO is the best way to go. You don't want pesticides and herbicides and genetically modified organisms in your food that are made to deteriorate your body, tear apart your blood stream, your lymphatic system, your immune system and are going to make you sick. Learning to cook from scratch, canning your own apples, learning to jam, milking your own cows or goats if you have the space, and really just being empowered to work with your own food, help create confidence in your children and create a better life for yourself.

JW: My biggest piece of advice is just considering any part of this lifestyle, a little bit or a lot. Just do it. Just jump in and take the plunge. You're going to make mistakes. You're going to forget what doesn't work but eventually you are going to hit your groove and you'll be on your way before you know it. Don't hesitate too long. Just dive in and I think you're going to be really happy that you did.

Nate's Notes

What are ideal things to look for in a homestead?

First of all, check what kind of growing season is in the area and the corresponding culture – from the farmer's markets to the local farmers you can work and partner with. Once you have the needed information, choose what you want to start with and put everything else on the backburner.

3 Benefits of Homesteading:

1. Empowerment that comes from working with food.

2. Being able to watch kids grow up empowered.

3. Creates confidence in children.

Why is modern homesteading becoming so popular?

People of all ages are taking part but it seems to be a generational thing where people want to get back in the garden.

How can someone living in the city become a homesteader?

You can start by getting acquainted with the food you're eating and seeking out local growers. In fact, just because you live in a small apartment or condominium doesn't mean you can't grow your own food. Grow whatever you can in windowsills, in your balcony, etc. Garden towers are a great opportunity for you to grow food without taking up too much space.

Take the opportunity to cook from scratch, can apples, and learn to jam. You'll not only save money but also learn new skills. Another way you can save money and be a homesteader is by drying your clothes on a clothesline outside or inside with a drying rack and even making your own soap from scratch.

If you want a challenge you can try milking a cow, a sheep or even a goat.

Jill Winger

Jill Winger is a wife, mother of two, author and modern-day homesteader who lives on a Wyoming prairie. She firmly believes that anyone can embrace the homesteading spirit, regardless of where they live. When she's not writing on her blog, The Prairie Homestead, you'll find her milking her cow, trying to make things grow in her garden, chasing kids, or making a mess in the kitchen.

Learn more at www.ThePrairieHomestead.com.

Emergency Home Power.
More Electricity than you
need in a Disaster.

Steven Harris

Nathan Crane: Steven, is it true that anybody can have power and electricity off the grid? And can they do it easily?

Steven Harris: Yes and most people think that when the power fails they need a generator. No you don't. You have a $30,000 generator sitting in your driveway right now and it's called your car. You probably have two of them and they are both full of gasoline. A car has a fifteen to thirty gallon fuel tank, it has an engine that has an alternator, it has a power generation system and it will sit there in idle for a very long time if you need it to idle. All you have to do to harvest power from your car is have a simple inverter that'll plug into your cigarette lighter.

You don't usually need more power than what's coming off the inverter. You can plug that into your car, run that into your house and off of that you can power your cellphone, your laptop, your iPad, your LED based lights and compact fluorescent lights (preferably those that are seven watts in size and lower). Now that's not the equivalent size - that's the actual draw of the light.

People just get stuck in this mindset, "I can't power my refrigerator!" "I've got to power my freezer!", "I have to bring back everything that just went away." You don't. You don't need to bring back everything, just the essentials. That would be your television, your radio, your phone, your illumination, and your lights. That does not include refrigeration because your refrigerator and your freezer are insulated boxes that will stay cool for a significant period of time.

There are so many things that can be done that people just completely ignore and they think they need to have a big generator. The thing is their car is ready to be the generator right now. It's already paid for and it already works. Generally, a car will idle for about 24 hours on a full tank of fuel because smaller cars have smaller fuel tanks but they're more efficient and so they idle with less gas usage. A big truck has a bigger tank but it's less efficient so it has more fuel so generally it idles for about the same amount of time. So the rule of thumb is you can generally idle for about 24 hours on a full tank.

If you're running just 10 watts of lights and a small fan and when I say a fan I mean a little 6 inch or 8-inch fan you buy for $10 or $15 from Walgreens or Wal-Mart. You point it right at your face because the idea is not to cool the house or to cool the room but to cool the person.

So let's say you are running less than ten or twenty watts total off of your inverter which could easily be LED lights from Home Depot that are 2, 3 or 4 watts a piece, a couple of little fans and a portable emergency TV. You don't need to idle your car. You just plug it in and leave it on all night. When you're done with it you go out in the morning and you idle the car for about an hour to put the energy back into the battery.

If you do end up powering things that are bigger and larger like a 150 watt inverter in the cigarette lighter of your car to plug in your television that you have rabbit ears for, you're going to maybe draw 5200 watts. You're going to go out there and you're going to idle the car half on and half off. I would count for 30 minutes, keep it off for 30 minutes, idle for 30 minutes, keep it off for 30 minutes. That way the alternator is continuing to replenish in the car battery what has been depleted. But, it's amazing what a little $20 150-watt inverter will do for you. The answer is it will give you back everything that you need in communication and illumination that you just lost in the disaster.

NC: What type of inverter should someone plan on getting?

SH: From the cigarette lighter of your car you can only draw up to a maximum of 150 watts and that's because you're limited by the 15 or 20 amp fuse that is connected to the power outlet/cigarette lighter outlet of the vehicle. Generally, those inverters cost $20 to $30 a piece to plug into there. You can either buy it through Amazon, your local Wal-Mart or Radio Shack. Home Depot sometimes even sells them.

One of the brands I like a lot is Whistler. They have some really nice features on them. They're worth a few pennies more than you would get with a cheaper Cobra but if Cobra is all you can afford, it's better than nothing. These bigger inverters will clamp onto your battery and they have big alligator clips that clamp onto the top or the side posts of your battery. Once you get above 750 watts then you have to actually screw them down to your battery post. They will have eyelets on them and they will go over one of the bolts sticking out of your battery and you get another nut that's the same size as the nut that's already on there and you screw that down to hold the inverter down. This is because it draws a lot of current and it needs to have very solid contact.

Sump pump as most people know pumps water out of the basement, out of a hole in the basement through the outside of the house. Sump pumps generally draw about 750 watts, some draw 500, some draw closer to a thousand. But they only run for 30 seconds and they might only run for 30 seconds every 5 minutes or 30 seconds every hour depending upon how fast the water is coming into your basement. Even though it's a big load for a short duration, you would need a larger converter on your vehicle in order to do that. I think anyone out there who's been in a disaster with a sump pump and taking 5 gallon buckets up and down the stairs to haul out the water, would really appreciate the benefit of having a vehicle with an inverter to run a sump pump during a disaster.

NC: If you need more power obviously you go to a higher inverter but that's going to draw more power from the battery. So is your battery life going to be less?

SH: If you're drawing more than the 150-watt inverter the car will be in idle all the time. Let's say you would move everything out of your refrigerator into your freezer and then you would power your freezer. The thing most people don't realize is you don't need power all the time. You only need to power it for an hour two or three times a day depending on how hot it is outside. You just need to keep it below or at 32 degrees.

Let's say you had a 750-watt inverter and you clamped it onto your battery underneath the hood of your car. You would run the cable to your freezer and you'd need to take all of your sleeping bags off the freezer because there's a hot side to the freezer that needs to cool-off. So, you pull off all your sleeping bags and everything out of the freezer and you idle the car for an hour. Then you unplug it, turn off the car, you throw all your sleeping bags and blankets and everything back on top of the freezer to keep it cool.

Another thing is it's better to cool the freezer than the refrigerator because it's what we call, all the Ping-Pong balls don't fall out. Let's say you had your refrigerator full of Ping-Pong balls and those

Ping-Pong balls represent cold air. When you open the door to your refrigerator what happens? All the Ping-Pong balls fall out.

However, if you lift the top off your freezer, all your ping pong balls pretty much stay right where they are. So always better to cool a chest type of freezer than a refrigerator in that type of situation. It's a big pet peeve of mine when people get stuck in refrigerator mode. I've seen people run generators for two days just to keep hooked up to their refrigerators. Then they run out of fuel after two days and they can't do a thing. A refrigerator can stay cool for about two days and you've only got two days worth of food in it. So the first thing I tell people when the power failure happens is open up the freezer and start eating the ice cream. Just a good way to start off a power failure.

NC: If someone's using the basic minimum amount of wattage and amperage for illumination, communication, and etcetera, what do you think the average car will last somebody in terms of power generation on a full tank of gas?

SH: Let's say you need to have more power at different times in your house three times a day. In the morning when you wake up and start making breakfast, in the evening when you're making dinner and late in the evening before you go to bed you need to use some hours. Let's say you need to use some hours worth of power three times a day because you want to have the car idling to give your inverter more power to run your sump pump, cool your freezer, maybe even run the coffee maker.

So, it could be for an hour three times a day and since you have 24 hours and a full tank of gas, that would get you through about eight days or more of a power failure. Most people's power failures aren't lasting more than a day to three days at most. If you live in an area where you have power failures that go longer, you're going to want to have a generator. The next question you're going to ask me about is if I have my car, I only have 24 hours of gasoline in it. What if I want to store more gasoline, right?

Well unfortunately your first option is those horrible 5 gallon cans that are mandated by EPA that are hard to pour gasoline out of, that leak, and that stink your garage. If you want another way of storing fuel that works exceptionally well it is by purchasing 15-gallon HDPE (high-density polyethylene) drums. They will be either blue or translucent white in color.

High-density polyethylene is the same plastic that gas cans are made out of. So it would be the regular 5 gallon one but these are 15 gallon. They will pop up on Craigslist every now and then or you can go to yellow pages online and look underneath barrels and drums. You'll find every city has a barrel and drum supplier in it and someone who buys used drums, cleans them out, and sells them. You'll pay between $15 and $40 for a 15-gallon drum and also get a good bung wrench from them. A bung wrench is what opens the bung, which are the openings on the top. A good bung wrench is important because it'll have a tight seal.

The good thing about 15 gallons of gas is it's going to weigh around 80 pounds, which means you can move it. You can pick it up and put it in the back of your pick-up truck, you can move it around your garage, and you can roll it around. You can do whatever you want with it. If you got a bigger drum, like a 30-gallon drum or a 55-gallon drum, you'll have to have a drum cart to move it around. You couldn't put it in your pick-up truck and fill it up at the gas station and then put it into your garage.

NC: Aren't there pumps for sale that go into the barrels so that you can pump right out of it into your gas tank?

SH: Yes they do but the cost is like $50 to $100 and it depends where you find them since they're not easy to get. Many times you have to go to Grainger.com in order to find them. Those do work for getting fuel into the vehicle but my siphon is the squeeze bulb that you have on a boat fuel tank to prime it and a 3/8-inch fuel line from the automotive store. You get a six-foot piece of 3/8-inch fuel line, you get a 4-foot piece of 3/8-inch fuel line, and you have a bulb with

3/8-inch prongs on each side of it. You just stick the fuel line into the bulb and you stick the short end into the drum and you got the bulb at the top. You stick the long end in your fuel tank and you squeeze the bulb a few times to prime it and it will suck down 15 gallons of fuel from the top of your pick-up bed and into your pick-up truck. It'll do that in about 20 minutes.

NC: Fifteen gallons is about the average size of a small to midsize vehicle gas tank, right? So you're probably looking at another eight days of power with one 15-gallon drum.

SH: You got that exactly. If you're idling for one hour three times a day and that's three hours a day, 24 hours idle time on a full tank with your big truck or small car, that puts you at about another eight days from another 15 gallons of fuel. What did that cost you? It cost you between $15 or $40 for the drum and between $3.50 and $4 a gallon for the fuel so you're in to it for about a $100 and $100 gives you another eight days of power. You didn't have to go out and buy a generator that cost $600 or $1000 to do that same job.

NC: What about for the people who are trying to get more off-the-grid?

SH: First regarding storing gasoline, you can put a stabilizer in it called STA-BIL from Wal-Mart but the best stuff is PRI-G. If you put that in every year, you can literally keep your gas almost indefinitely. We have people who have gasoline that's over ten years old that they've put PRI-G in every year and it lasts.

Now regarding solar panels and energy independence. Solar power will never save you money. You will never get your money back on the panel ever because it's a fundamental thing of how solar panels are made. They're made with a great deal of electricity and it costs a certain dollar value in order to make that. There are people who live in artificially price inflated places like California that do come close maybe after a decade of getting their money back because California has artificially, through socialism, raised the price of electricity from our nationwide average of eight to ten cents per kilowatt-hour to 24 cents a kilowatt-hour or more. So the rule is solar electricity is the most expensive type of electricity you will ever have period.

There's one thing more expensive than solar electricity and that is no electricity. What I mean by that is you might want to live off-grid so you may want to setup a permaculture homestead. You might want to be completely away from everything and from the Man. You might want to have your own water well and have your own septic field. You might want to generate your own power because you want that power and energy independence. For that, solar panels are going to be the best thing for you. Obviously it can be an issue like in Washington

State where you have three months of clouds and no, your solar panels don't work when it's cloudy. They also don't work when it's raining and they don't work when it's nighttime.

Generally, I tell people if solar panels were for preparedness people, where you and I live on-the-grid, don't even consider getting solar panels unless you have at least three to four months worth of food. It's more important for you to put the money into your food and water for your house rather than trying to put the money into some gimmick to keep your phone charged. As I said, you are much more economical by spending a hundred dollars on fuel and putting that fuel in your car to power your house because I showed you with $100 you can have now two weeks worth of fuel. One week with refueling your car, one week refueling your battery. That will get you through most disasters. Don't even consider solar unless you want the power independence and/or you have many months worth of food storage and you want to supplement your power by that method.

That being said, there's a new type of solar charger out there that's very affordable called MPPT which stands for multi-point power tracking. What it does is it basically says I don't care what voltage you are giving me as long as it's over 13.5 and less than 150 volts. I'm going to take that voltage and I'm going to convert it so it'll charge your batteries perfectly at between 13.8 and 14.2 volts depending on the charge state of the battery. It's a very intelligent modern computer controlled three-stage charger for your batteries because there's three steps in charging a battery. There's bulk charging, absorption charging, and float charging. It's really important to have a modern computer controlled three-stage battery charger. It's also important if you're running solar panels to have the same thing.

NC: What kind of life can you expect out of a typical homemade battery bank?

SH: First of all you're going to want to have a marine grade battery or a golf cart battery. Golf cart batteries are generally called GC2s. You can't use starting batteries because the chemistry is completely different. Ammonium batteries have a higher-level antimony in the plate, which allows you to have a greater depth of discharge of the battery without hurting it. You kill your batteries every time you use them. You take a little bit of the life of your battery every time you start to discharge it. Generally, most people with a solar system try not to go between down below 50% depth of discharge. You start off with a 100% depth of discharge you go down to 90% then you go down to 80% depth of discharge, so people try not to get their batteries below half way down because below that level, you start doing incrementally more "damage" to the battery, which has to do with the sulfates on the plates. There's salt sulfation which can be removed by de-sulfatoring your battery charger and then there's hard-crystalized sulfation, which is not reversible. Generally, a battery sitting there completely kept at charge at the top, ready to go when you need it is going to stay good for you for about five years for a lead acid battery.

And then there's the whole issue of nickel iron batteries but I'm just basically telling people don't bother with nickel iron batteries. They're very inefficient, they're very gassy, and in addition to that they are five times the life of a lead acid battery, so 25 years but you're paying nine times the price for them. So that's five times the life and nine times the price and that doesn't make financial sense.

But the basics of a home solar system is basically you put the panels on the roof or you put them outside and you angle them at fifteen degrees past the point of what your longitude is. Then you run the wires into the house to a solar charge controller and the solar charge controller goes to your battery and on the batteries you have the inverter. Those are the basic steps of a home solar system. So if you're running an MPPT solar charge controller, like I said will take any voltage between 14 and 150, and you got four panels up there and they're 24 volt panels, you can run those four 24 full volt panels in a series instead of parallel. Since the size of your wires is dictated by the amount of current or amperage that's running through it, you can get away with running a smaller cable from your solar panels down to your MPPT charger when you put them in a series because they're 100 volts. That means you get less left current with the same wattage flowing but the cable is smaller going down rather than if you put all the panels in parallel.

So there are lots of little details that go into stuff like that and there's also the size and the distance of the charger from the battery is the size of the cable going to the batteries and hooking up to the inverter. Then you get into full renewable energy system where the charger and inverter is all built into each other and the full renewable energy inverter charger system. They generally cost $800 to a $1000 and can hook directly up to your electrical panel. They take the input in from the solar panels and have another output that goes to the battery that keeps the batteries charged up and when the power fails it switches over automatically and feeds your entire house. Or if you're off grid they're hooked up to your entire house to your entire electrical panel to start with. Again, a solar power system in itself and how it's going to be working for you whether you want to be a homesteader, an off-grider or you just want to be a prepper and have better power for your home when a disaster happens.

Nate's Notes

What's most important in a crisis:

1. Communication
2. Illumination
   - 7 watt lights or lower are best

Your car is the first source of power for electricity.

1. Has gas, engine alternator, etc.
   a. To harvest power from your car you only need to plug an inverter into your cigarette lighter.
   b. Don't run more than 10-20 watts off inverter at a time.

2. Generally a small car will idle for 24 hours on a full tank of fuel because its engine is efficient.

3. You can get an average of 8 days of power with basic usage.

4. You only need to recharge the car battery for one hour in the morning with an alternator.

What kind of inverter do you need?

A 150 watt cigarette lighter inverter that retails at around $20-$30. This can be purchased at www.battery1234.com. Keep in mind, the higher the wattage of an inverter the more current it will draw from the battery.

Powering Your Freezer:

Put everything in the freezer and turn it on. Once it has run for an hour, unplug it and put sleeping bags on top of the freezer to keep it cooler longer. Also, a good idea is to fill up soda bottles with water for thermal mass.

If you need to freeze items for an extended period of time, purchase a generator.

How to Store Fuel:

a. 15 gallon HDPE drum in either blue or white. Blue drums are food grade drums.
b. Get a bung wrench.
c. Get a rotary pump form Grainger.com or you can make a syphon according to Steven's instructions.
d. PRI-G (gasoline stabilizer)

Different Classes Of Generators:

2 stroke generators, regular generators, inverter generators, trailer mounted generators, and etc.

Solar Panels – Energy Independence

Solar power will likely never save you money because it is the most expensive electricity. Solar panels, however, are the best thing for people who want energy independence. You can learn more at www.Solar1234.com.

New Type Of Solar Charger

The old solar charger is the PWI. The new better solar charger is called the MPPT (Multi-Point Power Tracking). This will convert over 13.5 and less than 150 volts. It's a very intelligent charger for batteries

3 Types Of Charging:

1. Volt charging

2. Absorption charging

3. Float charging

Making A Battery Bank

To make a battery bank, visit www.batteries1234.com. You'll want a golf cart GC-2 battery or a marine grade battery. As time progresses, you're killing your batteries because you're taking away a little life every time you use it. The key thing to remember is to try to not to get the batteries below 50% of discharge otherwise they start getting damaged quicker. These batteries will last if charged most of the time for a period of about 4 years. However, don't bother with nickel iron batteries.

On your roof, place the panels and angle it at 15°. You can run four 24v panels in a series rather than in parallel, which is better. Then run the wires into the house to a solar charge controller (MPPT charger). This will then be connected to the batteries and your inverter will be attached to the battery bank.

Full Renewable Energy Systems

A full renewable energy system charger and battery is built into each other. This costs at around $800 - $1000 and can be used to hook up to an electrical panel.

1st day - fuel, 2nd day - water, 3rd day - food, and 4th day - riot.

Steven Harris

Steven Harris is a consultant and expert in the field of energy. He is the founder and CEO of Knowledge Publications, the largest energy only publishing company in the USA. Mr. Harris came to his current position to do full time work on the development and implementation of hydrogen, biomass and solar related energy systems after spending 10 years in the Aero-Thermal Dynamics department of the Scientific Labs of Chrysler Corporation, where he was a pioneer member of the group that developed and implemented successful Speed to Market development concepts.

Mr. Harris has become a nationally recognized expert in the preparedness field. He is the #1 all time appearing guest on The Survival Podcast with Jack Spirko. His hands on, no-nonsense approach to DIY home energy for disasters and family preparedness has helped hundreds of thousands of people in times of trouble.

His energy books can be found at www.KnowledgePublications.com.

His free preparedness classes are at www.Steven1234.com and more about Steve can be discovered at www.StevenHarris.net

Mr. Harris also provides detailed training classes on batteries, energy and power of all types for the US Military and Department of Defense.

What most people don't know about self-reliant living and preparedness

Mike Adams

Nathan Crane: What are the biggest threats to society right now?

Mike Adams: At the moment, we're dealing with the Ebola outbreak in Africa and there's a very strong chance that it is going to spread to a major European City. If and when it does, it would probably be impossible to contain and it could spread worldwide. The human population is ripe for a pandemic spread because we're at the highest population density that we've ever been in the history of the world. Our cities' infrastructure is failing. For example, in Los Angeles the water supply isn't reliable anymore and police and emergency services' budgets are being cut because of the collapsing economy. We also have rapid air travel that allows people to spread diseases very, very quickly and the head of the CDC and the WHO even admit that there are no antibiotics that can treat the superbugs that are now spreading like wildfire throughout hospitals. Drug companies aren't working on new frontline antibiotics because it's not profitable to treat people only when they're sick. They want to sell drugs to people for chronic ailments because that's where the money is so they're not investing in research on antibiotics.

The human race today is the weakest that it's ever been in the history of humanity. People live indoors and don't go outside much. Some people never even exercise. The only exercise they get is walking across the parking lot. They take their car to drive-thru fast food establishments and the pharmacy. They're not getting any exercise at all. They couldn't garden if their life depended on it and it may depend on it. People are immuno-suppressed because of the medications that people take to suppress their immune function. The additives that are in the food suppress immune function and all the chemicals that are in the food, the pesticide, the herbicide, and the glyphosate make weak immune systems.

NC: What are some action steps people can take to prepare themselves?

MA: The right attitude is very important. There are people out there who are saying, "Well, I don't want to talk about that. It's too scary." Those are the words that are uttered by the people who will die in a crisis because they can't mentally grasp the importance of real optimism through preparedness. A real sense of optimism is when people anticipate what's coming and they take action to bolster their position so that they make it through any challenge. Right now there is something called the normalcy bias. People begin to think that because something functions this way over and over again in their day-to-day life that it will always function that way. If they go to their kitchen and turn on the tap, water comes out. They think, "Why wouldn't water come out of the tap? It's always been there for the last 35 years. What could possibly make it not work?" The problem is they don't think about where that water comes from. They don't think that human beings, who are vulnerable to pandemics, staff the water plant. So if Ebola or a superbug were to get into a major US city, one of the first things the government is going to do is call for a quarantine. Who's going to run the water plant? Who's going to run the power plant? What if somebody infected goes into the water plant and accidentally gets the Ebola virus into the water supply? One way or another the water supply is going to be disrupted and as a result someone will go to their kitchen tap, turn on the faucet and when no water comes out they have no idea what to do because they haven't stored any water. They don't have any water filters. They never thought, "How do you get water out of the lake or a stream and make it drinkable?" So now they are completely helpless and become a problem for emergency services. On the other hand, a prepared person will say, "Oh wow. The water tap isn't working. No problem. I've got a 500 gallon rainwater storage tank out back. We'll start tapping into that. We'll use these gravity filters to filter out any bacteria that might be in there. We could use these other techniques to clean up the water or even boil it if it comes to that. We know how to make water drinkable and safe." That's a person who will survive in a crisis.

NC: What are some of the things that you have found most people might be forgetting in their preparedness plans?

MA: A lot of people are very gear-centric and supply-centric. They've got the seeds for their heirloom garden that they're going to grow one day, they've got night vision goggles, and they've got plenty of ammo for a Glock 26. The problem is they don't have the physical fitness that they're going to need to deploy all of this. Physical fitness and stamina is so crucial. Most people live in the city. They're living in an apartment or a suburb, they have seeds, they have tools but when the power grid fails they have to go from their sedentary lifestyle to an active lifestyle of digging soil, pulling weeds, growing food, and carrying water buckets around. It's not realistic. You can't go from a sedentary lifestyle to an active pre-1900 lifestyle overnight. Many Americans and other first-world citizens around the world are extremely overweight and obese. It's going to take time to drop those pounds through physical activity and during that time, you're going to need more calories just to move your body around. So if you're extensively overweight you'll have an increased caloric need that's going to tap into your food supply right away from day 1. People are thinking unrealistically because they believe they can easily grow a garden from a bunch of garden seeds. The physical aspect is what most people are putting off and that could be a very dangerous mistake.

Also a lot of people don't think about the leverage that is provided by fossil fuels in agriculture. Food production today is driven by mechanized equipment like tractors that are running on diesel fuel. That same fossil fuel is a great multiplier of effort allowing one person to have the output of hundreds of people. When the infrastructure fails that leverage vanishes. Now, you are one person producing the output of one person and suddenly food becomes very, very difficult to produce. So what do you do? The best root crop to grow so you can survive is a potato. Throughout history nations have actually survived on potatoes. Just figure out how to grow a potato and that will keep you alive.

NC: What are the other foods that people should really consider growing?

MA: You need to grow fruits and unless you have an orchard already going, your options are limited. A good option to grow is strawberries, which are pretty simple to grow. Fruits provide a lot of water-soluble nutrients that are immune boosting and when you're dealing with any kind of a break down in society, you're going to have outbreaks of infectious disease no matter what. The fact that the infrastructure is failing will lead to outbreaks of Cholera because of failed sewerage processing centers, failures of personal hygiene throughout high population density centers. So you've got to be dealing with a lot of infectious disease. Most people aren't that healthy and they're going to be carriers of disease. You need to be able to grow your own fresh medicine and you can do that with things like strawberries, blackberries, goji berries, pomegranates, and etcetera. Pomegranates are incredibly rich with nutrients. The pomegranate seed even contains medicine. It tastes awful but it's very, very healthy and it boosts your immune system. No matter where you live, whether you're in a tropical environment, a desert environment, the Great Plains, or a forest, there is a lot of natural medicine out there that you can use.

NC: What options do people have about storing organic, freeze-dried food?

MA: One of my criticisms of the survival food industry so far is that so much of it is really genetically modified, soy bean derived texture vegetable protein with a lot of MSG added. A lot of chemical additives, a lot of GMOs, and a lot of pesticide are laid in food. There are some suppliers out there but they're very rare because the demand for really clean, organic, freeze dried fruits is so small. The most important thing is to have the tools and the skills to be able to start growing your own food because no matter how much food you store, that stored food runs out eventually. You need to start creating a sustainable food system. The name of that food system is called permaculture. Permaculture is when you create a food forest in a multi-layered food-producing plot of land that's producing food at any physical layer from low to the ground, medium level, and high level. It's conserving water, naturally resistant to pests, and has a high diversity collection of food producing plants. This is not something that is rolled out overnight.

NC: What would be the easiest way people can grow their own food?

MA: A multi-layered system would be the best. You start with sprouting because spouts can be ready to eat in 3 or 4 days. In a crisis, you start rolling out your food production even if you don't already have it in place. Start your sprouts on day 1 and you're going to have something to eat from your sprouting a few days later. At the same time, you should be planting in the soil things like potatoes and long-term orchard type of trees. These can be nut trees or pomegranate plants, fruit-producing trees, something that would give you food over many years. Most people have enough stored food for a year and that's great. But what are you doing during that year? You should be planting your garden. You should be sprouting, growing food, and planting orchards during that year because that stored food is really like a battery of food and that battery is going to run out of juice sooner or later. If you don't use that resource to invest in other food resources, you're going to find yourself starving and dead. So use what you have to leverage yourself into a sustainable future.

NC: How do you sprout?

MA: You don't need a sprouting machine of any kind although you can get some but you can sprout in jars or cans. All you do is you put a seed in the bottom of the jar, put some water in it, put a cheese cloth over the top so it could breathe and rinse it out a couple of times a day to avoid growth of mold. That's all there is to it. You can even use a sprouting bag. Some people use a hemp bag or a cheese cloth bag. You put seeds in it, soak it in water several times a day and the sprouts will sprout inside the bag and you'll have food in a few days. The fact that the bag has access to oxygen and air helps keep it clean, avoids growth of mold or anything like that. So sprouting should always be step 1 in a crisis.

NC: Why do you think most people do not prepare for the unexpected to happen?

MA: One reason is the mainstream media is telling them that there will never be any emergencies, the government will take care of you, people who are into survival are nuts. It's convenient to believe that you don't need any stockpiled food because you can go down to the grocery store or that you don't need a firearm in your house. You can call 911 so the police will show up and they'll defend you. Those are convenient but lazy beliefs. What we're seeing in society today is a temporary insanity of delusional thinking among the masses. The reality is people that prepare are the future of the human race. They and their children will survive and go on to represent humanity.

NC: What areas of the USA are best for self-reliant living?

MA: You need to have a place that has soil and water in order to grow food. Once you have established that simple criteria, the choices become very, very obvious. On the West Coast you can go into Southern Oregon, Eastern Oregon, and Eastern Washington. Idaho has a lot of great self-reliant people in that area but it's a colder region and a little more difficult to grow food. Wyoming is very cold but has a culture of self-reliance. A better choice would be to move down into Colorado or Utah. You have no water to really speak of in Southern California, Arizona and New Mexico. In fact, you really don't hit water as you're moving east until you get to Austin, Texas. Once you get to Central Texas, rainfall starts to vastly and sharply increase until you get into East Texas where you're in a really wet environment. I'm in Central Texas. Texas has a culture of self-reliance and independence and you can buy acres of soil at a relatively affordable price. Florida is a great place to grow food especially in Central Florida in places like Gainesville but you also have the hurricane risk. As you move up the coast, there is a lot of fruit producing regions but you still have the hurricane risk. In South and Central America, you're the foreigner and in a collapse it's not a necessarily safe place to live because the locals know you have valuables. New Zealand is a great place so check it out if you're going outside of America. Australia has its challenges since most of it is a vast barren desert but the coastal regions can be very, very fruitful in terms of food production. Canada is very, very cold most of the year so green houses are crucial for food production there. But along the boat-coast, you can extend that growing season quite extensively. So wherever you go, you're going to have to think about rainwater collection. You're going to have to think about soil quality and the growing season.

Nate's Notes

Possible for global pandemic

- Potentially could exceed health containments.
- Could spread worldwide if not contained.
- We are at the highest population density ever in the world.
- We have failing infrastructure like in LA, water supply isn't reliable, and police and emergency services are being cut because of finances.
- Superbugs are resistant to every chemical drug created.
- Our population is weaker than our ancestors have ever been.
- Chemicals in food and water suppress the immune function.
- Before World War I, all food on the planet was organic food.

Having the right attitude

- Need to focus on what is real and possible.
- Grasp real optimism through preparedness.
- Be ready to make it through any challenge.
- Having an honest assessment about the threats that face humanity.
- The normalcy bias – belief that everything will function the same as usual.

What are most people forgetting in their preparedness plans?

- Most people are very supply centric.
- Most people aren't physically fit, stamina wise.
- Stamina is very critical for survival.
- If you are extensively overweight, you will tap into food supplies.
- You need experience growing food, collecting water, and being physically fit

Food production

- Food production today is mostly run on oil.
- 1 barrel of diesel fuel is similar to 700 hours of human labor.
- Get really good at growing potatoes. It offers one of the very greatest returns on caloric needs. It can be white potatoes, sweet potatoes, or red potatoes
- You also need to grow fruits like strawberries. Fruit trees are a source of fresh medicine. Any kind of berry that is a nutrient dense fruit such as pomegranates, nopal cactus fruits, and goji berries. You will need medicine and calories.
- Wildcrafting is going to be your healthiest option.
- Storing food – needs to be organic and no genetically modified food.
- NaturalNews.com has organic freeze dried fruit.

- Better to store whole grains, dried organic fruit, and have tools and skills to be able to grow food.
- Need to create a sustainable food system.
- Permaculture
  ‣ How you stay alive year after year
  ‣ Creating a food forest with layers.
  ‣ Monoculture always leads to disease wipeout of the crop.
  ‣ Florida oranges are threatened to wipeout, bananas, etc.
  ‣ Permaculture resists infection and disease wipeout
- Create natural pesticide using cayenne and tobacco plant.
- Start with sprouting. You can eat this in three to four days.
- Non electric hydroponic systems.
- Can grow lettuce in 30-45 days.
- Plant potatoes in soil.
- Plant long term orchard trees, fruit trees, and nut trees.
- What can I eat a few days from now, a few weeks from now, a few months from now, and a few years from now?
- Sprouting
  ‣ Can sprout in jars or cans
  ‣ Put seeds in bottom of jar
  ‣ Put water in it

- ‣ Cheese cloth over top
- ‣ Rinse out a couple of times/day
- ‣ Can use a hemp bag, soak in water several times/day
- People have a lot of dead stored food but no living food.
- You need living nutrients in food to enhance your health.
- Body needs raw enzymes to help immune function and help digest food.
- Aquaponic systems can be too dependent on electricity to be effective as they are dependent on the grid.
- Low tech non-electric food production is ideal.

Why do most people fail to prepare for the unexpected?

- Mainstream media is telling people that the government will take care of them.
- We all come from survivors as ancestors.
- Human history shows that crazy stuff happens from time to time.
- It's convenient to live in a delusional world.
- Distractions keep people distracted from the reality.
- It's convenient to believe mainstream media
- Modern America has become very lazy about taking care of its own health and safety.
  - ‣ We have delegated these responsibilities to others.

- The reality is that people who prepare are the future of the human race. They and their children that survive will go on to thrive.
- We are a very young species that needs to grow up and mature.
- We have built societies that are dependent on power grids and the same power grids will fail us.
- Societies will learn to not depend on vulnerable power grids.
- Las Vegas is about to run out of water and will become a ghost town within a few decades. The same could happen to LA someday if people don't find a way to get more water there.
- Human Civilization has not been good at thinking long term.
- Need to look at the future of our grandchildren's children.

What areas of the country are best for self-reliant living?

- Arizona has a lack of water.
- You need soil and water to grow food.
- On the west coast, you can go up into Oregon, Washington, Idaho, Wyoming, Colorado, Utah, Austin, Texas, and Louisiana. In Texas you can buy acreage and soil for relatively low prices. East coast is good for food but

carries a hurricane risk. South and Central America can be good places, but you would be foreigner. New Zealand would be a great place whereas Australia is mostly desert but coastal areas could be fruitful for food production.

Fukushima

- Mainstream media will not share the truth about disasters.
- The damaged reactor buildings continue to spew extremely high levels of radioactive isotopes into the ocean.
- This has already exceeded levels of the Chernobyl disaster.
- The real risk from Fukushima is the structural failure of the above ground containment pool.
- If the pool fails, fuel rods would achieve massive criticality and nuclear fuel would release into the atmosphere
- Should this happen, it would make west coast uninhabitable

Mike Adams

Mike Adams, known as the "Health Ranger," is an outspoken consumer health advocate, award-winning investigative journalist, Internet activist and science lab director. He is the founder and editor of www.NaturalNews.com, which is the Internet's most-trafficked natural health news website. He is also the creator of www.CounterThink.com, www.FoodInvestigations.com, www.HealingFoodReference.com, and several other websites covering natural health topics. Mike is a prolific writer and has been called "the best health and natural products writer on the scene today."

Learn more at www.NaturalNews.com

The intersection of self-respect and well-being

Gerald Celente

Nathan Crane: Some of the trends that you predicted are incredible. How was that even possible?

Gerald Celente: The first big one that really put me in the limelight so to speak was when I called the 1987 Stock Market crash and I did it in January of 1987. I said this was the year it was going to crash and it did and then, I saw the Asian Currency Crisis happening in the 90's, the break-up of the Soviet Union in the late 80's, and I predicted a new third party. I wrote about it in Trend Tracking in 1988 and I said that someone like Ross Perot is the type of political maverick that the nation was looking for and that came to pass along with a whole bunch of other things. I coined the term "clean food" back in 1993. New York Times did a big story on it and I was talking about organic and bottled water back in the mid-80's before people were really having anything to do with it. And I also have an honorary doctorate in integrative medicine for the work that I've done in that field over the years. One of the books that I worked on early in the mid-80s was Natural Healing by Dr. Jack Soltanoff. My former wife was dying of Colitis and in those days there was no such thing as vitamin therapy and whole health healing. I went on a crusade to save her life and I did. I learned about all the different methodologies of looking at the world rather than through the eyes of conventional wisdom.

NC: In the Trends Journal you talk about the "I Don't Care" trend. What exactly is that and why do you think people should be concerned?

GC: We say, "Don't blame Obama Care, blame I Don't Care" and look at what the people have become. Crap in. Crap out. I have offices in Colonial Kingston, New York and it's a former supermarket like the old A & P's in the 1920's and 30's with big windows and I see people walking by all day. Look at how obese they've become. I'm old enough to remember when I was a young guy people weren't riding down the aisles of supermarkets in electric cars because they were too obese to walk. Obesity has become the norm. I remember getting on an airplane in the 70's and how people were dressed, the service in the airplane, and how people love to fly. Now it's a flying circus. Look at the way people go on the plane. There's no self-respect, there's no dignity, there's no concern about others, and there's no integrity. This is what I'm going to do. If you don't like it, too bad.

NC: Do you see this trend mostly in America? Do you think it's distinctly American or you think it's a trend throughout the globe?

GC: It's becoming global. It's the virus of multi-nationalization. Now it's a big deal in America when somebody opens up a butcher shop. It's all a big deal. Oh, a butcher shop! They're doing something that's a specialty that isn't a part of the multi-national insignia because that's the future. The multi-national companies are so fragile that if they don't meet their quarter expectations and their stock starts going down, people bail out on them. So if you really wanted to break the chains, that's the way to do it. You boycott them. Don't go to the chains and the chains will break up and then you'll have a society where people can open up dress shops and haberdashers. The reason this happened is because slimy politicians took away the laws that were put in place that prohibited this from happening.

NC: Is there any hope in the future ahead? Do you see any possibility for change? Any possibility that this "I Don't Care" mentality will be reversed in some way?

GC: Hope and change you can believe in. Hope is the most negative word in the metaphysical dictionary. It means wishing for something to happen without taking any action to do it. Can it change? Never before have Americans been so disillusioned. When the vacuum is this big, it can be filled with anything. It could be filled with greatness, it could become a renaissance, it could become a new age of spiritual enlightenment or it could become anything. It's up to the individuals to make it happen and everybody has that special gift. With the tragedy going on with Israel bombing Gaza, I've been looking up Zionism and how it started and

I read about Theodor Herzl. They call him the father of Zionism. So I said to myself, "Okay, one guy made a change." So if Obama can, if Bush can, if Clinton can, if Herzl can, you can. There's an individual out there that could change the world. Don't believe me? As I said, if Bush can, if Clinton can, if Obama can, if Herzl can, you can.

NC: What's your prediction for the future of this country?

GC: Well, if nothing is done, it's going to be hell. If the trends continue on the way that they are going, it's going to get worse. Let's not call this the United States because of the militarization of the police, the continued lower standard of living, the economic decline, the growing underclass, the violence, the pollution, and the multi-national take-overs. Rather, let's call it Slave-landia because that's the direction it's heading in unless people change course. Look at the tragedy being committed in the Middle East. Go over to Syria, the Civil War; take a look at Iraq, wonderful. It's better off without Saddam Hussein, isn't it? Take a walk over to Yemen and the never ending Civil War. You see the economy collapsing over there in Brazil and in Argentina they're going to default next week. How about Ukraine? Isn't the civil war started by the United States and Europe wonderful? Don't believe me? Do your homework. Listen to the audio tape of Assistant Secretary of State Victoria Nuland in February of 2014 with the

American Ambassador of Ukraine, Geoffrey Pyatt plotting the overthrow the Yanukovych government. It's there for everybody to listen to. Not enough for you? Go to YouTube and type in Victoria Nuland Washington Press Club December 12, 2013. There she is giving a speech saying how Ukraine should follow the path set forth by the International Monetary Fund. As she's giving a speech sponsored by Chevron, who just cut an $11 billion deal to frack away at Ukraine. Industrial production in Germany is down to its 2011 levels, Italy entered back into a recession, over in Indonesia things are getting a lot worse, India had to raise the interest rates again because there's a run on the Rupee, and it's one country after another. We're heading to World War III with all the pieces in place. And what is it going to look like? Ask Einstein. He said, "I don't know how the Third World War will be fought, but I do know the fourth one will be fought with sticks and stones." The Great War destroyed Europe at the time when it was blossoming and it set the stage for the following wars and the wars that we have now.

NC: What are some things that individual people can do right now to make a difference for their life and for the potential lives of the future of humanity?

GC: It all goes back to the individual. Nothing's going to change until people find the courage, dignity, self-respect, and passion to change themselves. Until that changes, nothing will change.

NC: Those 4 pillars are the pillars of living a fulfilling life: Dignity, self-respect, caring about ourselves, and being passionate about health, change, peace, and courage. It requires courage to stand up for what you believe in, to think for yourself, to go out into the world and make a difference and live your truth. Those 4 things aren't going to be acquired overnight but certainly with desire, willpower, the want to change, and some practice, any person can cultivate those four qualities within themselves and I agree those are great qualities. People around the world are wanting change, they're wanting peace, they're tired of war, they're wanting health, they're tired of disease, they're wanting good and clean food, they're tired of genetically modified organisms that are made in laboratories causing cancer and tumors. People are starting to wake up to the idea that the way that we're doing things in the world is not working and if we want to change things, we need to do something about it now.

Nate's Notes

Gerald Celente coined the term "clean food" back in the mid-eighties before Organic Food was known. He looked at the world rather than the eye of conventional wisdom and works based on the premise of, "Stop repeating what everyone else is saying. Think for yourself."

Current facts turn into trends – as well as making connections between various fields because all things are connected. As Celente said, "All things are connected like the blood that unites us all."

Celente's definition of Hell – "Taking the last breath and knowing you weren't the person you said you were or could've been."

Critical health nurses said, – "The biggest regret was never living their life to the fullest, to the way they should have."

The Virus of Multinationalisation – "The I don't care trend" is spreading globally. What goes in is what goes out. For example, obesity has become the norm.

We have to take back control of our lives by being responsible and voting with our wallets. Never before have Americans been filled with dissolution. It is possible that this is to become a part of a spiritual revolution. In fact, this could have the potential for the "Great Awakening".

If any person can do it, so can you. One way is to sign up at Occupypeace.us to support peace on the planet. If nothing can be done, it's going to get worse and it's going to be hell. Economic decline, growing underclass, violence, pollution, multinational takeovers, "slave-landia," and etc. will continue unless people change the course.

Einstein once said, "I don't know how the 3rd World War will be fought, but I know the 4th one will be fought with sticks and stones."

So what can people do right now? It all comes back to the people. Each individual person must promote peace, not war, promote health, not death, and promote love, not war. People must find the courage, dignity, self-respect, and passion within themselves if they want to change. The opportunity has never been greater than now and it's up to the people to do it.

Anything you do, do it with quality.

Gerald Celente

Forecasting trends since 1980, Gerald Celente is the publisher of The Trends Journal, Founder/Director of the Trends Research Institute, and the author of the highly acclaimed and bestselling books, Trend Tracking: The System to Profit from Today's Trends, Trends 2000: How to Prepare for and Profit from the Changes of the 21st Century and What Zizi Gave Honeyboy: A True Story About Love, Wisdom, and the Soul of America. Gerald Celente and The Trends Research Institute have earned the reputation as "today's most trusted name in trends" for their accurate and timely predictions of hundreds of social, business, consumer, environmental, economic, political, entertainment, and technology trends. Using his unique perspectives on current events forming future trends, Gerald Celente developed the Globalnomic® methodology, which is used to identify, track, forecast and manage trends.

Learn more at www.TrendsJournal.com.

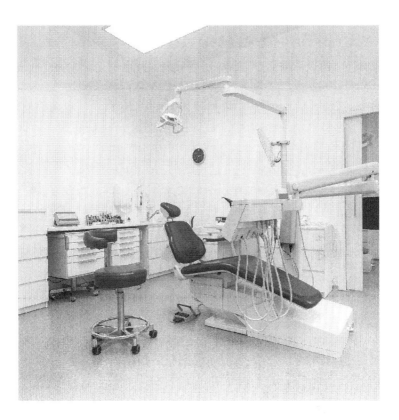

Alternatives to Dentist –
How to Prevent & Heal
Common Tooth Ailments
Doug Simons

Nathan Crane: You've said in your classes that our teeth are alive and what exactly do you mean by that?

Doug Simons: Sometimes we carry perspectives that we just have without knowing why and one of these perspectives that we often carry is that our teeth are dead. They're like a piece of rock and if they get chipped or cracked all they need is glue. Stop and think about that. It does not make any sense. Our teeth are alive and that means they have an entire system for maintaining their integrity and an entire system for repairing damage that might happen to them. In holistic medicine, our goal is always to support what the body is already doing. By support, I mean we learn the things that don't support and the things that offer extra support. Over a long period of time, I've developed an understanding of how they work so that we can maintain integrity and inspire them to heal themselves when there's damage.

The best medicine is good food and if we hope to supplement or drug ourselves to avoid eating well, it's never going to work. Our body runs well on good food and understanding what good food is takes a little bit of time because there's a lot of information out there and not all of it of course is correct in content. But basic understanding regarding nutrition will always help the body run well. So we begin with just that foundational understanding that we need to take care of our bodies for our bodies to work well.

When we move to talking about the teeth, there are certain things that damage the teeth and certain things that give them the nutrition and strength they need. We hope that basically people will eat well enough and that's a demonstration that we get to watch. People are not just losing their teeth in a very short period of time. They are strong, bone-like structures that take a while to deteriorate and if we begin to understand how to take care of them, they don't deteriorate at all.

To begin we need to understand the basic structure of a tooth. There's enamel on the outside and it's very, very hard. A matrix under that is a structure of the tooth and that's a bone-like material but of a different structure than bone. Then there's of course the nerve and then the teeth themselves are held in. They grow into the bones but tendons also hold them in. And when we're thinking about the teeth we want to take care of both, we want to take care of the entire system, which means the jaw bone and the entire tooth. So we begin to consider the teeth as alive and what we can do to help maintain that integrity. The teeth have a circulatory system in them. They're living and they maintain themselves. Much of the re-mineral maintenance and the re-mineralization of the teeth come through the saliva. I had for a long time felt that toothpaste was not helpful to my teeth and that it had a detrimental quality. Not knowing why, I just stopped using it and formulated a really amazing tooth batter, which is something anybody can do or you can purchase it. Very recently we learned that perhaps the detrimental part of toothpaste is that they use a substance, glycerin that some people don't necessarily consider as a detrimental material. But in this instance it coats the teeth and that coating sticks for a long period of time. So when we brush our teeth that re-mineralization that's happening to the saliva gets blocked. Again, remember I said that we look for things that damage the teeth and things that repair or allow them to maintain their integrity.

NC: Does that mean that the minerals are simulated through the actual teeth themselves? It doesn't come necessarily through the gums into the roots? It actually comes through the enamel like from an outside going in approach or how does the teeth actually get the minerals?

DS: There is re-mineralization and maintenance of the re-mineralization of teeth coming through the saliva and we would be foolish to assume that the same process of nourishment isn't coming into the teeth through the bloodstream. We know that the matrix of the tooth is amazing and a single tooth is said to have literally miles inside of it. Inside the tooth the structure has many, many, many miles of tubes. Each tube is so tiny and nutrients actually flow through the tiny tubing. Of course there's something going on there and it's all very complex. I'm only saying that I believe most of the mineralization of the enamel probably comes through the saliva.

NC: What can you do to maintain the quality of your teeth?

DS: I want you to understand how to maintain the quality of your teeth. How that's done then how to work through all phases of degeneration that happens to teeth, how to repair cracks, chips, cavities, abscesses, and perhaps talk about root canals. In general maintenance we want to maintain the integrity of the teeth and we want to especially maintain the integrity of the enamel. The enamel is actually an easily changed layer and it's very close in a certain way to calcium and calcium is an incredibly important part of the human body. So many things depend on exact calcium levels in the bloodstream including heartbeat and temperature. To ensure that never varies the body has many ways of maintaining that level and you have to be extremely at a balance for that to be effective in a way that it affects things that are very important like the rhythm of the heart. For example, if there is a lack of absorption of nutrition, which can be caused by a chronic condition or stomach flu, the body is not going to have the calcium levels changed in the blood because of that. So one of the places that the body will go is to remove some calcium and remove some enamel and bring that into the bloodstream. So if you think about it when there were times when your teeth were sensitive to hot and cold or that you felt like you questioned your ability to bite into a really crisp carrot, your teeth were weak. This is demonstrating the aliveness of the teeth.

One of the main plants that I like and use for maintaining high quality tooth character is a plant called horsetail. Many people know that it's a very revered herb. It's a well-known and well-used herb. It's very high in silica and has always been known as the plant that can be used to help with kidney maintenance, kidney health, bone medicine, and also tooth medicine. In Chinese medicine the kidneys rule the teeth, the hair, the bones, the nails, the knees, and the lower back. We need to nourish the kidneys anytime any of these are out of balance. There are a number of species of horsetail and the one we want is a species called Equisetum hymale. If you read about horsetail you will find cautions such as can cause headaches and disrupt digestion. You can have those experiences by using other species of horsetail and they won't necessarily give the medicinal quality that the Equisetum hymale will. So it's important when using these medicines to make sure you have the correct species of horsetail. Once you have the correct specie of horsetail you don't make a tea out of it but ingest about a teaspoon a day from four to six days and take couple of days off and continue again. The days off are always important because it has a catalytic reaction in the body and it makes it work better and faster. You'll start to notice a difference in about ten days to two weeks. You'll notice that your teeth and nails have grown more, that they're stronger, and that your hair has more quality to it in just that short period of time.

We often carry perspectives about the use of herbs that are not necessarily correct. An example of that is for an herb to work it has to be of high quality. Much of the herbal medicines that are available are not of high quality and so we feel that the herbs aren't powerful or don't work well. That's not a fair representation of how they might work. Herbs are about creating harmony and balance. We have forgotten that many herbs are a fantastic example of food medicine and that they should be eaten in a regular way so that the body has access to the nutritional qualities and magic that they carry.

NC: Why don't you like to use toothpaste?

DS: What we discovered is that among the thirty-four different toothpaste brands, only one doesn't carry glycerin. Whether that toothpaste has used something else that might also coat the teeth, I don't know. We've discovered that glycerin gets in the way of the re-mineralization and maintenance of the minerals.

NC: How does a tooth repair itself?

DS: Let's begin with something small like a very small chip. The way that the teeth will heal that is the chip is just in the enamel layer and the enamel will fill back in. If you get a larger chip, the enamel will take over that chipped area. It will repaint that area until it has a thick layer of enamel over it again. So be very aware that your teeth are changing and what you want to do is maintain their quality and not allow it to get so weakened that they might start to decay.

We take responsibility for the health of our body but we forget that we can do that with our teeth. So you want to look at them. Get yourself a dental mirror, some good lighting, and check your teeth. Get familiar with them and remember that all decays start with a very, very small spot and the sooner you see it the sooner you can do something about it. Let's say you have a tiny, tiny dark spot on your tooth. Maybe it's brown or black and it's the very beginning of decay. The first thing to do is carefully examine all the rest of your teeth, make sure your diet is in some sensible order, and start taking horsetail. The next procedure is to use a hard wooden stick and scrub that spot. Do it very consistently a number of times throughout the day. The wood will absorb the qualities out of the tooth that we don't want and that scrubbing cleans the tooth. So clean it very thoroughly with a stick, using tooth powder instead of toothpaste if needed. Since your diet is in order and you're using horsetail, you can rub the color out and it will literally disappear. Now if we move up to a bigger cavity where it's darker and has affected the structure of the tooth a bit, you might even see a bit of a hole. The procedure is exactly the same with the small spot: quality of diet, ingesting the horsetail, avoiding things like glycerin in the toothpaste, and examining your teeth with a mirror so that you can keep ahead of any other spots. Now if that hole is large enough, you'd chew some of the stronger PH balancing and harmonizing or what I call boundary medicines. You chew those and pack them in that spot that's decaying. You'd also scrub it consistently with the wood and if it's not being scrubbed it's being packed with the herbs. All we're doing is stopping the decay and to allow the enamel to regenerate. Once your teeth get badly damaged, it can be harder to repair.

That stick is always a dry twig; a quarter to 3/8 in diameter and each tooth is touched and scrubbed. It feels wonderful and teeth need pressure. They get invigorated, enlivened, woken up by pressure. A lot of our food is very soft and our teeth don't get the invigorating quality of the stimulation caused by pressure. Cleaning your teeth with a stick offers that pressure. Some people love to clean their teeth with a stick and do it exclusively without ever using a toothbrush. Other people tend to clean their teeth with a stick for a while and then do it two to three times a week. They'll switch back and forth between the stick and tooth powder and a toothbrush. It works really well but knowing that invigorating your teeth with pressure is very important.

NC: Are there any twigs or sticks that we should stay away from because they would not be good for the teeth?

DS: You don't want anything poisonous but what you want to avoid is something like metal. It's much too hard and potentially damaging to the teeth. Any dry wood will work. My favorite is probably something like cottonwood or willow. We use everything like mesquite, oak, pine is slightly too soft but it works and fir is the same thing. Any of these woods that are slightly hard like willow and cottonwood is fantastic. It's also better to break a small dead twig out of a tree where you're sure that the dogs haven't urinated. The most important thing is that it's a dead hard piece of wood since a living green one is too soft, too flexible, and too mushy. It won't give you the same experience that you want.

I think one of the things that might be helpful for people to remember as well is that you really need time to try these methods. Remember that each time you get a filling, you're losing a part of your tooth that you're never going to get back. So work at avoiding fillings.

Nate's Notes

Natural Dentistry

Your teeth are alive

- Nutrition is always critical
  - ‣ The best medicine is good food
  - ‣ Let food be thy medicine and medicine be thy food
  - ‣ Basic understanding of nutrition will help the body run well
  - ‣ While we are alive, we hope to have a type of balance that doesn't have big sways to it – such as the Red road or the Little Path.

- Certain things that damage the teeth
  - ‣ Begin by understanding basic structure of the tooth
  - ‣ Enamel on outside, matrix that is structure of tooth underneath kind of like bone, then the nerve, then held in with tendons to grow to the bone.
    - You want to take care of the entire system, including the jawbone and the entire tooth.
    - Teeth have a circulatory system to them; they are living and take care of themselves.

- Much of the remineralization of the teeth comes through the saliva.
- Toothpaste which is bad for the teeth is glycerin because it coats the teeth and stays on for a long time so remineralization gets blocked

General Maintenance:

- Maintain the integrity of the teeth and the enamel
  - The enamel is a very changing layer. Very close to calcium. So many things in the body including your heartbeat depend on the right amount of calcium.
  - If something in the body is out of balance such as bad absorption of nutrition, the body won't have calcium levels in the blood change, so what the body will do is go to the bones and enamel to remove calcium and put it into bloodstream.
  - When you feel like your teeth are weak or sensitive, it is because THEY ARE weak. It is because your teeth are alive.
  - Never want your teeth to stay sensitive or feel weak.

- One of the main plants to maintain health character is Horsetail.

- Well-known and well-used herb. Easy to understand, very high in silica, always has been known as a plant to help with kidney maintenance and kidney health, and also bone and tooth medicine.
- In Chinese medicine, the kidneys rule the hair, the teeth, the nails, and the lower back.
- Horsetail is very important to maintain the quality of the teeth. The species you want is: Equisetum Hymale
- Want horsetail to be done correctly so it tastes sweet, is bright green, and is the correct species.
- Horsetail needs to be very dry to grind it.
- Ingest 1 tsp./day, not in tea, for 4-6 days. Then take a few days off and continue. You can continue taking this forever.
- Know where the horsetail comes from. Don't be downstream from agricultural spots because it can absorb the toxins.

Using Herbs:

- Not about war against something but more about creating a balance.
- Herbs are a food medicine and should be eaten in an ongoing way.

- Some herbs are used for an imbalance situation and many herbs are about maintaining balance and health.
- The liver has evolved since the dawn of time with herbs like Dandelion, Burdock, and Milk Thistle. Herbs that are used for tonifying and nutritional way. The liver is used to having these and need these in the diet.

Want to maintain a living balance:

- We are balancing, not creating balance. Balancing is a forever part about being alive. We CAUSE a balanced life by what we do.
- Treat the plants well. We support their continual existence. You want to make sure their wellbeing comes first because with that attitude, you'll never have any problems with the quality of the plants and the quality of your environment.
- The plants are living beings and they are relatives in this magical world that we walk in.
- Plant communication – understanding that plants are here to support us. Treating them with respect is key.
- Plants can be considered like our parents (Native perspective)
- Invited to the much richer world when connecting deeper with plants.

Toothpaste

- Whatever you use to clean your teeth, make sure it doesn't put a gloss on the outer layer of the teeth such as glycerin.

- A single tooth is made up of many miles of tiny tubing, which is where nutrients flow through.

How does a tooth repair itself?

- **Chip in tooth** – The way to the tooth will heal if it's only in enamel layer, the enamel will fill back in. If it's a larger chip, the enamel will take over the chipped area. The healing of a chip happens with the enamel repainting the area until it has a thick layer over the chip.

- Need to remember that we can take responsibility for the health of our teeth.

- If you have a cavity, it just means your teeth are weak, and you need to strengthen them.

- You have time, you don't have to act immediately, you have time to try and improve your teeth without getting them drilled.

- **Small brown spot on tooth such as decay** – make sure to examine diet and make sure it is in balance.

- Start taking horsetail.

- Then start using hard wooden stick to scrub the spot fairly consistently throughout the day. The wood absorbs qualities out of the tooth that we don't want. The scrubbing cleans the tooth.

- Using tooth powder instead of toothpaste.

- If it's small enough, you will rub the color out, it can disappear.

- **If you have a large cavity that's larger decay** – procedure is same as above.

- **If hole is large enough,** then need to chew stronger ph balancing herbs, then pack them in the spot that's decaying, and scrub consistently with the wood in between packing.

How to clean with a stick:

- Teeth need pressure. They get invigorated and feel enlivened with pressure.

- Use a hard twig or stick and scrub all the teeth or the effected areas.

- Holistic medicine is based on participation.

- Any dry, dead, piece of wood will work such as dry cottonwood, twig or willow. Any dry twig that is hard and is not poisonous will suffice.

- Each time you get a filling, you are losing a piece of your tooth you will never get back.

Doug Simons

At 11 years old, Doug Simons began learning about the native plants of Colorado from his mother. His awareness, knowledge, and connection to the plant world has only grown stronger through his life and his travels across the American continent. Doug has also gained a vast amount of firsthand knowledge with regards to edible/medicinal plants and primitive skills through his experiences living primitively in the Sonoran Desert and Gila Wilderness of Southern New Mexico for over 20 years.

Learn more at www.chanchka.com.

The New Homesteading Movement

Laurie Neverman

Nathan Crane: How did you get into self-reliance?

Laurie Neverman: I was raised on a small dairy farm in Northwest Wisconsin so it's always been part of my upbringing to be working outside, doing something with the animals, the garden, and that type of thing. My mom had a huge garden, we raised big flocks of poultry, and we had dairy cows so I started out there. Then I went away to college, got my degrees, and once I finished school I worked at what was at that time, the world's largest flat plate collector solar water heating system. We used to heat over a million gallons of hot water every year. About the same time as that I was expecting my first son but unfortunately the plant ran into some trouble and they ended up pulling it down so I came home to be a full time mom. As the kids got a little bit older, we were initially living in the suburbs and we decided we really wanted to get back to a more rural setting. So nine years ago now we built this place out in the county on thirty five acres and we have about an acre garden. We're working now more on permaculture plantings like trees, shrubs that sort of thing and taking advantage of the native growth here too. And for the blogging aspect of it that kind of started back in 2008 when my husband lost his job that he'd had for about sixteen years. He ended up working part time odd jobs for the better part of the year and my health kind of went on a downward spiral. I went into depression and my weight ballooned up. It was a rough patch but we pulled together, made some changes in our lives, and I did what I could at home here to provide for our family. My husband ended up getting a job a couple of hours away and we pulled together and made it work. Thankfully after five years of being apart, he got a job back in the area so we got our happy ending and we're all back together on our homestead but I wanted to share some of what I learned during our rough spot with everybody else and that's where the blog came about.

NC: What are some things that you might suggest for people who are looking to start to become more self-reliant?

LN: One of the simplest things you can do is just start paying attention to what you eat. It can be as basic as reading labels or looking at preparing your own food from local ingredients. It can be that you start growing some of your own ingredients or join a CSA if you don't have room to grow your own food. CSA stands for "Community Supported Agriculture". That's a really good place to start because everybody has to eat.

Another way is to look at the things that you enjoy or are interesting to you. A skill set that's a hobby would help you to be more independent and self-reliant. There's so much you can do with woodworking, repairing, sewing, crafting, and other kinds of skills. Take your basic starter skill, build on that and turn it into a tool for your life.

NC: Is growing your own food the key step to becoming self-reliant?

LN: Some people aren't going to be able to grow a large portion of their own food. If you live in an apartment you can do things with container plants and you can get really creative but you may not be able to grow the bulk of your food. Still, it's very therapeutic to get your hands working with the soil. A big step in the right direction is connecting with your local food sources. It's cheaper to buy food that's travelled for thousands of miles than it is to buy something produced within a hundred mile radius from most of us. The reason for that is bulk commodities are subsidized, they have cheaper labor in other countries because they don't pay decent living wages, and they can spray things that aren't allowed in this country. So you can either grow your own food or connect with a local grower. You can ask you local grower questions and you can know what's going into your food. I personally find it comforting to have a well-stocked pantry. It's a great sense of security.

NC: Do you live off 100% of what you grow? Do you have extra that you share and sell at the farmer's market?

LN: Keep in mind that I am in Wisconsin so we're under snow for a good portion of the year. Most of what I do grow gets preserved to use year round.

It's not fresh eating throughout the season and I do have two teenage boys who eat like four normal people so I have that to keep in mind too. The reason that I have so much area under cultivation is so that I can get enough from one picking to make sure it's worthwhile preserving. If you're going to can it's much easier to just set up the table, do the picking and do a bunch of processing in one day and have multiple quarts of canned goods afterwards to show for it rather than to do just a little bit, just a little bit, and just a little bit. I keep a little notebook where I keep track of what we have preserved and once I hit the tally where I know that this will keep us through the next growing season then we just eat fresh. I also barter with neighbors using the excess produce for the other things that we need. For example, I have one neighbor that I can swap milk with, another neighbor that I can get eggs from, sometimes they have produce that I don't have, pears off another neighbor's trees, piano lessons with another neighbor and so it's a very handy bartering tool out here in the country.

NC: Have you ever had anybody experience getting in over his or her head?

LN: Absolutely. One of the biggest mistakes people can make is taking on too much and then just feeling overwhelmed and giving up. I've seen some big gardens put in and then as the growing season progresses it gets taken over by weeds. I can tell when they just abandon it because the weed whacker comes through. It's really, really important to not get overwhelmed because it's so easy to get a gorgeous seed catalogue in the middle of winter and you decide you want this, this, and this but when you dig in you realize that there's no way you can keep up with it. You have to keep in mind the time you have to allocate for gardening or other self-reliance things in your life. If you start small you can get a feeling for how much time X amount will take you and then once you have that metric in your life then you can decide to add another one or another two. It's definitely a great idea to start small and then build on it.

NC: I've heard that certain weeds can help pull different toxins out of the soil. What can you say about that?

LN: People worry that they're going to suck up all the nutrients out of the soil. If your garden soil is healthy, the weeds are not going to make it worse. In fact they can actually protect the plants. Some people have argued and have the data to support it that certain weeds can actually transmute elements in the soil to provide themselves the nutrients they need in poor soils. So if it's not there they can make it out of other stuff. Weeds just might actually be enriching the soil, which is pretty cool.

NC: How can someone get started in wildcrafting?

LN: It would be best if you can find a local mentor because plants will be varied around the country and there's nothing as definitive as having someone who knows and can say, "Yes, this is the plant." Many wild plants don't have toxic look-a-likes but some do so you need to be careful and make sure you get a positive ID. There are local cooperative extension offices for most areas in the United States so you can take a plant sample there to help you get an idea if you're right. The main thing is to start looking around, paying attention to your surroundings, looking at online references and a lot of different guides books. You do need to be cautious so make sure you check out a couple of references because some people will say one thing and someone else might say another. Any plant could potentially cause a reaction in somebody so it's always best to sample a little bit even if it's not something that's normally a problem since different food allergies can be set off unexpectedly. Always use caution and common sense when you're getting into this.

Sometimes you don't want to eat a lot of wild edibles, because along with that potent nutrient density is a potent flavor. For example, with bitter herbs, a lot of them are very strong flavored, especially depending on the type or time of year you pick them. If under dry conditions, that bitterness gets turned all the way up to an eleven. So you definitely have to be mindful of that when you're foraging. I do know that a lot of the wild greens are significantly higher in their nutrient density than their domesticated cousins because those stocked in supermarkets are over watered and oftentimes over-fertilized because they want it to grow big and fast.

My neighbor has been cutting shrubs down for years because he said they were Russian olives and that they're an invasive species. He didn't want them and given that he worked for the local conservation office I figured he knows what he was talking about. After I did a little more research it turns out they weren't Russian olives. They're autumn olives and the berries have a hundred times more lycopene than tomatoes do and they're tasty. He's not cutting it down anymore. Instead I make them into a jelly or fruit leather and things like that. It's interesting that a lot of things that we think are weeds were brought over from Europe and Asia because they were used for food and medicine. It's all a matter of perspective.

NC: Do you have a favorite wildcrafting recipe that you like to make very often?

LN: My sons like spanakopita. The dish with spinach and feta cheese between the puff pastry. I change that up with lamb's quarters. Lamb's quarters is heat tolerant and drought tolerant so we cook that up and sauté that with some onions. So that's one of our summer staples.

NC: What are some of the things that you've been able to do to reduce your energy usage?

LN: My house is built Green Certified and Energy Star Certified and in the building process we were able to incorporate a number of green technologies. An example of one is that the house is super insulated. There is concrete sandwiched on the outside walls of the house, there's insulation, concrete with rebar, and then another layer of insulation so that it's air tight and extremely weather, heat, and cold resistant.

For the average homeowner, one simple thing that you can do is an insulating shade. We have insulating cellular shades over all of the windows in the house. There are layers of air trapped in the shade itself and then that drops down over the window. Insulating window covers can block the heat or the cold and trap the temperature you want inside. You need to take the steps to turn off the lights when you're not in the room to cover the blinds, to cover the windows at night with insulating shades, to not use excess water, to not brush your teeth with the faucet running, and to keep a basin in your sink to catch your dishwater that will be used to water your plants outside. Little everyday small things add up and make a difference.

Also look at improving your insulation. Check your weather stripping because a lot of houses have poor quality windows. If you look at an infrared shot of the house the windows will be glowing brightly because they're losing a lot of heat or losing a lot of cold. Make sure that you have good quality windows and doors and that everything is properly insulated.

Another thing that we've been doing in the house is slowly switching to LED lighting in our most used areas. There are some sales and rebates available from different stores and utilities. Even if the bulbs are expensive, we definitely noticed the difference in our energy bill.

NC: Have you experimented at all with solar power at all?

LN: We do have passive solar heating and solar water heating. The house is sized with large south facing windows and then we have an overhang. The main story overhang is where the roof goes a little bit further so that it doesn't keep letting the heat in during the summer but as the angle of the sun drops in the wintertime, it allows it into the house. We have two four-by-eight hot water heating panels for solar hot water. We would like to add solar electric. The cost is always a consideration so that would probably be the next area that we'd like to enter.

NC: What are some important skill sets that people could develop on his or her own towards becoming more self-reliant?

LN: Definitely be able to prepare your own food from scratch. It's stunning to me how many people eat out so frequently. That's a big first step because it's also a great money-saver. Don't be one of those people who store their books in their oven instead of using it for cooking.

Another great skill is simple home repair. Anytime you have to call out the repairman, holy smokes! I don't know what the rates are in your area but they start at $80 an hour out here for most types of repairs. If you have a clogged drain or if your appliance has stopped working, you can use the power of Google and You Tube. You'd be amazed at what you can fix. Make sure you also do the maintenance on your belongings otherwise you'll be paying to replace it. So don't ignore upkeep and general maintenance on your home, your equipment, and anything like that - otherwise you'll be paying more in the long run.

Nate's Notes

How to become more self-reliant:

- Pay attention to what you eat.
  - ‣ Preparing your own food
  - ‣ Reading labels
  - ‣ Grow your own ingredients
  - ‣ Join a CSA
  - ‣ Look at things that you most enjoy and are most interesting to you such as skills, hobbies, woodworking, crafting, sewing, etc. that can help you turn into becoming more self-reliant.
  - ‣ Connect with local food sources
  - ‣ Preserve food via canning, storage, etc.
  - ‣ Start small, grow from there

Wildcrafting

- Creating your own medicine from wild edibles (Weeds)
  - ‣ Weeds can enhance the quality of the soil
  - ‣ Learn which weeds are medicinal and edible
  - ‣ Mushrooms can help clean the soil
  - ‣ Fungi under the soil allows plants to communicate
  - ‣ Healthy soil is very much alive
  - ‣ Make sure to cross reference a couple of sources when sampling wild edibles

Reducing Energy

- Incorporate green technologies
  - Insulated concrete
  - Green star certification
  - Insulating cellular shade over the windows – double honeycomb
  - Take the steps to cover windows at night with insulated shades, don't use excess water, turn off lights when not needed, use dish water to water plants
  - Switch to LED lighting
  - South facing windows
  - Large overhangs to keep sun out during the summer and allow sun in during the winter
  - Solar panels for heating water
  - Energy efficient windows

Developing Skill Sets

- Food
  - Cooking at home, growing food, buying local
  - Don't store cookbooks in your oven

- Home repairs
  - Learning to repair items on your own
  - Use YouTube to learn

- Learning to fix tools
  - Mowers
  - Hand tillers
  - Don't ignore upkeep

Laurie Neverman

Laurie Neverman, creator of Common Sense Homesteading, has a BS in Math/Physics and an MS in Mechanical Engineering with an emphasis in Renewable Energy. She is a wife and mother with a passion for natural healing, homesteading and gardening. She and her family live in a Wisconsin Green Built and Energy Star certified home. Her interests also include herbalism, wildcrafting, homebrewing and live culture foods.

Learn more at
www.CommonSenseHome.com.

Creating Sustainable Food Forests, Building Community, and Staying Warm

Paul Wheaton

Nathan Crane: How important is community in a self-reliance scenario?

Paul Wheaton: Community is complex. It has to do of course with the psychology and humanity of all the people. So how can you have all of the upside without any of the downside or at least mitigate most of the downside? If you have twenty people living together under one roof then your cost per person is half, maybe even a third of what it would be if a person were living by himself or herself. Or if it's a place that's rural where you're trying to do a bit of homesteading, permaculture, and if you're going to buy a new tractor, it's like you get 95% off on your tractor purchase. There are some real clear benefits to community but then there's that whole side of the drama and the crazy that comes from living with other people. How do you mitigate that? How do you make decisions? How do you move forward? How do you have full velocity despite the consensus process? Most importantly, how do you go to a community where there's somebody icky there, live in that community so intimately with him or her, and later on have the icky people expelled? Oh wait, what if they decide you're the icky person? You don't want to stay at some place and put your life into it only to get thrown out. So you want to get the upsides and mitigate the downsides.

I very much want to see where permaculture will be in the future. So the idea of incubating twenty people with twenty different visions for the future and giving them each their play space to demonstrate their vision in seed and soil. Then one person can see the others and being human, they would've observed that that person is doing it all wrong. They'll decide they're going to do that thing on their piece but they're going to do it right and do it better. Ideas feed ideas that feed ideas and that will accelerate our future. That's the kind of community I'm attempting to build.

NC: How can you serve everybody the best in spite of a hundred different people in the community trying to do different things? You're never going to get anything done.

PW: How do you get twenty people to live under one roof without stabbing each other? The drama can be really extreme. There are ways and I've come up with something that I think is very helpful. For me, one way to thin the herd is if someone can tolerate listening to all of my podcasts. There's a bit of a gauntlet that people have to go through and when they've listened to all of the podcasts then they have a pretty good understanding of what I'm all about, how I'll make decisions, how I'll behave, and what it will be like there. That's proven to be extremely effective. We already have a hive mind and a similar goal when people arrive.

The next thing is that the decision process is an independent-thought-consensus-dictator hybrid. Some people say, "Oh then you will be the benevolent dictator." No. I make it very clear. I am the evil dictator. The problem is when you use the term benevolent dictator, certain people will have an idea of what benevolent means and then they'll hold me according to their interpretation of what benevolent means. So now, I must do what they say or they're going to take away my license to use the word benevolent. If I say evil dictator then I can do whatever I think is best without having to be considerate of having my license revoked. I'm very adamant about that.

The process I dominantly use is independent thought. Eighty-five percent of all the decisions that are made because people think no one's going to care and they'll move forward with their own vision of how things ought to be. The next stage is consensus where we check with some people. That takes time or if it's not working out then you take the final 1% or 2% of the decisions to the dictator who will make the final call.

NC: What are the things that someone should look for if they wanted to get involved in the community?

PW: A good place to start to get involved in a community would be ic.org, which is intentionalcommunity.org. There are thousands of communities and most of them are going to be consensus based. It's good for people to explore the idea of a community. If you want to go along with the flow, a consensus-based system is lovely. They do require that you have to participate in the meetings and understand what's happening.

If you want to innovate, blaze new trails and do some new things, a consensus-based community would not be a good choice because what you're doing is considered by most to be crazy. If you're doing one thing and somebody else is doing something you think is crazy, you'd prefer to not have that in your community.

When you're going to a community, how do you really know what they're like? When you interview them they're also interviewing you trying to decide if they like you and want you in the community. You're trying to decide if you want to go through all the trouble to move there. So everybody's putting on his or her best face. In the end you've been there for over a year and you're thinking, "What have I done?" How do you make it so somebody could be comfortable and happy for decades as opposed to mere months?

The thing to look for is what are the community's values and make sure there are values. A lot of times a politician will say, "I stand up for good things and I'm against the bad things," and you say, "Where do you stand on abortion?" "Well, let me tell you about abortions. I stand up for good things and I'm against bad things." That's all you can get out of them. It's not until you move in that you discover out the real story. "Yes, we do eat babies. They've got everything a human person needs to eat and they're made out of it."

NC: What are some things that someone in a leadership position should consider to help make their community run sustainably?

PW: People have to be able to count on you to solve problems. You have to make things move forward and say, "We're going to drive you into town and get you a ticket to wherever it is that you want to go from here." It's like in a company where you have to work with somebody for forty hours a week. If that person is a drama queen then you're not moving forward. It's not pleasant. You have to be able to let that person go. On the opposite end of the spectrum, you need to be able to find ways to be able to support your community so it can grow and be a more beautiful place. It's your responsibility as a leader of the community you have to hear out everybody's opinion. It also helps to share the reasons why a decision was made so that when other people make suggestions they are well-informed suggestions. Communication is a big factor.

NC: Do you recommend that leaders of communities create podcasts or blogs to help people decide joining their community? Does it add to their leadership style and decision making process?

PW: Projecting the message of what you're doing here, why you're here, how you go about things and being very thorough is important. A lot of people think you need to have this book of rules and it's not true. In my community, we've got a sheet of paper that we call the choreography document. It basically says, "Let's be quiet after 9:30" but we crank up the music at 6 am. We're an early-to-rise community. There are a lot of communities where everyone sleeps in until 11am. That's a different style. It's helpful and smart if you can project your personality and vision so that people can know what they're getting into.

NC: What is a food forest and why should people consider having one?

PW: A food forest is a collection of diverse plants that include a lot of trees. Permaculture systems end to be very tree-heavy. There will be the high canopy, mid canopy, shrubs, and then the low growing annuals. These are the different layers of systems. Food plants actually do better in a food forest where there's some shade than an open field with 100% sunlight. One of the best permaculture DVDs out there is The Grid by Geoff Lawton. The great thing is it shows him building a food forest. He plants things in a certain way and suddenly all sorts of food starts coming out of it. He spends about one day a year tending to it and food keeps pouring out year after year after year. He doesn't irrigate it and doesn't have to replant it year after year because the annuals will re-seed themselves. He starts off planting it very heavily in nitrogen fixing plants, which provide the dominant amount of fertilizer for latter years, and the soil becomes incredibly rich and supportive of this new system.

NC: Is there a minimum amount of land that somebody needs to consider starting a food forest?

PW: In order to build a food forest it needs to have trees, which eliminate the whole permaculture on the balcony. Can you have a food forest in a very small backyard? You can. Not a magnificent one but a food forest. The key is not to have a lot of the same species. A lot of people gravitate towards hugelkultur beds. It's just soil on wood. A pile of wood covered in soil and as the wood rots it becomes like a big sponge for water and nutrients. Then all the winter and spring rains get stored in the hugelkultur and provide ample water for the plants throughout the following summer.

What you do is place a bunch of wood on the ground and dig up the soil right next to where you placed it. Put the soil on top of the wood, add more wood on top of that and add another layer of soil. Once it's three feet tall, the trenches next to it are three feet deep so your hugelkultur is actually six feet tall. Now you start planting and mulching it. That's all there is to it. Usually, the first year's harvest is not so good because everything hasn't rotted appropriately yet. The second year is quite good and the third year is magnificent.

NC: What are rocket mass heaters?

PW: People who switch from a conventional wood burning stove to a rocket mass heater often report that they heat their homes with one tenth of the wood they used to use. Normally you're using eight to ten cords of wood to heat your home and that's a lot of wood. But now you're down to just one cord of wood a year and that's turning out to be plenty. The problem people have with a conventional wood stove is they might experience a chimney fire, which can burn down your whole house. A rocket mass heater tries to have a chimney fire every time it burns. There's a truncated chimney inside of it that's incredibly insulated. With a conventional wood stove you try to get as much heat out of the fire as you can right away. With a rocket mass heater, the fire needs to be far hotter than a conventional stove because all that heat goes through the short little stubby chimney and burns all the smoke, creosote, and everything else that could possibly be burned. The heat is then released into the room. That heat is called exhaust because usually there's little to no smoke. Then we run it through a mass, and then we run the exhaust outside. So a rocket mass heater keeps more of the heat inside and people will often have a fire in the evening. Usually the wood feed is tiny, about one fifth of a standard wood stove. It's filled with wood, the fire burns, and then the fire is out. If you get up in the morning and the fire went out with a conventional stove, you would be really cold. But with a rocket mass heater, it's still exuding heat for days after the fire.

NC: How easy are these for people to build?

PW: There are some designs that are faster and easier than others. The most popular designs are using cob, which is just clay and sand that you pull out of the ground. Some are built with the pebble style. They're typically built over the weekend and most people spend about $200. Others have been able to scrounge around for parts and get it down to under $20. That's a lot cheaper than a conventional wood stove.

Nate's Notes

Community

Community is the most complex in permaculture. Deals with the psychology and the humanity of all the people. It's simple and complicated at the same time. How can you mitigate most of the downsides? Cost per person is much less if you are living with 10-20 people per household. Cost savings is one major clear benefit to a community.

- Want to get upsides and mitigate downsides.
  - Exploring the visionary process. One person with a vision and then allowed to proceed.
  - Want to accelerate learning more about permaculture. Can you incubate 20 people with 20 different visions for future?
  - Comes down to the leader. Leader must be effective and care about the people.
  - When people arrive they should already be in alignment.
  - Independent thought dominant process. People make 80% decisions because of how they want it to be.
  - Then next stage is consensus. Final decision comes down to a "dictator" – "central leader"
  - Drama is 1/100 of drama in a consensus model.

- Things to look for in getting involved in a community:

  - Go to www.ic.org and start shopping.
  - Good for people who want to get out of the rat race and get onto a farm without wanting to pay for expensive land and massive work.
  - Consensus based systems can be difficult and challenging.
  - If you want to innovate and blaze new trails and do new things, a consensus community may not be the best bet.
  - Decision making process becomes critical. When you show up to interview, everyone is putting on their best face.
  - People who were leaving a community found that the main cause for leaving was drama. Wanted to get away and be by themselves.
  - What are the true values in the community? Look for real values.

- What to look for in starting and running a community:

  - People have to be able to count on you.
  - You're going to solve problems and make things move forward.
  - Got to be prepared to send people away.

- May not be the best idea to have people paying rent and being dependent on income from community members.
- Suppose the property is entirely paid for so when people come by, you don't need rent from them.
- Many people looking to get out of the rat race and have a little bit of garden space, maybe build a little thing here and there, cook a little bit, and grow in the space of permaculture, self-reliance, etc.
- If a person is not a fit, if they have too much drama, then you need be ready to send them away.
- You are the CEO and the President. It's your responsibility.
- You have to hear out everybody's issues and ideas and then make decisions.
- Choreography document (similar to book of rules but not so rigid; just outline expectations)

Food forests and forest gardens

- When we make a permaculture food system that is done really well, it will pump out food year after year and we won't have to do anything except harvest.
  - You won't have to irrigate, fertilize, pest control and you will have food year after year.

- If you have to leave or choose to go away, you can leave your food forest and not worry about it.
- You will want to build mega resilience into food systems so it's still pumping out food and still very healthy
- Food forest is a collection of diversity that includes a lot of trees. You have the High Canopy level, the Mid Canopy level, the Shrubs, and then the low growing annuals.
- Food forests fit in well with low sunlight.
- A DVD by Geoff Lawton on food forests is recommended viewing.
- Form of horticultural that permaculturists modeled after.
- Yes you can have a food forest in your backyard
  - Don't have a lot of the same species
  - Mix up your species a lot
  - Standard small is going to be a backyard
  - Add texture to the backyard
  - Introduce a little pond
  - Want to go up and down
  - Don't want it to be flat
  - Want hugelkultur beds – Put a bunch of wood, then when wood rots, it provides water, texture, and nutrients

- Hugelkultur
  - Soil on wood
  - Plop a bunch of wood on ground
  - Add more wood
  - Add more soil
  - Once it's 3 feet tall
  - Dig trenches next to it 3 feet deep
  - Now just plant and mulch it
- World domination gardening

- Permies.com/wdg
- Richsoil.com

Staying warm

Rocket Mass Heaters (RMH)

- www.Stoves2.com
- How to heat your home more efficiently
  - Switching from a conventional wood-burning stove to RMH. It's reported you can heat your home with 1/10th of the wood compared to a conventional wood-burning stove.
  - Maybe down to 1 cord of wood per year.
  - Wood stoves have burnt down whole houses with chimney fire
  - Truncated chimney inside RMH that helps get as much heat out of fire right away.

- Try to get the RMH far hotter then direct all heat through a short stubby chimney, which burns all smoke and creosote and then it releases heat into room. What's left over is typically very clean. Pretty much just steam and carbon dioxide with usually little to no smoke.
- It can heat your house or Teepee for days.
- Uses radiant heat and conductive heat
  - Usually takes about a day and a half or a weekend to build
  - Level of DIY is not major but you do need to have some ability to think in 3D.
  - Most popular designs are using Cob – Clay and sand.
  - Can be built with pebble.
  - Most people spend about $200.

Paul Wheaton

Paul Wheaton is the creator of the largest permaculture forum on the Internet, www.permies.com. He has been crowned the "Duke of Permaculture" and also referred to as the "Bad Boy of Permaculture". He has released over 290 podcasts on many permaculture topics ranging from eco-building to frugality to cast iron cookware. He is an Advanced Certified Master Gardener, permaculture design guru, farmer, community leader, and repository of well researched opinions.

Learn more at http://www.permies.com.

Emergency Herbal
Medicine Storage
David Christopher

Nathan Crane: What critical herb should someone have on hand in case of an emergency?

David Christopher: The most important herb to have on hand is cayenne pepper. After that would be garlic and then comfrey. Another really good one would be slippery elm bark powder. There are 25,000 of these herbs and we cannot focus on just a couple hundred of them. Start with cayenne pepper because that will stop bleeding. It also helps blood flow, helps it circulate better, and thins the blood if you have thick blood. A student, who had learned the benefits of cayenne pepper, heard a gunshot at the next door neighbor's house. The kids were home alone and the 4 year old had found the parent's gun and had shot the 6 year old brother right in the abdomen. It hit the spine and ricocheted so there were two holes pumping out blood. She called 911 and was informed that it was going to take half an hour for the ambulance to get to that location. What does she do? Well she mixes a heaping teaspoon of cayenne in water and had the boy drink it. She also took the cayenne and put it right on the hole and applied pressure. So it's cayenne, cloth and applying pressure on both of those holes that allowed him to survive until he got to the hospital. Everyone was amazed. Cayenne is amazing at stopping bleeding.

Herbs that have dual purposes are called tonic herbs and cayenne is an example of a tonic herb. One other thing it does besides stopping bleeding is it will stop a heart attack. If someone's going into a heart attack, the first thing to do is to give him a cayenne pepper and water mixture. Have him drink it and it will go into the heart within one or two heart beats. The cayenne is one of the plants that are highest in vitamin C as far as medicinal plants are concerned. Vitamin C is one of the things that is definitely needed with a heart that's failing. The stimulating properties of cayenne stop people from going into a heart attack.

It's also one of the best things for a stroke. My neighbor's mom had a mild stroke and her face drooped, her right hand didn't work as well as before, and she limped on her right leg but still got around. I advised her to use cayenne pepper among some other herbs. She started on a plant based diet with a lot of fresh fruits and vegetables and she didn't have any signs that she had a stroke. It was amazing. However, the particular program she was on helps you get rid of excess weight, which ended up being a problem. She was looking a little skinny and frail according to her relatives and they were concerned so they convinced her to start eating meat. She started eating a lot of meat and she had a major stroke when she was home by herself. She was eventually found and her relatives took care of her but because she didn't go back to the diet she died from that stroke.

Cayenne is also helpful with hypothermia. When you wrap a blanket around someone with hypothermia you are only compounding the problem. It's like a refrigerator. You have the cold in the refrigerator and by putting the blanket around it you're just going to keep the cold in there. It does no good to put blankets around someone with hypothermia. The core is cold and you need to heat up the core. What better way to heat up a core than to swallow a furnace? Basically, you swallow cayenne and it heats your body. To give an example to that my little daughter was on a children's choir tour and they decided to visit an Oregon beach. They had to go through trees and nature to get down to this beach. Now the Oregon water is not the same with California water - it's a lot colder. A little girl in particular started turning blue so she was given cayenne. Immediately her lips turned red, her face got flushed and she started throwing the blankets off. The hypothermia is over.

It's also useful for taking you out of shock. I was shoveling my driveway and sidewalk when my feet gave out from under me. After I finished, I went back to the house, took off my snow clothes, and my white long johns were red from my right knee down to my foot. I had a long cut on my shin and there was a white thing sticking out so I touched it and it caused my toe to move. Any rate, I started going into shock and my wife grabbed the cayenne extract and had me ingest it, which immediately brought me out of shock. We cleaned it, stopped the bleeding, took garlic to get rid of any infection, and put comfrey on the wound.

Cayenne is also good for stimulating the production of hydrochloric acid. The whole purpose of hydrochloric acid is to break down all those proteins into chains of amino acids. It then goes into the intestinal tract and then the pancreas releases enzymes to break it down into individual amino acids and then into individual components. As you get older you produce less hydrochloric acid so that's when cayenne comes in handy.

Another thing cayenne is good for is strep throat. As far as antibiotics are concerned it can take 10 days to get rid of strep throat. I'd advise that you take a tablespoon of honey and you mix into it a quarter teaspoon of cayenne pepper. Then take four cloves of fresh garlic, press it, and let it set for 4-5 minutes. You'll then mix that into the honey and cayenne mixture. Honey with its propolis, cayenne with its rubefacient quality, which means that it brings blood to the surface, and the garlic, which is the antibiotic herb, will all assist in healing your throat. Take the combination of honey, cayenne and garlic, swish it around your mouth and swallow it. It will coat the throat with the honey and the cayenne will cause the blood to get in the area. This simple combination will get rid of the strep throat usually within a day. Sometimes it might take a couple of days but usually within the day. Keep in mind that if you drink milk after taking the mixture it will nullify the effect. Since we are on the subject, milk is a carrier for strep. There is a book by Frank Oski called, "Don't Drink Your Milk." He noticed that those patients that drink milk were the only ones getting strep throat. Milk is a carrier for strep, especially pasteurized milk, because pasteurization doesn't kill the bacteria that cause strep throat.

It even works for little things like headaches, getting circulation moving in numb fingers and toes, and getting blood to the brain.

NC: Do you recommend that people buy cayenne from the store or should they make it at home?

DC: You can get good results no matter where you get it. It's always good to get something pure and doesn't have preservatives in it. If you are going to get cayenne from a store, I'd get it from a health food store rather than just the regular grocery store. If you store them in the proper condition, out of light, away from moisture, and keep them in an air tight container you can store those herbs away and probably they will still be good in five, ten, fifteen, twenty, or even forty years.

NC: You mentioned earlier that garlic is the antibiotic herb. How would people administer garlic as an antibiotic?

DC: What you can do is take 17 cloves of fresh garlic a day and I'm not talking about the bulb. I'm talking about the little sections of a bulb. Take 17 cloves and it sounds like a lot but once you put it into a garlic press that reduces the amount quite a bit. You can then mix it with honey to make it easier to ingest. One way that I enjoy is to make up a really nice onion soup using vegetable stock and when the soup has cooled down enough to eat you put the already pressed garlic that's been sitting for the past 5 or 8 minutes. You'll want it to sit for a few minutes because it creates a new sulfur compound that's even more potent that the other compounds put together and it's only in fresh garlic. You'll want to eat 4 bowls a day with 4 cloves of freshly pressed garlic per bowl of soup.

Another method is to break up a head of a cauliflower and put it in water in a blender. Blend the whole thing until you have a cream of cauliflower soup. You can even add some salt to make it taste a little bit better. Once it's down to a temperature that you can bear, you put the 16 cloves into that. The cauliflower annihilates the strong flavor of the garlic so it's a lot easier to take that way.

Another really good herb is goldenseal. It's really expensive but it's antiseptic so it can be put right onto wounds or taken orally to help get rid of bacteria or viruses. A substitute for goldenseal can be barberry or Oregon grape. Comfrey is the main healing herb and it is absolutely amazing in its healing properties. It's called cell proliferant, which means it encourages healthy cells to grow and helps to regenerate cell structure that's been damaged.

NC: Regarding comfrey, is it better in powder form or liquid form? Or what should people look for when storing comfrey?

DC: I would recommend growing it in your backyard. Once you get comfrey planted it's not going to die on you. In fact the problem is containing it because it takes over everything. I'd grow a good batch of comfrey in your back yard and have fresh comfrey available. Then if you can't use it, pick it, dry it and store it. Do that as much as possible. When you pick it right off the plant you can put it in a blender with some juice and have a green drink. If it's dried it makes a wonderful tea. You can even add Stevia to your comfrey tea it tastes really good. It's probably the best way to use comfrey.

NC: Lastly, could you talk a bit about slippery elm?

DC: Slippery elm doesn't work well in water because it's hydrophobic. It repels water but that's exactly how you want to use it. You'll take the slippery elm and mix it with water and this will take a long time to mix. So you mix and mix and mix and mix until it finally turns into a slime. It's that slimy texture that coats, soothes, and heals tissue. This can heal any GI tract problem whether it is an ulcer, damaged tissue, hemorrhoids, or etcetera. Slippery elm is the herb to heal and stop internal bleeding. I knew someone who was having 27 bowel movements a day, which were mostly water, but she was taking a cortisone enema on a daily basis to keep her from bleeding to death. She began taking a 70/30 combination of slippery elm and licorice. 70% of slippery elm and 30% of licorice. She no longer needed any cortisone enemas and it healed her problem.

In fact slippery elm is an herb that can be taken orally or applied topically. It's one of the herbs that can be used for bleeding gums. A lot of people have their teeth taken out even if they don't have cavities. They have their teeth pulled because their gums are weak and loose. I find that a combination of oak bark and slippery elm makes a really nice poultice for your gums. You put enough water in it to make a pie-like dough and you put it right on your gums and the lip and cheeks will just hold it there. This will take care of pyorrhea. A 60% wild oak bark powder and a 40% slippery elm bark powder combination is amazing and will heal those gums quickly.

Nate's Notes

What herbs must you have on hand when an emergency strikes?

1. Cayenne pepper

- A first aid herb that heals cuts, bruises, and etc. It will stop bleeding, help circulate blood better, and thins blood. Blood clotting is very specific. When you get a hole in your vascular system, blood is used to fill up the hole. Onion will make blood less sticky and help it flow. You should eat food as it's grown, which is the healthiest way to eat. Eating properly to start with is best advised.

- Very high in Vitamin C

- You can get good results from any kind of cayenne but what you find in the health food store is the best.

- Doctrine of Signatures – herbs can give you clues as to what it's for.

- Ways to administer Cayenne pepper:
    ‣ Mix teaspoon in cayenne with water then drink it.
    ‣ Put cayenne on cloth onto cut and put pressure.
        - Cayenne is a tonic herb because it will go either way

- Uses for Cayenne pepper:
  - Heart attack.
    - Give it in liquid form and it will help stop heart attack and protect the heart.
  - Strokes
  - Hypothermia
    - In cases of hypothermia, don't wrap a blanket around a person because it compounds the problem. The core of person is core and you have to heat up the core. Cayenne BTUs is same as a furnace.
  - Shock
    - Cayenne can take you out of shock.
  - Migraine headaches, numb fingers, and toes.
  - Helps blood to circulate properly
  - Helps to get blood to the brain.
  - Gastro Intestinal Reflux Disease
    - Most people go on Prilosec, which reduces hydrochloric acid. You need enough Hydrochloric Acid to break down proteins because its purpose is to break down protein down into it's component parts such as amino acids and then uptake those component parts. However as people get older they make less Hydrochloric acid instead of more.

- Cayenne stimulates the production of Hydrochloric Acid.
- You need to taste the cayenne in your mouth to affect the sensors. Swallowing a capsule of cayenne won't work. It's best to eat cayenne when you have food in your mouth.

  ▸ Strep Throat
  - Antibiotics can take ten days to get rid of strep throat.
  - Cayenne can get rid of it almost immediately. Take a tablespoon of real raw honey, ¼ teaspoon cayenne pepper, and 4 cloves of fresh garlic (that have sat for 4-5 minutes). Mix the garlic into the honey and cayenne. Put the mixture in the mouth, swish around, and swallow. Don't wash it down because you need to let it stick and coat the throat. Take every half hour or so and it will get rid of strep throat in about a day.
  - Milk is a carrier for Strep

- Storing herbs:

  ▸ Keep out of direct light.

  ▸ Keep out of moisture.

  ▸ Keep them airtight.

2. Garlic

- Known as the Antibiotic Herb
- Gets rid of infections.
- 4 cloves of garlic per unit of antibiotic.
- Garlic has at least 28 different natural sulfuric compounds.
  - Used as an antibiotic.
  - Won't cause problems similar to sulfur drugs.
  - Gets rid of bacteria without getting rid of all the friendly flora.
  - Destroys viruses.
- How to use Garlic:
  - Take 17 fresh cloves of garlic per day for viruses. Put it through a garlic press and let it sit for 5-8 minutes.
  - You can mix it with honey and water.
  - You can make onion soup with cooled vegetable stock. Add in 4 cloves fresh garlic and eat 4 bowls per day.
  - Cauliflower soup works as well. Just add in 16 cloves of garlic.
  - Fresh is best, dried will work as well. It's important you don't cook the garlic.

3. Golden Seal

- Very antiseptic:
  - ‣ Can be taken orally to get rid of bacteria and viruses
  - ‣ Can put right onto wounds.
  - ‣ A substitute is Oregon Grape.

4. Comfrey

- Used for healing wounds
- This is your main healing herb because it has very profound healing properties.
- Cell proliferant
  - ‣ Helps to regenerate cells that are damaged.
  - ‣ Can grow up to the waist, then cut down to the crowns, and will grow right back up in a few weeks.
  - ‣ We capture the fast growing quality when we eat it.
  - ‣ Big difference between the whole and the part. Can't go wrong using wholesome herbs and wholesome foods.
  - ‣ Isolated chemicals outside of herbs can be toxic, which is why you need the whole herb.

- Grow it in your back yard for a multitude of uses:
  - Eat it fresh by ingesting it in a green drink. Add to water and blend with honey
  - Use fresh Stevia Leaves; not the white product.
  - Dry it and use it as tea.
  - Store it.
- Pain
  - Pain is just a signal that something is wrong.
  - For massive pain, take a heaping spoonful and mix it with water. Drink this mixture 3-4 times per day.
  - Then drink a quart of comfrey tea per day thereafter.

5. White Willow Bark

- Helps with pain.
- This is what aspirin is made out of.

6. Slippery Elm Bark Powder

- Hydrophobic (repels water)
- Mix it in water and it will turn into slime.
- The slimy texture coats, heals, and sooths tissue.
- Great for GI tract issues because it stops internal bleeding.
  - Great for Hemorrhoids, ulcers, and internal bleeding.

- You can also use a combination of Slippery Elm and Licorice for internal bleeding.
- Works great for bed sores.
- Can be ingested and also applied topically on wounds.
  - Turns into a nice poultice
  - Works great for bleeding gums
    - Put it right on your gums and line with it
  - White Oak Powder and Slippery Elm Bark Powder

BUYING HERBS

Dr. Christopher Herb Shop

888-372-4372

www.drchristophersherbshop.com

David Christopher

Having been raised in the simple ways of natural health, David's interests grew beyond his university study. In 1974 David Christopher, M.H., took his place by his father's side at The School of Natural Healing. David's book entitled, An Herbal Legacy of Courage, is a loving tribute to his father. In 1979 he became a Master Herbalist and the director of The School of Natural Healing. Today, thousands safely apply the Christopher methodology thanks to his directorship.

Learn more at schoolofnaturalhealing.com.

Survival In A Nutshell

Daniel Shrigley

Nathan Crane: What are some of those things that people really need to focus on first in any survival situation?

Daniel Shrigley: First you need to evaluate the situation you're in, you need to be levelheaded, and you need to remain calm. Don't let fear defeat you, defeat fear. Fear is just a feeling but you can get past it. But fear can be a good tool if you use it the right way by staying alive, staying alert, evaluating your surroundings, not running around in a panic, not getting scared, slipping and falling, getting bitten and etcetera. Once you get past the psychology of survival, you need to evaluate your environment and determine what you need to survive to defeat the elements. For example, if you're in the desert you're going to need shade, water and after that, you can worry about fire at night. You're going to need fire depending on how bad the temperature drops. The things you want to protect yourself from are sun, sand, wind, rain, and if you can defeat those by making proper shelter, water proof shelter or just a sun shade, then that will really go a long way. The priority of survival is water and it's always either number one or number two. You always need water. It doesn't matter if you're freezing in the winter or in the Saharan desert because water is essential. So it'll be shelter, water, and then food; or it could be fire, water, shelter, and then food. Usually food is last and there's clothing, bush craft skills and tools and other things that you add in after that.

NC: Can you share some examples of people being able to find water or collect water in different kinds of environments?

DS: You always want to treat water by boiling it and if you cannot boil water at least know how to make a primitive water filter. Layering sand, charcoal from your fire pit, a layer of gravel, and fill the bottom of the filter with some green vegetation to act as a screen or a piece of your T-shirt so you are not getting any sediment in it.

Another common way you can get water is by solar stills in the ground. People know you can wrap plastic or even a 2 liter bottle around a branch you can get some condensation during the dew point hour as the Earth is rotating and the thermal blanket is being pushed down by the sun. This dew point collection hour usually starts anywhere between 2 hours to 1 hour and half before the sun typically rises. That is why when you come out in the morning you see windshield condensation. You want to collect that off green shrubbery, leaves or even use your cotton shirt as a sponge. Run through the tall grass and wring your pants afterward. You want to use that dew collection because you do not have to filter or boil it.

In addition, don't stock pile all your stuff in one location. Go geostash it because you could easily lose your inventory all at once. But if you geostash it, use 55 gallon drums and put rice in the bottom of it. You can hold a lot of stuff and the rice will suck the moisture out. All it takes is a larger invading force to come in and you'll lose all your stuff. They could be law enforcement, military or a band of misfits but all it takes is an organized group. A good plan would be to have waypoints where you stash your stuff. So if you lose it you don't lose it all. You may want to cache your stuff and have it mirror each other so one cache has the same as the last cache unless you have progressive caches where you try to pick up more units as you get closer to your bug out location.

NC: If somebody lives in a city, where would they geostash their inventory? What are some examples of stash waypoints they can utilize?

DS: When pandemonium is going to set in on a major population, you need to remove yourself from that city. You need to do it before it sets in and not wait for the last minute. There is always a telltale sign that something bad or imminent is going to happen and it is going to happen. Hurricane Katrina was an utter flop. FEMA failed, our government failed, and a lot of bad things happened because people did not listen to the telltale signs. People did not take proper precautions and we learned how much of a struggle it was for FEMA to get in there and render aid to the citizens of New Orleans. Imagine if that happened in San Francisco or in Los Angeles where there is an even larger population.

NC: Do you believe it would be a good idea to not only be dependent on yourself but having interdependence and social support in local communities and neighboring cities too? In fact, a community garden would be ideal because you'd have a sustainable food source supporting one another.

DS: A community garden is fine when it comes to food but you need to have a wild garden. A wild garden has the benefit of being hidden because the average person will walk right past the potatoes and carrots if it's not organized. People will steal food in a crisis. If they walk by a garden, they are going to raid it. You are going to have 50 people out there digging up everything and taking it. You can't shoot them all. All they are trying to do is eat food and you are going to murder someone for eating food just because it's your garden? So what you can do to alleviate that is to make your garden hidden. Learn about hidden gardens, hidden wild edible gardens, hidden domesticated gardens and other things like that because it will blend in.

NC: How can someone have a scavenger mentality? How can they be resourceful in nature and have everything you need around you?

DS: The thing about scavenging is you have to get into the right mindset and absorb and meditate in your surroundings. You have to let your eyes become detectors for what could be a tool resource and to think outside the box. For example, what can I use a flat rock for? What kind of rock is it? What is obsidian rock? Why would I want obsidian rock versus flint? What would I use flint for? Is sand stone useful in my situation? What can I do with obsidian rock? What would I do with flint? When you know these things you can centralize and organize what you want to do when you are scavenging.

Do you know the 5 major poisonous plants in the local region where you live? It's important you know what are the edible plants and the poisonous plants. Mushrooms are too much of a difficulty for a commoner that doesn't have any formal training with eating mushrooms so it would be best to stay away from it. Stay away from bright colored berries because if that's a warning to birds then it should be a warning to you. Now there are other bright colored berries that we are used to eating like raspberries, strawberries and cherries and all that. But predominantly in nature, berries that are brightly colored are not good to be eaten. A useful rule of thumb is to only eat dark colored berries.

Scavenging also includes edible insects. There are 1,900 edible insects that we know about. If you can get past the yuck factor, there's more protein in the insects than there is in red meat. There are a lot of health benefits to something that has so much nutritional value. Go take a survival class that has a good reputation. Avoid those pop up schools that have only been around since Man Versus Wild hit the airways. Go to a real school that has been around for 30 or 20 years. You can also join groups. There are foraging groups that go out and do foraging.

NC: What are some key tips for people who are looking to take their survival skill set to the next level?

DS: Be willing to learn from anybody and not just who you look up to. You can even start fire with ice. If you shape the ice into the shape of a magnifying lens and use it in the same way you would if you are trying to cook ants with a magnifying lens, it is going to work because it's going to offer the same thing that the glass does. It's all about shape. Think outside of the box. Did you know that if you scrape out shavings of aluminum, you could use that to catch a spark? Be willing to go outside. Carry a cigarette lighter if you own one. It is not cheating to keep a cigarette lighter on you. You don't have to rely on primitive skills to prove yourself as a valid survival expert. Think smarter so you don't have to work harder. But in the event you don't have a cigarette lighter, it is critical that you know how to start a fire, that you practice it beforehand, and that you know how to collect and gather the right resources. Waiting until you are in a survival situation is the wrong time to practice this.

My favorite survival object on the face of the earth is bamboo. Bamboo will feed you, you can create weapons and shelter with it, it boils water, it makes filters, and etcetera.

NC: How big does your bamboo need to be?

DS: If you want to boil water in bamboo or use it for a filter, it needs to have 3 cylinders. Bamboo is naturally chambered so you need to have 3 cylinders. It also needs to be at least 4 and a half to 5 inches in diameter. As a weapon, you want to have 2 and a half to 3 inches in diameter. You can make spears and arrows out of them. You can do everything with it. You can eat it, build a house out of it, and even make a boat out of it. There's a lot you can do with bamboo that will assist you with survival. Will you find bamboo everywhere? No but if you do you are fortunate because it has starch in it and your body needs starch. You can use it for hunting, setting traps and snares, spring snares, and deadfalls.

Nate's Notes

1. What does someone need to focus on first in a survival situation?

   a. Evaluate the situation first.

   b. Remove fear and do not panic.

   c. Do not run off in a panic

   d. Once you get past the psychology of survival, you need to determine the elements of your surroundings.

      i) If you're in a desert, you will need shade. If it's getting cold at night, you will need fire.

   e. You'll want to protect yourself from sun, wind, cold, rain, and dust.

      i) Can make a waterproof shelter or sun shade

   f. You will always need a water source.

   g. Average person getting lost in the wilderness is a hunter or a hiker.

      i) Find water.

         1) Treat water by boiling it or by filtering it.

            a) Charcoal, Sand, Green Vegetation, and a T-shirt is a good makeshift filter

2) Can use solar stills in green
   a) Can get droplets from condensation
3) Dew point hour
   a) 2 hours before sun rises. Can collect condensation with smooth rocks off of green shrubbery. Use shirt or pants as a sponge.
   b) Can tap vines, banana trees or bamboo

2. Psychology of survival is psychology of life
   a. Psychology starts at home
   b. Encourage community preparedness and not individual preparedness
   c. Forming community and neighborhood watch programs to support each other and expand to further level
   d. Can collect waste water and reuse it – not fecal matter or urine
   e. Power is in numbers in everything you do
   f. Start a community outreach program
   g. Come together to support each other
   h. Resourcefulness, education, skillsets, and inventory

3. Geostash Your stuff
   a. 55 Gallon drums
   b. Put rice in bottom of drums
   c. Bury in the ground
   d. You should have more than one bug out location
   e. Should have cache way points
   f. Somebody living in a city needs to leave the city as early as possible.
   g. Create wild gardens the average person can walk past and not notice.

4. Wilderness Survival
   a. Learn to utilize everything in nature
   b. Wilderness meditation
   c. Need to get into the right mindset. Need to allow eyes to become detectors to see resources.
   d. Centralize and organize what you need to do next
   e. Need to know poisonous plants as well as edible plants
   f. Take a survival class from a group that's been around for a long time.
   g. Join foraging groups to learn about edible plants
   h. Need to learn field hygiene

5. Take survival skillsets to the next level
   a. You can learn from anyone who knows more than you do
   b. If you shape ice in the form of magnifying lens you can use it to start a fire
   c. You can start fire with water
   d. Think outside the box
   e. You can scrape shavings of aluminum to catch a spark
   f. Be willing to go outside and experience what it's like to be in touch with nature
   g. You don't have to rely on primitive skills. You can have lighters or other tools with you.
   h. Do not wait until you're in a survival situation. You need to practice before you ever end up in a survival situation.
   i. Bamboo is a favorite survival object. You can make filters, drink water, food, tools fire, and everything with it.
      i) It needs to have 3 cylinders and be 4-5 inches in diameter to work for boiling water, filtering, and etc.
      ii) Can make weapons such as spears, arrows, and etc.

Daniel Shrigley

Daniel Shrigley is an 18 year multiple combat and service veteran of the United States Army with many years of experience in combat, survival, and policing/security as well. Daniel hosts Survival Talk Radio, a show that teaches survival related topics. He has attracted a following from across the globe and due to his high interaction with fans over his media accounts, Daniel is now seen as an icon in Survival. He also daily passes on his wisdom and knowledge to his fan base worldwide via his activities and online magazine. Daniel is the brainchild and creator of the new highly anticipated Survival Reality Adventure TV Show titled "Survival Trek Escape". Daniel also is an Ambassador for the Messengers Of Peace Organization, a mentorship program designed by the Worldwide Scouting Organization of over 30 Million Scouts.

Learn more: www.facebook.com/daniel.shrigley

Water: What to do if the
Tap Runs Dry

Scott Hunt

Nathan Crane: What can people do to be prepared to secure water in a disaster?

Scott Hunt: Our water plan is basically divided into 3 sections: water storage, water re-supply plan, and then ways to purify, disinfect or treat your water. Start with how to store water whether you live in LA or you live in Idaho. Even people that live in rural areas let their guard down because they think, "Oh, we have water everywhere. I don't need to store." That's a grave mistake because in Toledo, Ohio the water system was contaminated. If you have a small budget, you can start with soda bottles but 55-gallon drums would be best. Other storage containers are doorway storage tanks and water bricks. Water bricks are nice stackable containers designed for water storage. They can even become part of your furniture because you can hide them easily. Our standard is that you need to have at least 2 gallons per person per day for up to 3 months. There's really no excuse because everybody has water coming to him or her and they know they need to store a certain amount of water. Water can be stored up to 5 years believe it or not and I recommend rotating it out every 6 months. There are products on the market like Aquamira, which is a 2-part solution of chlorine dioxide, that can be added to your water and it will last for 5 years. Water storage is extremely, extremely important. You don't want to compromise yourself, your family, and security if you have to travel outside of your home or dwelling to get water.

Next, can you develop a way to get water on your property? That could be as simple as catching it off the roof and there are many ways to do it. It is relatively inexpensive to take your home and basically turn it into a catchment system for water. You can be real fancy or make it very simple. You can catch whatever's on the roof into barrels and filter it later or you can pre-filter the water coming off the roof with 8 levels of filtration so you can drink the water. If you can, a lot of people are drilling wells. Another option is solar water pumping.

NC: Do the different storage tanks determine the length and quality of the water? For example, if you have a clear see-through tank you want to keep it out of sunlight otherwise it will grow algae, correct?

SH: In terms of preparedness and self-reliance, storing water, food, and fuel will need to be in a place that is cool, dry, and out of the sunlight. The darker containers, the greens, the blues, and the blacks, will not allow the sunlight in and your algae growth is minimized. There are a lot of different types of containers so you need to look for polyethylene, BPA free, dark containers with a recycling symbol number 2 on it and then store them in a cool dry place. You can't afford to be sick so treat the water, put it away, and then when you use it, run that water through a filtration device before you drink it. If you're just using it for gray water then that's not a problem.

NC: What do you recommend if people live in a place that doesn't have enough sunlight to pump water into a tank all the time?

SH: Most of the places in the country have enough sunlight for water pumping but a lot of it depends on the shading, the location, and the time of year. The solar water pump should be designed for the worst-case scenario so there's no place in the United States that you can't pump water with solar. Some of the controllers even have an AC interface so you can hook up a little generator to the same system to get you through. It can also be interfaced with the grid as well so there are a lot of backups.

You're also not limited to a solar water pump. Mechanical pumps like the hydraulic ram pumps invented in the late 1700s use falling water to move water and can move an estimated 1500 gallons a day. That's how water was moved in the United States before electricity. Hydraulic ram pumps were around for a long time and any falling water can be used to run the pump. It's a great old school method to move water that isn't finicky. However, there are a lot of variables that have to be worked out to make sure that it will work efficiently.

NC: Since hydraulic ram pumps are outdated and really hard to find, where can someone get one?

SH: I sell and install hydraulic ram pumps at practicalpreppers.com.

NC: Is there a way to make your solar pumps protected against an EMP or a solar storm that might happen?

SH: You have this fancy solar pump and it's full of controls, it pumps water for a hundred feet but if it gets hit with an EMP, it's dead water, no pun intended. What do you do with it? You buy a pump separate from the electronics. There are two companies that carry this and they are Lorentz and Sun Rotor based out of Oklahoma. You should also have an extra board controller in a Faraday cage protected from an EMP. So if you do lose your board, you can replace it and it only takes 10 minutes or so. It isn't EMP proof but more of a plug and play approach to an EMP.

NC: What about wind powered wells?

SH: Ask yourself, what resources do I have where I live? If you live in Arizona, you've got wind and sun. Then that's the resource you should be maximizing to be self-reliant. It's a great thing whether it's making electricity or for pumping water. You can get away with pumping water with the windmill in an area that might not be good for producing electricity because you need high average wind speeds to make electrical power. A lot of windmill pump manufacturers and installers also make a provision to have a solar pump included with the system so at the very bottom of what they install in your well, when the wind is not blowing, you have a solar pump or generator. Seasonally in the summer, you get a lot of sun and in the winter, you get a lot of wind. So balancing out a system that uses both is a great approach to take.

NC: What tools should someone have in his or her supply?

SH: Being able to treat and purify water is a great thing. There are kits out there for $30 that are a ceramic filter with an impregnated carbon core in it so it will remove any bacteria and make the water taste better. Even cheaper than that are the life straws that are about $20. These are nice portable devices that you can throw in a bug out bag, keep in your vehicle, take with you camping, you name it and you're not afraid to drink any water. Most water in North America has no viral load in the water that we know of right now. It's all bacterial that we have to deal with: bacteria, protozoa, cyst giardia and these ceramic products, ceramic straws, and filters will take out all of that so nobody will get sick. It's great for kids because everybody knows how to use a straw. It's a fairly simple device to use and they're not too expensive and you can filter about 260 gallons of water through the one. The military uses a SteriPEN and couple it with a life straw because they don't know where they're going to be when they're dropped into an area. They do not trust the water. They're going to kill everything with that SteriPEN and then drink it through the life straw as a backup to make sure that they don't get sick.

If virus is a concern there are a couple of products out there. Buy a Sawyer and a LifeSaver. The LifeSaver products are standard military issue for the British military. They have it in their Humvees, on their person, and you can drink the nastiest of water. It has a nanotechnology filter and the pores are smaller than the polio virus. There are other ways such as distillation and pasteurization. You can also use chlorine. For about $4, you can treat 10 thousand gallons of water yourself by buying Pool Shock. Nobody's going to get sick. You can even make your own Clorox type solution.

There are a lot of solutions when it comes to purification for an individual or a family. There are even filters that will filter 500 thousand gallons of water like a community-based filtration system that LifeSaver makes. In fact, I once took a fish tank and I loaded it up with cow manure, chicken manure, and all sorts of things from around the farm and drank that through a LifeSaver. My lawyer said, "Are you insane?" But I did not get sick. I wanted to know if it would work. The sky's the limit on filtration and water purification.

Nate's Notes

In your book, The Practical Preppers Complete Guide to Disaster Preparedness, you speak about securing a water source— even in an urban area. Water is of course one of the most important things in a survival situation, what can people do to be prepared to secure water?

WATER

Everybody has some sense of water coming to their location otherwise you wouldn't live there.

1. Water storage
   a. No matter where you are you want to store water.
   b. Try to stick with Polyethylene potable water containers. Fifty-five gallon drums are best, doorway storage tanks or water storage bricks.
   c. You need at least 2 gallons per person per day for up to 3 months. That's 180 gallons per person.
   d. Figure out how many gallons you and your family need.
   e. Can get you through terrible drought conditions or emergency situations.
   f. Can be stored up to 5 years with a product like Aquamira.

g. Recommended to switch out every 6 months though.

h. Want to be cool, dry and out of sunlight

i. Opt for better containers like green, blue, black.

j. Looking for triangle with a 2 in the middle, which is Polyethylene and get BPA free containers.

2. Water resupply

a. Do you have a way to capture water on your property?

b. Catching on the roof such as rainwater catchment.

c. Catch what's on the roof into barrels and then filter later or you can use a filtration system right on the roof.

d. Drill a well if you can

e. Developing springs

f. Solar water pumping is a very efficient way to pump water out of a well

i) Want to pump into a tank or a cistern

ii) Most places in the country there is enough sunlight for pumping water

iii) You want a tank that's oversized for days when you don't have sunlight. Know what usage is, then size the tank appropriately.

iv) Always design for the worst-case scenario.

v) Can get a controller that is interfaced with an AC current

g. Hydraulic ram pumps can be used as well. Visit www.PracticalPreppers.com

h. Protect Solar from an EMP or a Solar Storm

   i) Pump should be separated from electronic controller. Buy an extra board in faraday cage to be able to be replaced as needed.

   ii) Lorentz solar pump is an example of a pump separated from the controller

i. Mechanical solutions like a ram pump, a wood stove, and a roof over your head is enough to be more prepared than most people.

j. Hand pumps are great as well for backup water.

k. Windmill pumps

   i) Piece of art. Windmills are incredible machines but very expensive.

3. Ways to purify water

a. Stay sheltered in one place if possible.

b. Being able to treat and purify water is a great thing.

c. You can buy filter kits and build them with 5-gallon pails.

d. Ceramic filter with core is about $30

e. Life straws or to-go filters is another good option.

f. Do not want to get sick.

g. Have multiple backups and extras.

   i) Steripen coupled with a life straw

h. Whole house water filter systems that don't require electricity but just run through a pump.

i. Lifesaver nanotechnology filter

j. Distillation, pasteurization, disinfection with calcium hypochlorite or chlorine. A good brand to look into is Pool Shock.

ENERGY

1. A little bit goes a long way.

   a. You will want to produce enough power for a well pump, a freezer, a few lights, and just the basic necessities.

   b. Start very simple such as fuel storage, batteries, human storage devices, and propane.

2. Energy Stored

   a. Fuel, wood, propane, and batteries.

3. Resupplied
    a. How to make own electricity
    b. Hand crank generators
    c. Thermal Electric Generators such as heat sources like a fire
    d. Little stoves you can put a power pot on
    e. Generators – Old school generators that run on old motor oil and are EMP proof.
    f. Some sort of solar panel system
        i) Something that will charge a battery because you can run a lot of things with just a battery.
    g. Solar oven works great for cooking
    h. Bio mass in rocket stove or gasification stove to cook
        i) You'll also want a mix of batteries.
        ii) It's also good to standardize equipment to a size.
        iii) Start with AA batteries and do as much as you can.
        iv) Stock up on rechargeable batteries that are really good such as Eneloop.
            1) Eneloop batteries and Tenergy
            2) These will be used to run flashlights, radios, and anything that runs on AA batteries

3) Duracell batteries are good too.

v) Absorbed Glass Mat (AGM) Battery –
You don't want cold cranking. What
you do want is a deep cycle battery
such as a marine battery.

vi) For as long as you take care of a
simple lead acid battery, it can last
you a long time.

4. Hot water

a. Simple ways using solar panels or solar
heaters

b. Amish use wood stove and range boiler

c. Heat pump technology

d. Also passive things like solar showers to
put into sun

GETTING STARTED

1. Food

a. Have enough food and the food you like

2. Water

a. Be prepared with storing, filtering, and
cleaning water.

3. Shelter

a. Be able to stay in the same place as long
as possible

Scott Hunt

Scott Hunt has worked for the last 3 years as a consultant to National Geographic and Sharp Entertainment on the shows Doomsday Preppers and Doomsday Castle. He has also appeared on the Sportmans Channel's "American Unplugged." Scott is the owner of Practical Preppers, LLC, which is a company that specializes in preparedness solutions, and he is a Mechanical Engineer who designs sustainable off-grid water and energy systems. He analyzes your chances of survival if your worst fears become a reality and you have to put your plans into action. Scott's extensive background in Homesteading, Sustainable Water and Energy systems is a key factor in his analysis of whether the proper infrastructure is in place should a disaster occur.

Learn more at www.practicalpreppers.com.

Sustainable Medicine before, during and after a collapse
Sam Coffman

Nathan Crane: You have a lot of military experience, specifically Special Forces experience, but what was it that drove you to start a school and to really start sharing empowering information with people?

Sam Coffman: Everything started for me when I was a Special Forces medic. That's basically AKA Green Beret medic and going through SS Medic school. Then going about a year and two months of drinking out of a fire hose, sleep deprivation, team work, and learning to be what will be the equivalent of like a third world or fourth world PA where you have nothing but what's on your back, what you've taken in on your back or what may be able to be dropped in. So you have to learn a little bit of everything not just for your team but also for indigenous people: family medicine, OB-GYN and delivering babies, minor surgery, and even major surgery like amputation and debridement, how to set-up a clinic, how to set-up an OR in the middle of a fourth world environment, and so all of this stuff was great but then I kept thinking, "This isn't it. There is more to this than that." And that for me keyed me back into my own fascination with the planet and with the plant world. And I always tell people, "The point where you really get into herbal medicine and understand it, is when you use it to deal with your own personal injury or your own personal illness" or something of that sort and it works. It absolutely works. And through that period of time I was teaching survival for my team and my unit as well as other military, law enforcement and civilians. It was just so important. But the thing that never really happened for me back then was I didn't really understand the big picture. It didn't have a context to put it all in. I was teaching primitive survival skills for instance and we'd go on a walk about. We'd make bow drill fires or hand drill fires and we'd make a fire bundle. We would walk two or three miles for our next campsite and have all the stuff. And we'd set-up snares and we'd fish primitively and setting up our shelter for the night. That was great but it was sort of like what I call, circus side show tricks. And so it took me almost 15 years of going through this to figure out how to put it together in this blueprint. And that's what I did. I came up with my own runic system to denote exactly what these different areas are of study, the five core areas, if you count leadership and teamwork, and how they work into even the elemental structures of them in terms of eastern or western elemental theory. And how they all focus together to not only be an individual training system but also as a group, as a team, and as a community. I literally took this and it became the logo.

And so it's been about 15 years of working through this system to where about 7 years ago I started the school here in San Antonio. We have a 50-acre campus north of town. It's just like a university. We have a core program and we have electives. We cover everything you want to learn, how to blacksmith and all the way to herbs. Whatever you learn though, you learn from the ground up. If you want to learn how to blacksmith, we have a yearlong program for you to learn how to make your own charcoal, your own bellows, harvest your steel from old farm equipment, how to create your own forge and then by the end of the year, you're making folded steel swords. And the same thing with herbal medicine. My point is that my idea of this school has to be deeper than just teaching a few skills. It has to become a blueprint of human cultural life and life changing in that regard.

It takes more care to understand how to use herbs in synergistic manners. And what I mean by that is there are strengths to herbs and the biggest strength is being able to get to the tissue that is affected in your body. That's why we have so many different ways of preparing herbs. Like syrups or tinctures or as even a dry encapsulated herb or as an ear oil or as a salve or a poultice or in the other end of your body, an enema, suppository or a douche. All are the different ways that we have and there's a multitude of ways to be able to get the herb to the tissue so that it acts on the tissue itself. And most of the time for acute illness and for acute trauma or even recovery from illness, it is, generally speaking, the mucosa. Over 90% of infectious diseases enter through our mucosa, whether the respiratory or the genitourinary or the digestive entrance. So if we can get the herb to that part of the mucosa, it's amazing how much we can help heal the body from the inside out rather from the outside in.

NC: What are some general herbs for overall immune function that you would recommend to people so they don't have to wait until they get sick to try and treat it?

SC: I'm not a big fan of long-term tonics. I'm not really a big fan of taking the same herbs for months or even years every single day. But what I am a big fan of is using herbs that are really pretty strong. Some of the really important herbs are on the toxic side. They can be a little toxic so you have to be careful how you use them. One of the most potent lymph movers that there is in North America is called poke. We use the root of it so we say poke root, Phytolacca Americana. It's an incredibly potent lymph mover and by this I mean, the actual fluid in your lymph system is not driven by a pump. What drives it is an herb like poke and muscular skeletal movement, which includes the diaphragm. So diaphragmatic breathing is for deep breathing exercises. The things that move the lymph as well are Qi gong, Tai Chi, working on the breathing and expanding the diaphragm to be able to really move those muscles, and a full body exercise like swimming. A gentle lymph massage will help move the lymph. The idea is to create movement in here and poke root is very good for that.

Another one that's very good is called Iris Versicolor. Its common name is the blue flag and it's also on the toxic end of the scale. And another one that's very good is called red root or Ceanothus species. It's also called New Jersey tea. There are several species and they're all interchangeable. Some of the gentle lymph movers are the flower of the red clover Trifolium pratense. We have Galium aparine, which is called cleavers. Some people call it Velcro weed.

Another portion we need to pay attention to is actually the white blood cells, both their count and their activity. What we can do there is we can increase the count and increase the activity. There are several herbs but two in particular are very good at this. One of them is probably something everybody knows, as I've already heard about it, Echinacea. And here we really want Echinacea angustifolia or Echinacea pallida, the roots. Or else you want Echinacea purpurea. The flowers also do this too. They increase the white blood count. In other words the count of macrophages and neutrophils that are in the innate immune system, they are the part of our body that deals with anything coming into our body and they raise up signals that say, "Hey we've got a problem here. Let's get the reinforcements for the other parts of the immune system, the adaptive portion, to respond." Another one that's good at that is called boneset, Eupatorium perfoliatum. It is very good at both at the same thing, which is raising the white blood cell count and raising the white blood cell activity. Those are strictly lymph things.

We also want to re-enforce and help nurture the liver and the urinary tract. And the reason is the liver helps break things down in the blood stream and breaks big toxins into small toxins so that it can pass into our bloodstream and excreted out of our body. This results in more waste products when we're sick. There's an old saying in any emergency room, the solution to pollution is dilution. Same thing for our urinary tract. We need to have more solution to be able to dilute and excrete. So if we can support liver function with a couple of good herbs such as burdock root, which is Arctium lappa and it helps stimulate another form of white blood cell that's called the Kuppfer cells. What those do is detoxify. The first part of the blood comes into your liver through this tube called the portal vein and these Kuppfer cells are out there like fish in the mouth of a stream waiting for food then they do their job. They break things down, they pick up the invaders, and they help metabolize what needs to be metabolized. Another good herb for that is dandelion root, which everybody's familiar with because it's considered a weed. Dandelion root, Taraxacum officinale, does not only help support the liver in that function but it is also a good diuretic. It will help you excrete those waste products. That's what we would do to help our body with herbs by stimulating our lymph, breaking down those toxins, and getting rid of them.

NC: In your experience, how effective is herbal medicine in emergency or post disaster type situations?

SC: Yes there are herbs that are extremely good in an emergency situation and not only that, they are available to us not only sustainably but practically. Think about it. If you are the person who stores a lot of antibiotics, that's fine but you are now in ration mode. Assume every time you use that, you are taking something that is not sustainable. It's going to go away and it's going to expire eventually. You're going to have to base everything on a sustainable product. If you don't already have either a medical degree or a nurse or PA or nurse practitioner, you don't know how to use that drug properly. You don't know how to recognize between an anaphylactic reaction, an infection or an inflammation. My point is that herbal medicine is something that anybody can learn, can practice, and can apply on him or her.

NC: What advice would you give somebody who's just starting out with herbalism?

SC: The first thing you really need to do is get some material that can teach you. For me, it's books. If you don't have a lot of money to spend on, a really good primer to start you off with everything is David Hoffman's "The Holistic Herbal". This gives you an overview of everything. It's not deep in any one area but it's a great starter to give you an idea.

Start reading, going to classes somewhere, and talking to somebody who not only has information academically but also has clinical experience. You also have to practice even on yourself. You just have to go out and understand what the herb looks like, talk to somebody, learn from herb walks. The way you get to this life is to taste the herb, smell the herb. Of course you have to learn your toxic herbs first and even the most toxic herbs, like oleander or datura. You can still get away with taking a small piece. You don't even have to eat it but just take enough just to get a taste in your tongue, spit it out and you're fine. It's the ones that have a contact dermatitis like poison oak or poison ivy that you need to stay completely away from but if you learn what those are first then you're just really safe and you go to an herb garden. And you take a taste of comfrey and you feel how it tastes and feels like. How does that make you feel? Is it heating? Is it cooling? Is it dry? Is it wet? All of these are ways to get in touch with the herb.

NC: Any final recommendations for people?

SC: One of the first things I tell for everybody is what I call the 4 A's of survival. That is attitude, awareness, adaptability and accountability. So have the right attitude and understand that attitude is everything no matter how many skills you have.

Awareness. When you have the awareness to know what's going on, the better prepared you're going to be. That's what scouts are all about. The scouts are the awareness for a community or a team. They learn how to reconnaissance. They learn how to go into the urban area and be the grey man and gather information. They learn how to hide. They learn how to be stealthy. They learn how to gather information for the community or for the team cause they're the eyes and ears of the team for the community.

And then adaptability. You never can predict what's going to happen. Not in disaster, not in life, and not in anything. So instead of thinking that you've got it all figured out, you got your bug out plan, your bug out bag, your bug out location, and all of this stuff. Assume the worst case scenario of what's going to happen. You have no idea and you're in an airport somewhere and you're a thousand miles from home and you don't have anything. So you have to be adaptable. You have to know how to work with what you've got.

And the final A is accountability and that is both for the good and for the bad. That's where we learn. We learn from mistakes. That's why we make mistakes in training so we can learn from them.

Nate's Notes

Herbs are a vitalistic bio form. It has the footprints and fingerprints of it's life.

Getting started with Herbalism:

1. Get material that can teach you about herbalism (books, videos, audiobooks, etc.)
    ‣ Recommended: The Holistic Herbal by David Hoffman
2. Enroll in classes.
3. Practice on yourself.
4. Learn as much about herbs by tasting, testing, and observing the effects.

4 A's of Survival:

1. Attitude
2. Awareness
3. Adaptability
4. Accountability

When the world runs out of pharmaceuticals, what are you going to do? Enter herbal medicine because it is the medicine of the people.

Examples of when herbs can be used as medicine:

For preventive medicine, use herbs that are very strong for short periods of time.

Lymphatic System in trouble? Powerful lymph movers include Poke Root, Blue Flag, and small amounts of Red Root. Some examples of gentle lymph movers are Red clover and Cleavers.

Echinacea root or flowers and bone set can increase the count and activity of your white blood cells.

Your liver helps break down the big toxins into little toxins that can be found in your blood system. Dandelion root can help reinforce and nurture your liver and urinary tract whereas Burdock root is an ideal blood cleanser.

Let's say you have a broken thumb. Mix 1lb of Comfrey and 1lb Horsetail together into a wet poultice and put on your thumb every 3 hours.

Sam Coffman

Sam Coffman is the founder and director of The Human Path - a survival school near San Antonio, Texas. Sam has over 10 years of military experience as a U.S. Special Forces Medic (aka "Green Beret" medic), an interrogator and a linguist. He studied botany and bioregional medicine both privately and at several outdoor schools in Colorado, and during his military service as a Green Beret Medic he logged thousands of hours in the field as a team medic, military emergency rooms and troop medical clinics. Over the past 25 years, Sam has not only taught wilderness and urban survival for military and civilian students, but also has focused on post- disaster and remote-medicine using primarily (if not exclusively) plant medicine. He has worked as a clinical herbalist on his own and in conjunction with functional medicine doctors (M.D. and D.O.) for chronic as well as acute illness and injury. Sam has been highly focused on bio-regional plant medicine for infection, injury and illness most commonly encountered in a post-disaster, remote or underserved environment when there is no higher definitive medical care.

Learn more http://TheHumanPath.com.

Weedcrafting: Sustainable and Safe Foraging

Nicole Telkes

Nathan Crane: What are some of things to get started in weedcrafting? What would you recommend people to do?

Nicole Telkes: My first recommendation is to turn off your phone and the computer and go outside. It's a great start to go to webinars and summits to get inspired to do things but the best teachers are the plants themselves. So going outside and sitting with the plants, walking around, learning how the land works, and what grows where is best learned in person outside. You will learn so much more outside than anything out of a book or on the computer.

Another way that you can start to get involved with learning about wild harvesting and foraging of plants around you is to find a space that is about recreating wildness around us and finding it in places that you may not have thought of as wilderness before. Start to recreate it by spreading seeds and going outside to your community gardens, to your green belts, to parks and different areas around you that you didn't really think of as wilderness. Before picking the plants, the most important part is going to be learning how to identify them properly so you don't make yourself sick or even kill yourself or others. Identification is going to be the first way to get started before you go out and decide to make something out of them. 95% of wild harvesting and wildcrafting or foraging doesn't involve picking anything. Most of the time you're going to be going out and learning about the natural world so you can be a better forager, knowing where things are and when they come up and this only happens by spending a lot of time outside with the plants. People get bogged down with Facebook groups for identification and foraging. That's the wrong path to go down if you're wanting to learn about plants.

Most people who do it as a lifestyle are picking something that they're going to throw into a salad or they make something with the plants that they harvested around them. And most of the people who are in that type of lifestyle would probably agree with me that it's going to be something you have to learn through experience and not by just reading about it.

What I've noticed is that a student's perspective of what it takes to wildcraft changes drastically when they realize that being outside and picking plants is not glamorous. It's fun but in Texas where I wild craft and forage, you're going to end up with fire ant bites, gluck all over your fingers, sweaty, burnt and it's just part of the whole deal. It's really fun and an enriching experience but it's not the same as sitting in front of a computer and reading about it or watching it online.

I had one student that was feeling really disconnected because she had to move to a trailer park in Colorado.

She felt that she was robbed of having this wilderness experience. After my class, she, her kids, and her husband went around the trailer park and picked up all the trash, started to sow seeds, and collected the wild plants that were growing in all the corners. They celebrated what was there. It completely changed her life and made her feel like this was something that she could do anywhere. That's part of my perspective that I'm trying to get across to people and that is you don't have to go out to the mountains or the deepest parts of the desert or somewhere in a big old growth forest. You can go anywhere and start to create diversity in your own backyards by spreading seeds or keeping seeds in your pocket and just throwing them out on really nice mono cropped Monsanto green lawns and just kind of letting everything flourish as though as it should and that you'll see pollinators come, critters come, and things change very quickly when encouraged. Part of weedcrafting and wildcrafting is we have to create beauty where we want it and not just expect it to be there for us so that we can just walk into nature's grocery store and pick things off the shelves when we feel like it because that's a very consumerous, consumptive kind of attitude. So we have to be active participants in creating the diversity and the foraging for the world around us, not just for ourselves, but to help critters and pollinators and other things that might be getting stifled by lawns and anything like suburban cement that goes down and covers up seeds.

This is not something that takes a master's degree but if you get inspired and you want to see things change, it's really exciting to see how fast you can encourage things to make more edibles and more medicine around you.

NC: It reminds me five or six years ago, I sponsored to bring out Kate Armstrong who is the Urban Forager out of Denver. She came to San Diego and we did harvesting weed walks in three different cities around San Diego. I was so amazed at how many wild edibles that were in people's lawns and next to sidewalks. Oftentimes, you walk right pass this stuff going through town or going through the suburbs. Most of the time people are unaware that there is so much medicinal food everywhere and you can eat for free or treat yourself for free if needed. It's quite amazing.

NT: On that note, I agree that you can eat for free and you can treat yourself for free but it's not really free because we have to give back in order for it to be there for our caloric needs. It makes me feel uncomfortable to think about everyone foraging for their food because there are just too many people, unless we did it in a thoughtful way. I've seen people foraging in the city and it's more about them being excited and just grabbing what's around them than being thoughtful about the way that they're grabbing it. So hopefully it's not telling anybody that anything is necessarily right or wrong but just having a thoughtful approach and being somewhat critical about the way you're going about harvesting plants.

When I first started getting involved with wild medicinals in the middle of the desert, there was nothing more exciting to me than being able to identify a stand of plants and then go out to that stand and make my own medicine. That was just so empowering and it really made me feel like it was something I do for the rest of my life and I would be happy. I've made that my life's work but I've also made my life's work to encourage and be a part of giving back to whatever plant community or ecosystem that I'm taking from. We have to always look at ourselves as being part of it and that this isn't a grocery store where you can walk in and just take things off the shelf. You're still exchanging money. You have to give something in order to take it.

I do want to get back to also giving skills to people who are wanting to move forward in doing wildcrafting. Some of the skills that I found that were really vital to what I needed to be able to do this safely and effectively were proper botanical identification skills. The way you get those skills, besides learning about them in books, is to find knowledgeable people to take you in plant walks. A lot of people will tell me, well there is no one in my area to take me on a plant walk. I beg to differ because what I found in my communities is that there are people. It's just that they're hard to find and they're usually older. Our culture tends to ignore the elders that have this knowledge and that are sitting right down the street from you and know everything about the local plants. It's just nobody's ever asked them. They may or may not be amazing botanists but they know the plants and they've been using them for many, many years. They'll likely even know everything about growing them and how to find them. That's another way to approach learning about plants. Go to your elders and go to the people in your area that may not have academic knowledge but have personal experience with the plants.

NC: What are some groups where you can find those people?

NT: Meetup and Craigslist are great for that. I have also found that the native plant societies are great places because a lot of retirees will join them. These will be people who've been using the plants for a really long time and they'll know everything about what birds like the berries of this one and what colors they come in. Native plant societies are a great resource and every single area of the country has a native plant society that meets up and has plant walks. They may not know the medicines and the foods as much but they do know the plants and you can always apply the medicinal and edible knowledge from the books that you have. You just have to be able to identify the plants of your region because a lot of the cousins and genera are similar.

There's going to be species that are similar looking in different bioregions or not if you don't have trained eyes. The more you're able to train your eyes to understand what the little differences there are, the more you're going to apply the medicinal and edible knowledge that you might have in some books to what you see outside. So the big thing is to join plant walks. I've seen so many different groups that come up on Meetup for different types of foraging and wildcrafting from different regions of the country. There's a Facebook group I started for locating medicinal and edible plants where people can swap plants across the country. It's called the Medicinal and Edible Plant and Seed Locator Group and nothing is advertised on it. It's only for people who are looking for things. It's not an identification group but if you're looking to get plants and you're not ready to do it yourself, you can get it from people who were on there. You can get seeds, plants, and simple medicines that have been made fresh and they're sent across the world. We have people all over the world that are sharing seeds and plants on there. There are over 5,000 members so you never know who's going to ask for what and it's usually an herbalist so it's some plant you never heard of that comes up there.

Another exercise that really helps folks a lot is plant sitting. You sit with the plants and you have to give at least 20 minutes of sitting there. Some people would draw the plant and others would just watch it but 20 to 30 minutes of just sitting with one plant and watching it is going to give you a lot of information.

NC: Would you recommend that you identify what plant it is first or just go sitting around a plant you don't know?

NT: I would sit with whatever plant interests you. It's more fun than going out looking for a certain plant and trying to make sure you have the right one.

As far as picking anything, one of the biggest things that come up with people is, "How much do you pick if you find something?" Maybe you're in your backyard and you've identified that you have plantain growing all over your yard. You've learned that plantain is a very useful medicinal plant and you want to use it. Or maybe you found purslane everywhere and you want to start using purslane in your salads or something. So once you've identified the plant, there's different ways to think about harvesting. A lot of people use the concept of only picking 10% of the stand. But I think this is not using your critical thinking skills because sometimes a plant is going to get mowed in a couple of weeks so you end up harvesting all of it for whatever you're doing. Maybe a cotton wood tree blew over in the rain and they're going to harvest and take the whole tree so you'll just take as much as you can before it's gone. There are some levels of how to decide what and how much of it to harvest.

NC: What are some resources such as guides and books that you would recommend people to use?

NT: It really depends on where you live and whether you're looking for medicinal or edible. So the choices are very different. A new book just came out that's fantastic called Foraging and Feasting. I highly recommend getting it for your library. It is a beautifully illustrated, beautifully written book that some herbalists put together and one of the women is a botanical illustrator. It has recipes and all sort of different weeds that are useful in cooking and it's just so well done.

For medicinal, it really depends on your bioregion because every bioregion has different kinds of plants. In my bioregion, there's lots of cactus whereas if you go up into New England there's relatively little cactus. They have a lot more things like Vaccinium or cranberries. You have to find out who has written a book for your area. In my area, there was no book so I created one, The Medicinal Plants of Texas which was all the wild, weedy, and common plants that you're going to run into and its materia medica. You're also going to find that Peterson's puts out some field guides from different areas. Peterson's is a common title that you'll see on different materia medica and plant books that are Peterson's guide.

And then there are different authors and herbalists like Michael Moore, my teacher who had put out a bunch of field guides for the desert Southwest and mountain west.

The way I would choose a book is based on who wrote it. Look at the author's bio and whether or not the author is somebody who has experience with actual collecting and using of the plants and not just studying the plant. As far as if it's for edible and medicinal, you'll want somebody with direct experience and then if you just want to learn identification tools, you would make sure that the person wasn't just learning through experience but they have some sort of training in order to produce a book that is botanically accurate. You want to make sure they have some training and know how to identify properly. That's usually people who have some botany background because a lot of things have changed in the botany world and now gene machines are outnumbering people who can actually do field botany.

NC: What is a gene machine?

NT: What's happening is that the skills of herbalists and foragers are becoming a thing of the past. Today's science wants to split everything up into a smaller and smaller piece so what they're doing is they're taking plants and putting them under microscopes and splitting them apart smaller and

223

smaller and smaller until they're just looking at the genes. And they're deciding where certain plants are going to be located botanically and taxonomically based on what they see under the microscope, not what they see when they go outside. All sorts of botanical names are changing right now due to the way science is starting to approach plants and the natural world. Those of us that forage and go outside are naturalists. We see things as a complex interrelationship and web where all sorts of big things and little things and everything comes together and we can be a part of that. What's happening in science today is everything's becoming more and more picked apart down to the tiniest neuron or gene and we're losing the bigger picture. Being a part of the foraging and wildcrafting world is reconnecting to something that we're losing in our higher education right now, which is going outside and learning things by walking around and looking.

NC: Our ancestors have always used wild edibles as medicine and they were able to identify it. How did they identify these plants without the books, YouTube, and iPhones?

NT: How they did it is by sitting outside and watching animals. That's why it's not just about staring at the plant but staring at how things are interacting with the plant, what's eating it, and how did they eat it. Somebody told me that I had ringtails on my property, which are a type of tiny little wildcat that live in the trees and eat mice and things. I was looking at videos of them and I noticed that the mice eat the prickly pears. It was funny because I was looking at my cactus and I noticed that a mouse had eaten the prickly pear because I saw the same little teeth marks. You can learn things both on the computer and in person. But it's interesting to see how you can tell what's eating things, why it's being eaten, what might be safe, and that's what our ancestors did. Some people learn through watching other critters and what they did and then experimented on themselves. So it's good to know the poisons first and then you learn how to slowly eat things and use things that are common.

NC: Is there a general way to look at certain plants that we should just leave alone or stay away from? What are the steps to take to develop that knowledge?

NT: What I found as a wild harvester is that there are a lot of plants that have trickster, poisonous plants that look a lot like it. Most things that are medicinal have some edibility to them so that's a spectrum more than anything. But just because something is edible doesn't mean it tastes good. You can eat them, you just might not want to. But there's something that the plant world does, I truly believe to keep you from being too brazen in your approach and that is have trickster poisonous plants that look very similar to a harmless plant. There are things like if you see a really bright shiny red berry that looks too good to eat, you don't probably want to eat it. Or if you see a really crazy looking mushroom that is just all sorts of spectacular colors, you probably don't want to eat it. There's no general rule though and be very, very humble on your approach outside. Until you're 100% confident about a plant, you don't eat it or touch it. So you have to get a book or a guide that can tell you what are the poisonous plants that are growing in your region that you really need to get to know.

NC: And would you recommend people cross-reference various books?

NT: Definitely. I have every single Texas field guide you can get because the plant pictures are different. The way they approach to organizing them is also different. Some species are found in some books but not in others. There's nothing wrong with having a huge collection of field guides.

NC: What are some other things that we as individuals can do to encourage more weeds, more medicinal plants, and healthier wild lands?

NT: First of all we have to get to the schools and start influencing schools with what and how they're teaching kids. Some schools have done really amazing things like in Germany, every single school child starting from age 5 has to do gardening from the minute they get to school until they leave. The best way to start learning about plants is to just have a small garden that you can tend and then start to understand them in a more direct way. Any kind of growing, even if you have to do it in a container, is going to change your relationship with plants. You have to be quite aware of what you're doing to grow something and harvest it and use it. It's very empowering and it makes you feel super.

Also just trying to encourage seeds anywhere you go. If there's something beautiful and lovely and you want to see it in other places, take the seeds and spread it as much as you can. I'm always carrying around seeds in my pockets and putting them in different places. So be the seed saver. In fact, a lot of cities are doing things like food forests. In Austin legislation was passed to encourage urban farming and forestry. So having weeds and foraging weeds out of the farms are much more sustainable than going out to the wild lands outside the town.

NC: It's a great example what you're doing. One person said, "Hey, I want to encourage organic farming and gardening," and that sort of thing. And some of these farms that she started with had just a couple of acres. And now some of them have over a hundred acres because of her doing that. So there are all kinds of things we can do on a personal level or a community level and even on a global level by just taking those little actions every day.

NT: I have one plant in particular that I'm celebrating as the plant of the year and I'm going to be spreading seeds of it everywhere. It's known in the New York Times as the Careless Weed but I know it as Amaranth. It's wonderful because it's a weed that is resisting Monsanto right now. They can't get rid of it and they've tried every pesticide possible. Here's this wild edible that, against all odds, is fighting against the most powerful corporation - and it's winning! They can't figure out what to do. I'm going to be eating a lot of Amaranth this year and seeding it all over my property because it's such a fighter. If the land is in balance one plant won't be able to take over everything. There are a lot of plants there and you will be able to eat healthfully and have a balanced type of nutrition because you have a lot of diversity. So we have to increase the diversity around us whether it's in a city or in the country.

Nate's Notes

Getting Started:

- Turn off the phone and the computer and go outside.
- The best teachers are the plants themselves.
- You need to go outside and get a personal experience.
- Recreate the wildness around you. Spread seeds and go outside to community gardens, greenbelt parks, and different areas around where you live.
- You need to learn how to identify properly.
- 95% of wild harvesting/foraging doesn't involve picking anything.
- It's mostly about learning about the natural world.
- It does require spending a lot of time outside with the plants and getting a firsthand experience.
- It's also important to forage in a thoughtful way. You need to give back as well.

Developing Skillsets:

- Getting proper botanical identification skills.
- Find people that already have the skills needed and can take you on plant walks.

- Native plant societies, Meetup, and Craigslists are all examples of places where you can find skilled people.
- Plant sitting
  - Sit with the plant for 20-30 minutes.
  - This will give you a lot of information.
    - Sit with whatever plant that interests you then try to identify it.
    - See things as a complex web that we can be a part of.
  - Sitting outside and watching animals as well will help determine edible plants.
- You can also experiment with plants on your body before ingesting.
- Learn poisons first.

Watch Out for Certain Plants:

- Some plants have similar lookalikes that are not edible.
- Learn the poisonous plants around you that you need to stay away from.
- If you see a very bright shiny red berry that looks too good to eat, you probably don't want to eat it. Same goes for very colorful wild mushrooms.
- Often, if it looks too good to be true, you don't want to eat it.

Resources to Use:

- Foraging and Feasting by Dina Falconi is a recommended book to use.

- Resources also depend on your bioregion. You should get specific books for your area.

- The Medicinal Plants of Texas by Nicole Telkes is good book for those residing in Texas.

- Petersons puts out field guides.

- You'll want someone who has training and experience.

- You can even search for local field guides.

How Can we Encourage More Weeds and Wildlands?

- Get into the schools.

- Any kind of growing will help, even in containers.

- Get experience in gardening.

- Encourage seeds. Take seeds from other plants and spread them everywhere.

- Create a food forest, urban farming, community gardens, or a co-op.

Veronica, Amaranth resists pesticides and is a great weed to make friends with.

It's also important to increase awareness around non-GMO crops and help spread wild edibles.

Nicole Telkes

Nicole Telkes is an educator, author, and registered Herbalist from Austin, Texas. She has a background in botanical studies, plant conservation work, community activism, and herbal first aid clinics. She published the first Medicinal Plant Guide for Texas in 2014 entitled "The Medicinal Plants of Texas" and strongly believes in herbal medicine being "the people's medicine." Nicole is the Director of the Wildflower School of Botanical Medicine in Austin, offering six-month to yearlong programs in community and clinical herbalism.

Learn more at:
www.wildflowerherbschool.com.

Back to the basics,
forward to the future
James Stevens

Nathan Crane: How long have you been in the preparedness and self-reliance field? What got you into this field?

James Stevens: Being a prepper is an active lifestyle. It's something you have to work at, it takes diligence, it takes commitment, it takes money, it takes time, and it takes energy. It will work you to death to become prepared especially with the pressures we feel today with the economic situation, with the political situation, and with the moral situation we're facing. It seems like the screws are being tightened virtually every day by stupid mistakes, gossips and all kinds of errors of judgment that we're seeing at the political level, at the financial level, at the economic level, and at the living level here in our country as well as throughout the world.

Now at 75 years of age I can look back and say, "Oh my goodness, maybe I could've done something really important." My generation has to pass on what we've gained, what we've learned, and what we've shared with others all this time. I think it was Plato who said, "Those having torches will pass them on to others." It's time we get some younger people who have the ability and the quality of information to share with others. We live in a new world of Internet technology and digital capability, communications and virtual stores, and electronically controlled food preparation appliances. Those are important things that you have to deal with today. On the other hand, what happens when that genius is no longer practicable or practical when the grid goes down or something happens?

Over the last 40 years I've lived through life being prepared and working at it every day today. Every day I add to my food storage. You ask me, "Why?" It is because I eat everyday. So what I take out today or yesterday I need to put back today or what I will use tomorrow, I need to create today because it is a lifestyle. A preparedness lifestyle really says I will be able to live in the future pretty much as normally as I live today. It may be in the dark, it may be in the cold, it may be in the heat, and it may be down there. Preparing a stove, a common stove or a jet stove is possible because I know how. It won't be a big deal. I can do it because I've already practiced it. That is the essence of the preparedness lifestyle. Being able to continue life as if virtually nothing happened.

The first major reason for a preparedness lifestyle is you are advised to be prepared. If you look in the Bible, you'll see that Noah, Joseph of Egypt, and in the parable of the 10 virgins they were all prepared. We know that we've been warned about being prepared and we've been given good examples. Secondly, we'd be critically wise if we prepared ourselves because luck smiles on those who are prepared. Thirdly, if you're the head of the household you have a patriarchal, matriarchal or a personal responsibility that's necessary to protect your family or yourself. That is part of your preparedness lifestyle. It allows you to control your environment, your food supply, what you do and how things affect you. That is the important part of controlling your environment and by being in control of it you're able to respond. So that is why preparedness is important and there are 3 paradigms that people need to look at. One of them is that you're going to be able to create a store in your home. An in-home food storage. Another word for it is an in-home convenience store. We need to be able to bloom wherever we are planted. Whatever you have is what you got. Deal with it. Make it work. If you live in an apartment learn how to use the bottom closets, under the bed, behind the couch, and make tables. Whatever it takes to be able to store food.

Now people say, "Why is food storage so important? I'd rather have a gun." No, you wouldn't. Everybody eats but not everybody shoots. And not everybody is going to get shot. If you have food, it doesn't matter how much gold other people have. They will come to you. I believe the future economy will be food-based because food will be in very short supply. When it's in short supply, its value goes up and whatever you have you'll trade for it to keep your family alive. Now, that's radical in many ways but to me it's reality and having lived through World War II and other situations, raising 6 kids in really tough times, some really tough economies, recessions and things like that, I can tell you that it really helps to have food.

If you like corndogs, you need to learn how to freeze-dry, how to dehydrate, jelly, and chill them. There are many, many ways to store food. I think there are 13-14 ways you can store food in your home and another 10 or so that are commercial. And then the third part is the fact that we need to be able to camp out within the lawns of our home. Our home has to be a safe haven that even without lights, without heat, and without fresh supplies of food coming in to the grocery store we can be sustained.

NC: What are some things people living in the city can do right away?

JS: My book was written for some of the population that live in the urban, sub-urban and even the ex-urban areas. It has charts and tables to help people to walk through all the decisions that they have to make. It's almost a decision matrix. It helps you write down to do the things that you need to do. I also have a DVD that just came out. So my book is a workbook. It teaches you how to determine what you want and what you need. What is the difference? My dad once said that when you can determine the difference between your wants and your needs you're on your way to success because we want a lot of things but we only need a few things. I think the important part the book tries to succeed at is to give people the guidelines for decision-making. There'll be a long list of things and a checkup and where do you get them? When do you have them? It's not just a list. It's tables and charts to help you chart your future. The tables merely organize the information. It even talks about everything from short-term use to long-term use. Everybody eats so I have three preparedness rules. First is storing what you'll eat. Second is eating what you store. And lastly, use it or lose it.

NC: How can people get food and store it properly?

JS: There are three ways that people can get food. There's the Pioneer Message. That means you plant it, you go out and you work it, and pretty soon you get a crop. You'll then save some seed and start over again next year. That was the agrarian society, which this country was built upon and it's the toughest one because it doesn't fit in very well with our current lifestyle. It takes work and it takes energy. The pioneer lesson is the toughest one because it's from scratch and it takes a lot of talent. Most likely in the first 2 years you're going to have crop failures because the ground wasn't ready. It didn't have the nourishment that it needed for the plant, not enough sunlight, and too much water. So pioneer has a lot of advantages and you're going to have control over your destiny. But the disadvantages are that you might not have enough space, you don't know how to work, you don't know how to care for it, you don't know how to share responsibility with others, and sometimes it costs more to produce an in-home garden. The second method is a "P" also called the

Package Method. It requires a little thinking and a little planning. So that is low-lifestyle modification required and preparedness requires lifestyle modification. And then if people don't get that they're in trouble. The final "P" and the third set is the Pantry Method. The rule for food storage is you have to be able to produce food, you have to be able to prepare food, and you have to be able to preserve food. If you want to produce food in the city, you go down to the grocery store, you grab a cart, you go through the aisle, and you pick out what you normally eat. You then go to the checkout, you produce your cart, and you produce the food. You can eat it and if that's what you are used to, what's wrong with that? Yes, you can have a sustainable garden but you cannot store that food in cans for a lifetime. I'd live out in the country. I can freeze dry in my own home, dehydrate food in my own home, and create jelly in my own home. Those are the things that you learn to do because it's possible. Did you know there are 14 ways to store food? You can salt down things, fry them if you want, sugar them down, smoke them, pickle them, and you can add lye to it. In order to store eggs for a long time you have to have lye and they're called century eggs. Then there's canning, bottling, jellying, jugging, putting things in jugs. How about subterranean burial like Kimchi in Korea? How about refrigeration? Did you know that refrigeration came to United States in 1923? In fact, Einstein was one of the people who helped create the refrigerator. Now that's 14 quick ways that you can store food. You see we have lots of resources but we just don't use them. We sit around telling each other how tough it is. It's just not tough at all. You just have to go at it. Again, excellence and preparedness is about attitude. Do you really want to accomplish? Are you really willing to be able to do it? Do you really care enough? Those are the questions you have to ask yourself.

NC: I was reading that back in the 70's your book started out as a couple hundred pages and now it's at well over a thousand pages. Why is it that it ended up becoming so thick and full?

JS: Nobody knows everything about preparedness. Nobody ever has and nobody ever will. I accept that humbly and recognize that this is a lifetime effort that has spanned about 40 years. My book is a guide and a handbook. It's called the Family Preparedness Handbook. It helps people do things. People need to realize they can do it one step at a time, just like eating. Take a bite, chew carefully, and swallow. Take another bite, chew carefully, and swallow. Stop eating when you're full. When you're hungry come back, take a bite, chew carefully and swallow. That's what it takes to be prepared. It is not science. It is law in motion and nothing else. It's nothing more natural than eating. If you store what you eat and you eat what you store, you can't go far along. Someone will say, "I love Twinkies. I'd like to have a one-year supply of Twinkies." Again learn how to dehydrate them, freeze them, refrigerate them, jelly them, pickle them, and freeze-dry them. All those things you see, learn how to do all the above. Canning is a very expensive way to store food. It's a very heavy way to store food and very vulnerable if you live in an earthquake zone. So there are, you know, there's so many ways to do it.

Personally, preparedness costs money. Let me say that again, preparedness costs money. Second one is that your lack of preparedness will cost you more money. Life says to you, pay me now or pay me later. I don't think I'm an expert at this. I think I'm good at it and a professional. I know how to do it. I can sit down with anyone and talk about it. Third is it's never too late to start preparing. We have to start somewhere. We were all embryonic at one time. And the fourth one is that you'll never be finished preparing. We're getting a day older every day. We're getting more skilled everyday or we're getting more stupid every day. We have more assets every day and we have fear assets every day. Every day is a new challenge. And so you'll never finish preparing. You can have a hundred years supply but when you eat one meal a day, you now have ninety-nine years and 364 2/3 day's supply. We are never totally ready for the future. Part of that is we don't know what will happen. And that's what preparedness is all about. It was Winston Churchill who explained it clearly back during the Second World War. He said, "Success is not final. Failure is

not fatal. It is the courage to continue that counts."
That's great advice.

My dad came along and taught me this. "Jimmy..."
he called me, "I want you to remember this forever."
And he said, "Here you are son. If you're doing
something, do it right." "Oh, okay Dad. I got that.
Okay, I'm going to be good. I'll be a good carpenter,
whatever dad." And he said, "No, son. I don't think
you got it all. If you got to do it, do it now." I said, "I
think I got it. I think you want me to take immediate
action." He said, "Son, I don't think you got it at all.
Listen to me." He said, "If it's worth doing, it's
worth doing right now." There's a whole different
emphasis when those terms go together. Not just a
matter of doing it right, not just a matter of doing it
now but doing it right now. It's fantastic advice.

You see the greatest gift we've ever been given is our
ability to choose. It was given to us by God and our
Constitution. We rankle when people want to take
away our ability to make a choice that is convenient
and particular to us. The second one is that there's no
fixed outline and there's no free program that fits all
family's preparedness. Now, see if you can accept
that. You can be comfortable going about doing what
you do because that's your choice. And then the third
one, part of that is if you progress with the choices
you made you become wiser. And you should
become smarter and your lifestyle will reflect your
previous choices. Isn't that neat? Isn't that so true?

Isn't that great to recognize that preparedness is merely about choices? But I think the greatest and higher authority is overcoming this personal family preparedness and help prepare mankind to have a better life. I call this my preparedness rules of three by Jesus. Ask and it will be given to you. Search and you will find. And last is knock and the door will be opened unto you. What better rules of three to follow than those? So to me it's just as simple as that.

Religion is another set of the rules that we impose upon ourselves and we live by it. These are traditional rules and that is not imposed on anyone else but us. I think the second most important thing is shelter because if you were in the Arctic or in Greenland, you'd need to have shelter before you worry about drinking water. Drinking water would freeze before you opened the top of the tin can. Hot coffee would freeze in 2 minutes. That's cold. So third of course is security. That's protection, it's defense, it's group dynamic, and it's a mutual assistance group. It's a lot of stuff but security doesn't have to be killing somebody else if they take your food. It's about security, giving your family a safe haven, and protecting them. So if you live on the mountainside you have to have seeds, tools, and equipment to deal with it. And then you need water but you have to know how to collect water. You have to know how to treat water. You have to know how to store water. If water is just water, you need to understand it.

Nate's Notes

Prime Rule of Three

1. Better to be prudent than wise

2. Providence smiles on us who prepare

3. If you're head of the household, you have a patriarchal, matriarchal or personal responsibility to protect your family

In home food storage/convenience store:

- Create in your home a store
- Whatever you have, deal with it and use it
- It's not about gold, it's about life
- Life is preserved by eating and drinking
- Learn how to freeze dry, dehydrate, jelly, can, anyway you can learn to store food

Need to be able to camp within walls of your home

- Even without light or heat we need to be able to sustain ourselves
- Do everything you can to to stay in your house in any kind of disaster

Bugging out is not what's important

- If you leave to early you could miss out on resources
- If you leave too late you could get stuck

You need to know the needs of your specific geographic location
- Preparedness is not about skills, it's about attitude
- Build your boat now while it's not raining

We have to take responsibility for our family.
- Provide water, shelter, food, fire, protection, and spiritual guidance
- Create a mutual assistance group/community
- If you can determine what you want then you can get it

Store what you eat; eat what you store
- Use it or lose it
- Food and water are most important
- Shelter and warmth

Need be prepared to deal with what you get
- That's what preparedness is all about
- Getting food
  - Pioneer method
    - Plant it, work it, harvest it, and eat it
    - Most sustainable but toughest one. It takes work, will fail a little bit but if you're going to fail, fail now when it's not critical to your life.

- Package Method
  - Stocking up with large amounts of packaged food
  - Need to eat it before it expires or lose it
- Pantry Method
  - A mix and match of the above. Canning, etcetera

- Have to be able to produce food, prepare food, and preserve food
- Hard to store enough food for a lifetime in cans
- Get a freeze-dry machine and dehydrator in your home
- You can salt, sugar, smoke, pickle, can, bottle, jelly, dehydrate, and freeze-dry food to store it
- Nobody knows everything about preparedness and we need to accept this humbly
- Preparedness costs money but your lack of preparedness will cost you more money. Life says to you, pay me now or pay me later.
- Each person's preparedness lifestyle is each person's own choice.
- Ask and it will be given to you, search and you will find, knock and the door will be open unto you.

DISCOUNT CODE TO OWN

"BACK TO THE BASICS BOOK AND DVD"

www.TheSelfRelianceSummit.com/james

Buy the book and get the DVD free with code: *srs2014combo*

50% off the DVD with code: *srs2014*

The Original

Doctor Prepper™

James Stevens

James Stevens, otherwise known as Dr. Prepper, is the owner of the Preparedness Radio Network. The Preparedness Radio Network is the leading preparedness broadcasting group on the Internet currently broadcasting on PreparednessRadio.com. James is a best selling author of Making the Best of Basics: The Family Preparedness Handbook and it is now in it's 11th edition selling more than 800,000 copies worldwide.

Learn more at www.PreparednessRadio.com.

What is the Grid?
Why and How you Need to
Get Off It Now

Jason Matyas

Nathan Crane: Why do you think it's critical that people should consider getting off the grid now?

Jason Matyas: As each day goes by there are more and more stories that demonstrate the wisdom of reducing our dependence on modern systems and the modern economy that in many ways has trapped and restrained our choices. And there are lots of things that people want to do in life but they just don't have the ability to do them because the system that they've grown up in or the system that they've chosen to be a part of in various ways limits their choices. Ultimately it's based upon your ability to improve the situation of your family by taking action to change your situation for yourself, to make decisions, and lifestyle changes that are going to enact change, make an impact on you and your family situation and the constraints that you are operating under.

NC: Our lifestyle is really dependent on our actions. Do you recommend that people go totally off the grid and quit on the spot or just start taking baby steps first towards being more self-reliant?

JM: Well, I think it's important to establish your priorities but it's dependent on the realization that these modern systems that most of us have grown up and viewed as normal are historically abnormal and often they are very prone or susceptible to systemic shock in various ways. Most people who realize a lot of these realties in the modern system see that with the electrical grid. The electrical grid is important obviously, because most of our basic life support systems are dependent on a safe supply of electricity. So going off grid in terms of electricity is important but there are other elements of the modern system that entrap people as well. Things like the food production in control grid. Your heath is directly related to the degree in which you participate in the modern food system or choose an alternative path which is more wholesome, natural, and preferably local in terms of sourcing so that you can know where your food is coming from and how it's grown. There are things like the financial and economic control grid. How our financial system, economy, and the wages in this economy severely constrain our choices unless we make a decision to seek an alternative income source as well as what we need to live and where we're getting those things from. A lot of people see government intrusion in various ways and are happy about it. Other people don't want the government telling them what to do. The problem is that many people, because of their political affiliations, often are not consistent in their understanding of how the government is trying to control them. They agree with some forms of government control but not others. And so, they like liberty in some occasions but not others. I push people to be consistent in pursuing liberty, which is basically what America was found upon. One of the things that many people don't ever think about is the cultural control grid. This is how our modern culture, particularly the entertainment-based consumer culture, really informs our priorities, our decisions, and our lifestyle in terms of how we spend our time and how we spend our money. If there's one thing that people take away besides, "Hey, take action!" is this: stop being just a consumer and make a decision to be a producer in whatever form that takes. Be a productive family because once upon a time, the strength of America laid not in the big corporations but in the productive capacity of households and families to not just grow their own food but to be industrious with the resources they had. And we need to return to that if we're going to see true change towards a more sustainable future rather than the unsustainable one that we're currently on.

NC: So you've got food production and health grid, the financial economic control grid, the government, and the modern culture consumer controlled grid. Are there any others?

JM: There are others. The health care system is a control grid and it's becoming increasingly more centralized especially as Obama Care gets implemented. And I think that the results of the modern "health care system" speak for itself. It reveals that it's really not a health care system; it's a sickness management system. For those who are unaware, the modern medical system in this country is for the pharmaceutical industry. This is why when you go to most doctors they're going to assess your symptoms and give you a prescription drug or a non-prescription drug to treat the symptom instead of addressing the underlying cause. That is the reason why pharmaceutical-related death is the fourth leading cause of death in America. So people are worried about Ebola today and rightly so but hello, people? We're killing hundreds of thousands of people with pharmaceuticals every year and nobody really cares about that. So to the extent that you can preclude having to participate in that system by having good health from natural living, eating whole foods, and having a healthy lifestyle. That's going to be liberating not just in terms of an impact on your health but also because you're not going to have to go and seek help from a system that is designed to entrap you and limit your choices as far as your health care.

NC: How can the food system have a negative or positive impact on people and what can people do about it?

JM: The people that have sought out whole foods and local sources of foods have probably come across some of this information. I just want to hit some highlights right here just to give people some context about our food system and just the enormity of the problem that we have. So the United States agriculture is still seen by some as a huge area of strength of the nation. The reality is that America in its colonial and in the founding era was an agrarian economy. In other words, the vast majority of production was agricultural and a vast majority of households were largely self-sufficient based upon their own production of what they needed in different terms of food. That system was a locally based agrarian system that has transitioned to an industrial and chemical based agricultural system over the past 60 years. So much so that family farms have decreased from about 7 million in the 1900s to only 2 million in 1997 and have continued to decline. The interesting thing to know about the statistic is that the vast majority of those 2 million family farms are not the solution for the future because most of them are not producing food for the local economy. They're at the behest of the big agriculture conglomerate because they're farming corn, soy or involved in the modern industrial food system that treats plants and animals like they're industrial machines which is not the way God created them to be managed. That's an issue of stewardship but a lot of farmers have transitioned from that industrial system where they're caught in a system of debt because the whole industrial agriculture system is all about bigger is better. You have to have bigger machines and far more acres because the margins are so slim. You can only do that with debt so they're always trying. They always have to produce more and more in order to keep up with the debt payment. So basically modern farmers that are doing industrial agriculture are basically like the serfs in the old feudal system. They're basically trapped in this system where they have to keep doing this system in order to perpetuate itself. It's not a very appealing career choice for most and that's one of the reasons why so many family farms are being lost. On the consumer side, spending on processed foods has doubled over the past 30 years. The reason for that is because of government involvement and intervention in the economy in the form of subsidies for things like corn and soy and other seed crop inputs. Those provide key inputs for food producers to make "cheap food" like boxed, processed food products that are denatured and don't have any nutritional value. The output of those food products is what leads people to consume them because they think they're cheap. They take food-like products and make those the staple of their diet instead of real food.

Every county in the state of California is in extreme or greater level of drought. The reason why this is important is because the vast majority of fresh fruits, vegetables, and nut crops in the nation come from central valley: 99% of almonds, grapes, and walnuts, 97% of apricot and plum, over 90% of broccoli, garlic, and celery and over 70% of spinach, peaches, avocadoes, leaf lettuce and strawberries all come from California. This is an example of how centralization leads to big problems because the California water board cut off irrigation supply to a lot of areas. The ultimate result is that the availability of a lot of fresh fruits and vegetables is going to be reduced because of the reduction of supply, which is going to cause the price to go up. And if anybody's been paying attention to their food budget some of the biggest increases in prices over the past year have been fresh fruits and vegetables, particularly ones that are grown particularly from California. The big impact from this drought is not going to be seen until later in nut trees like almonds and walnuts. If you stop watering an almond tree and it dies, the production from that tree is not coming back for 30 years. It's not like you can replant it next year and have a crop. We have huge problems with the production system and with the consumption side where people are buying cheap food-like products that is not real food. And then we have this problem with the distribution system which the average grocery store only has about 3 days supply of food for a normal consumption rate. So, it's very vulnerable to shock in supply or demand. A good example of this every time there's a hurricane or when a storm is coming, you see pictures on the news that grocery store shelves being completely cleared out of water and other staples because people don't have food storage in their house. And so when they see that they're not going to be able get that in a few days or a week because the power is going to be out, they all rush to get it at once and it clears the shelves. Since people don't have a food storage pantry anymore, people's homes are using a just-in-time supply system, which means that the entire food distribution food system is just in time. If you don't have any food storage, you're going to be in a world of hurt if there is anything that disrupts the availability of food with that distribution system. So these are all areas where from a production perspective, a distribution perspective, and a consumption perspective, our entire food system is unsustainable. It is extremely unhealthy and it is prone to shock, which is one of the reasons why if you want to have freedom of action you need to take steps to secure food supply that is reliable and preferably local. You can grow your own garden and that's as local as you can get. If you can't grow food in your garden, maybe you can grow some of it. Get all that you can from local sources and know your farmer. That's the best way to assume the quality and know what's in your food, much better than a USDA label on something that you buy in Wal-Mart.

NC: Why do you think most people who know this stuff aren't taking enough action?

JM: It's a cultural thing. Again it goes back to that consumer culture that we've been indoctrinated throughout our lives that convenience and low prices are the two primary objectives. Those are highest and best goals to attain so that's the way that people live their life. If that's the way you live your life and make your choices and particularly with respect to food then most likely you're going to go to the Wal-Mart organic labeled produce and without knowing it you're contributing to the problem. It's largely being grown in the same manner as non-organic produce. The only difference is that they're not spraying it with chemicals but they're still doing monoculture. They're still doing very large production facilities. It's all centralized in terms of production and distribution. Ultimately you still don't have any control over the reliability of that food source. The best way to assure not only quality but also availability of food is to go local. Grow it yourself. Know your local farmer and his production practices. He doesn't even need to be a certified organic for you to trust him. You don't need the government being the middleman to trust your farmer. Go into the farm and see what his production practices are, know your farmer personally so you can trust him, and if you can trust him then you can trust his production practices. You'll be able to interview him and talk to him and see them first hand. So I think a lot of this is taking action on our own hand by re-localizing a lot of things. Food is the one area that we're most advanced in because the local and organic food movement is the most progressive of all the movements related to re-localizing economy. So I think that's one reason why people who want to build a local community and a local economy should be looking to get plugged in with their local food economy first.

NC: That's a great piece of advice to get plugged into your local food community. What are ways people can do that other than farmer's markets?

JM: Farmer's markets are especially good because you have a collection of farmers all in one place. It's one way that you talk to different farmers, interview them to understand what their production practices are like, and determine if this is somebody who's trustworthy. In that regard, it's a great way of networking and getting to know your local food producers.

There are also food co-ops and buying clubs, which are a way for people to pull buying power and to buy locally produced food as well as food that may not be grown in your local area. This is one way you can buy in bulk and get significant cost savings for items like grains, spices and other products that you want organically but are hard to find in your local grocery store or even in a health food store. You may buy those through a buying club.

But the model I think what works best is a Community Support Agriculture (CSA) program. A CSA program is when a farm sells a share of the production of the farm and usually they'll have different choices: a small vegetable box, a large vegetable box, a green vegetable box, and other options. The idea is that every week you get a delivery either to your home or to your drop point near you containing some of the production of that farm and you are essentially subscribing to that service. You pay a deposit upfront and then you pay over time. What it does is it allows the consumer to share the risk with the farmer and allows the farmer to plan their production based upon the demands of their consumer members. So if you really want to support your local farmer, I highly recommend that you look for a local CSA program to be a part of because it's the best way to help farmers to do a good job in producing the right amount and types of crops for the local food community. That way he doesn't end up giving away or composting the excess produce because he has too much or can't use it all. It's a way of more efficiently allocating resources and sharing risk with the farm. I would encourage people to look for CSA programs in their local area if they can find one.

NC: Jason, you say that the financial system siphons off people's wealth and limits their ability to accumulate wealth. What do you mean by that?

JM: It's important to understand what our financial system is and what our currency is, right? So a dollar is not really a dollar. If you take out a dollar bill of any denomination and look at what it says at the top, it doesn't say anything about a dollar certificate or silver certificate. It says Federal Reserve notes. A federal reserved note is a debt instrument. It is debt-based money, which means that your currency is not issued into the money supply. It is borrowed into the money supply. So there's always more money owed than is physically existent in the economy. What that does is it creates a gigantic vacuum that's sucking the wealth towards the banks in the form of interest and most of us never think about this because they don't think of the dollar as being a debt instrument. That means that the entire financial system, a fiat currency that is a debt-based centralized banking system, is a vacuum that's sucking wealth to the financial institutions - into the banks. On top of that, you have the fact that over time through continually printing and issuing debt into the system, the value of those dollars will continually decline in such that since the Federal Reserve was created in 1913, the dollar has been devalued over 96%. Let's think for a second. In just over a hundred years, the dollar has lost not just the majority or the vast majority but over 96% of its value. Another thing that is more impactful is that since 2000, the dollar has lost over 26% of its value. I think it's close to 28 or 29% now. Within the past 14 years, we've had over a quarter of the value of the currency devalued. So a dollar that you had in 2000 is now worth less than 74 cents. This explains why it is more difficult for families to make ends meet because inflation is constantly tapping their buying power.

Another big trend that happened in the 1980's and in the 1990's is in the financialization of our economy. What I mean by that is that there's more and more economic activity in the financial sector but not in the real economy. The Gross Domestic Product

(GDP) is the measure of national output. Inflation-adjusted gross domestic growth, as reported by John Williams of www.shadowstats.com, has been negative with the exception of one slight lift into the positive since the year 2001. For 13 years we had real economic growth that's negative. Despite the nominal numbers that the government reports when you factor in real inflation, it is actually negative. This explains once again, why families are finding it hard to make ends meet because their purchasing power income is being tapped. The economy is contracting and there are fewer and fewer jobs. Since Congress authorized the Federal Reserve, which is a private banking cartel that loans money into the money supply at interest, it is creating a vacuum effect where wealth is constantly sucked to the banks. The important thing to know is even if things are going well you're still being robbed every minute of every day because they're constantly inflating away the value of the dollar.

This is one reason why re-localizing your economy is extremely important. To be able to minimize your exposure to this wealth sucking system that is the dollar, which is the primary means of economic transaction, it is essential to barter goods and services with other families or with other service providers. It's also noted that foreign nations are trying to minimize their use of the dollar because we're able to export our inflation to them. The dollar is a world reserved currency and other nations have to use the dollar for buying things like oil and for many other international trade transactions. Many countries such as Russia, China, Brazil, India, and many of the gulf Arab states are starting to make agreements between individual nations, even sometimes groups of nations, to make transactions in currency other than the dollar. Those are all signs that the dollar's world reserved currency is limited in terms of how long it's going to continue. We can't keep feeding, not just our own people, but every other nation on earth by exporting our inflation to them without doing anything about it. This impacts people individually because if you're not taking steps to minimize your exposure to the dollar-based system you're constantly losing the value of your assets over time. You need to look at ways to protect yourself against that and ultimately it's about having your wealth acquire assets like gold, silver, and productive farmland. If you're going to be trading in the stock market do the things like commodities other than the underlying asset value.

These are all things to be aware of in regards to the financial system so people can make strategic decisions to minimize their exposure and to not continue participating in a system that is continually robbing them over time.

NC: I've seen a lot of controversy regarding gold and silver. Do you really think that we would go back to a gold and silver scenario as we have a couple of times in the past or do you think something else is ready to emerge?

JM: Well, there are a couple of things to note here. The first to note is that the National Constitution requires that dollars be redeemable in gold and silver. In other words, our current form of money is unconstitutional. As soon as President Nixon took us off the gold standards in 1971, we ceased to have constitutional money. It's as plain as ink written by a quill on the handmade paper that the Constitution is on. In other words if you look at the spring of 1971 you'll see that on the bill it says silver certificates or something to that effect. What we currently have is potentially fraudulent and unconstitutional. The second is I think that we can go back to a gold-silver standard. But the question is what form does it take? Gold and silver has been money for a bit since the beginning of human history for at least 4000-5000 years of recorded history. You see it in the Bible constantly whenever it talks about money it talks about gold or silver as the form of money usually in terms of coins but nonetheless it's based on some asset of actual value. It continues to have recognized value. The current system of the fiat-based currency has no precedent in human history. It's the first time that we've had not just one currency but that most of the currencies in the world are un-backed by anything of value whatsoever. It's just that they can trust the United States government in being able to redeem a government bond. That's the only thing that essentially gives the dollar any value but the way the government is spending shows that it is becoming less and less likely in the future.

I think we dream about gold and silver and we need to because it's required by the Constitution. Ultimately what we've see through history is that the banks will not only rig the system in their favor but often the system leads to a crisis. Then they offer a solution to the crisis, which means more control for them. Again, take action, limit your exposure for the system you currently have and build your local economy.

Franklin Sanders has had a newsletter for 30 years that analyzes financial markets and he's a precious metal broker. He did a webinar and he said, "Build the new economy now." In other words, don't wait for things to get better for you. Change it. Replace the current failing system with a better, just, and proper system that's based on real value with people actually caring about their neighbors. Create that system now in your local area and don't wait for the centralized system we have to somehow improve or collapse so we can pick up the pieces afterwards. That's foolhardy. At some point there's going to be a change. There's going to be a tipping point and people are going to give up on the old system and join you in your new system. We're going to have vibrant flourishing local economies because people like you took action to create them before they were needed. Don't wait for things to get so bad that there's no other choice but for the centralized system to offer you one option and that is more control for them and less liberty for you.

NC: Have you seen successful models that people should consider researching or looking into in terms of building a new economy such as a trade-based economy or an economy that is fairer and just in their local environment?

JM: Re-localize your food supply. The ultimate re-localization is exploring that on your own land. I think this is where the burgeoning homestead movement is coming out of because people are sick of being dependent upon the consumer economy for the basics of life and they want to be more self-reliant. They want to produce not just their own food but raise animals that not only produce milk, meat or eggs but can actually accomplish work. In many cases, produce manure that can contribute to their gardening and their crop production. People are looking to produce more using natural systems. So all of these things are ways that we can try to directly produce more of what we have and not rely upon the outside system.

How do we rebuild local economies? I think one thing is to look for local businesses to buy products and services from. So instead of going to the big, huge big box stores to buy things, try to find local providers for those products and services that you need and localize through your spending that way. There are a number of alternative currency systems that rely on some form of hour-based unit of measure. I went to Cornell University in Ithaca, New York and for about 20 years they have had a system called Ithaca hours. Ithaca hours is an alternative currency system and people get paid in these units, which are linked to a fair wage. People need to just think outside of the modern economy. They need to think of creative local solutions to re-localize not only their purchasing but also their production.

NC: It's wonderful work that you're doing and you're part of an incredible film. How can people get involved? How can they support? How can they get connected with you and with the film? What are some things that people can do today?

JM: The website is www.beyondoffgrid.com. Last fall we started a webinar series and we invited experts. We interviewed them for the film as well as other experts not featured in the film but had expertise in a certain area related to these topics of being less dependent on modern economy and being more self-reliant. Last week we had an interview that was relevant to current events. We had an emergency medical physician talk about Ebola and dispel the mystique about that disease so people can be informed, make informed actions, and make life preparations for what is coming. It's only by being informed and prepared ahead of time and making conscious decisions to be less dependent on these modern systems that are prone to failure or to shock that we can be in a position of strength for our families and our local community.

We've done 23 webinars now and they're all designed to dive deep into individual topics. We touch on a lot of those topics in the film at a high level and start to pull them out together. But the webinar is really about providing more and more in-depth coverage.

The webinars are free when they're live and then we make the recording available. People can register about week afterward. So you can get information on that on the website. If you're interested in supporting the project, we do need additional funds to complete the project as we're in postproduction and editing is some of the most expensive work that needs to be done. You can click on the support link on the website and learn how you can support the project and we've got some great supporter rewards available. We have topical eBooks from some contributors to give to the supporters at various levels. We've also got all the uncut video footage from the film. You will be able watch all the uncut interviews, the site visits we did, the homesteads, and the farms. Lastly, we have the webinar recordings from all the past webinars we've done. Go to www.beyondoffgrid.com to learn more about that.

We'd also appreciate it if you can follow us on social media. We're on Facebook, Twitter, Google plus, and YouTube. And when you go to the website, sign up with our email list because that's where we're most active. We want to have some of a conversational interaction with our audience and so email is a great way for us to reach out and touch people. I really love getting replies back with what people are working on or how they were inspired or just ways that they appreciate what we're doing.

Nate's Notes

Reasons why people should get off the grid now:

- The system we live in limits our choices.

- Waiting around for things to get better does not work and won't get us anywhere.

- Need to establish our priorities.

- Most modern systems are susceptible to shock and crashing.

Reasons why people should get off the grid now:

- Food production and health grid

  ‣ Health is directly related to food production

  ‣ Need to source where our food is coming

- Financial economic control grid

  ‣ Wages and goods economy severely constrain our decisions.

- Government controls the grid

  ‣ Most people don't want the government telling them what to do.

  ‣ Most people don't appear to be consistent in pursuing liberty.

- Modern Cultural Consumer Control Grid
  - Culture determines how we spend our time and money.
  - Stop being just a consumer and make a decision to be a producer.
  - Be a productive family.
- Healthcare System Control Grid
  - It's becoming increasingly more centralized.
  - The result of modern healthcare system reveals that it is not a true healthcare system.
  - Modern medical system is a dispensary for the pharmaceutical industry.
  - You will be given a prescription drug to treat the symptoms but it won't address the underlying cause.
  - Pharmaceuticals kill hundreds of thousands of people each year.

How does the food system negatively impact us?

- America was mostly agrarian in the beginning with most people self-sufficient food wise.
- It has even transferred over to the industrial system over the last 60 years.
- Most family farms are not producing for local families. They are usually farming corn or soy for a large industrial food system.

- Farmers have to produce more and more to keep up with debt and production needs of food.

- On the consumer side, you have the spending on processed food doubling in the last 30 years.

- Processed food is fueling chronic disease epidemic.

- California is in extreme drought and yet most food comes from California.

- Price is going to go up because of the lack of production.

- Grocery stores only have about 3 days worth of food.

- Shelves can easily be cleared out during any kind of natural disaster.

- If you don't have food storage you can be hurt if the system goes out.

- You need to take steps to cultivate your own food supply.

- Grow what you can and get everything else from local farmers.

- You need to take action now!

- Everyone has been indoctrinated throughout their lives that convenience and low prices are our primary objectives. We need to change this thinking!

- Buying organic produce from Wal-Mart is contributing to the problem. This food system is largely grown in the same manner as monoculture and large production facilities. Ultimately you still don't have any control over the reliability of the food store.
- Need to go local for assurance of quality.
- Need to get plugged into the local food community first.
  - At farmers markets, question farmers about their food practices.
  - Look into food co-ops and buying clubs.
  - Community Supported Agriculture – CSA
  - Really helps local farmers in many ways

How does the financial system siphon off our wealth and limit our ability to accumulate wealth?

- A dollar is not really a dollar says the Federal Reserve note on the dollar.
  - It's a federal debt note, which means there is always more money owed than in actual existence in economy
  - This creates a vacuum in the economy.
  - The entire financial system, which is a debt based centralized banking system, is a vacuum sucking the wealth to the financial institutions and banks

- The value of dollars are always declining. The value of the dollar has lost 96% of its value in 100 years.

- Since 2000, the dollar has lost 28% of value.

- Inflation is constantly capping families buying power.

- More and more economic activity in the financial sector but not in the real economy.

- GDP is a measure of output but the real economic growth has been mostly negative since 2001.

- The economy has been contracting and there are fewer and fewer jobs since the Congress authorized the Federal Reserve.

- Relocalizing your economy is very important.
  ‣ Bartering goods and services with other families means that you will minimize your exposure to the wealth sucking system.
  ‣ Foreign nations are trying to minimize dependence on the dollar.
  ‣ Russia, China, Brazil, and India are starting to make agreements with other nations to make transactions in currency other than the dollar.
  ‣ Need to minimize exposure to dollar.
  ‣ Constitution requires that the dollars be redeemable in gold and silver.

- In 1971, Nixon took us off the gold standard. Since then we have no longer had constitutional money.

- The money we currently have is illegal and unconstitutional.

- It is possible to go back to a gold and silver economy.

- The current system of Fiat money has no precedence in the human system. This system often leads to a crisis. The banks then offer solutions to the crisis, which supports the banks.

- It is the centralized banks that are actually the problem.

- Need to build your local economy.

- Build the new economy now by replacing the current failing system with a better, just and proper system that's based on real value and people actually caring about their neighbors. Don't wait for the system to collapse or improve. Instead, start to create the replacement now.

- People will look towards those who are building a new economy.

- Relocalize your own "needs" supply. Do that in other ways as well such as your clothes, homes, food, and other needs.

- Look for local businesses to buy products and services from.

- Need to localize purchasing and production.

- Take action now to help your family to be more productive.

- Create a food production and a trade based system in your local area.

How can we go about seeking true freedom in light of these aspects of the modern grid?

- We can build our own future right now by taking back control of our economy.

- You can help pull people into the new system and as it grows we can replace the system with a more community-based system to create freedom.

- Small actions now can have a huge impact in the end.

Jason Matyas

Jason Matyas is a lifelong gardener, a 17 year Air Force veteran and is the founder of a family business with his children called Seeds for Generations that provides heirloom garden seeds and inspiration for gardening as a family. He is the Co-Founder and Executive Producer of the Beyond Off Grid project, a documentary film and media project devoted to inspiring and equipping you to reduce your dependence on the modern economy and seek true freedom by returning to the old paths of productive households and community interdependence.

Learn more at www.beyondoffgrid.com.

Ongoing Training and Community

Would you like ongoing support, guidance, inspiration, and practical how-to information each month to support you in becoming more self-reliant?

Join Self Reliance Mastery today to learn from the leading experts how to live off-grid, be more self-reliant, and experience sustainable living for yourself and your family.

Each month you will have access to cutting edge information from new experts on dozens of life-saving topics related to self-reliance.

You will learn through videos, audio recordings, transcripts, ebooks and more.

Visit www.SelfRelianceMastery.com to set up your account and join thousands of people around the world who are dedicating themselves to a more self-reliant lifestyle

www.SelfRelianceMastery.com

About the Author

Nathan Crane, is a highly sought after lifestyle entrepreneur, speaker, award winning author, and conscious filmmaker. By the time Nathan turned 26 years old he published, shared stages with, and worked with dozens of world renowned experts and best selling authors such as; Dr. Gabriel Cousens, Gregg Braden, Jeffrey Smith, Sonia Choquette, Alan Cohen, Mike Adams, Guy Finley, and many others. He is the Founder of The Panacea Community, President of Panacea Publishing, Inc., Director of Panacea Life School, President of Integrated Health International, Director and Filmmaker of the Search for Sustainability Documentary Series, and serves on the board of California Citizens for Health Freedom. Nathan is dedicated to help all people experience higher levels of health, happiness, and fulfillment through online and in person educational conscious publishing programs, events, conferences, expos, projects, documentaries, books, and experiences. Nathan enjoys growing organic food, outdoor activities, time traveling with his wife and daughter, speaking to thousands of attendees at conferences and expos, and producing life changing events around the country. Connect with Nathan by visiting www.NathanCrane.com.

Printed in Great Britain
by Amazon